THE HARDER LIFE KICKS YOU
THE HIGHER YOU CLIMB

THE HARDER LIFE KICKS YOU
THE HIGHER YOU CLIMB

A. R. McKnight

authorHOUSE®

AuthorHouse™
1663 Liberty Drive
Bloomington, IN 47403
www.authorhouse.com
Phone: 1-800-839-8640

Published by AuthorHouse   11/19/2012

ISBN: 978-1-4772-9182-5 (sc)
ISBN: 978-1-4772-9181-8 (e)

Library of Congress Control Number: 2012921833

This book is dedicated to the memories of
My mother and father
William F. and Willie D. McKnight
Mom once told me "Life is going to kick you no
matter what you do, but if you stand up rather than lie down
The harder life kicks you the higher you climb"

Prologue

I WONDER WHAT OLE POP AND JESSE ARE THINKING NOW

It's been two weeks since I was sworn in as the President of the United States and I am still adjusting to having that title attached to my name. In just a few minutes I will address the nation for the first time in my new position. My good friend Senate Minority Leader Walter Bowens steps to the podium.

"Ladies and Gentleman, the President of the United States."

I watch as all the people in the room stand and applaud. This is all still very new to me. I stand in the wings with my wife listening to the applause not realizing Walter is talking about me.

I feel as if I am watching a scene in a movie from someone else's life. My wife has to gently nudge me toward the stage. As I walk out into the flash of cameras the reality of the moment hits me.

Two weeks ago I became the second African American to hold the office of President of the United States. The fact that I am African American is no longer a big deal for America. Since the election of our first African American President our nation has gotten over the awe of the ethnic background of their President. They simply want to know what a candidate's plans are for governing this great nation. I however am still amazed at all of this.

I never consciously thought about the Presidency, nor had I ever thought I would even be in politics and I definitely didn't think I would ever run for this office. However here I am standing before the

American public with the spot light and history waiting on my first words.

I walk to the podium with my thoughts on Ole Pop and Jesse. Even though they have passed on to glory I can still feel their presence here with me and the influence they've had over my life. I am not perfect but thanks to them I am so much better than I was.

I bet Ole Pop and Jesse are both looking down on me and getting a kick out of all the commotion their nephew has caused. In fact they are probably tickled at the thought of this boy they raised being asked to lead this great nation. I can almost hear the laughter coming from deep inside Ole Pops chest, sounding like the rumble of a rolling freight train in the distant night.

For a few seconds as I stand on the podium, my life to this point comes into focus. The importance of the values Ole Pop, Jesse and my mother worked so hard to instill in me have proven to be the rock I needed and will continue to need to survive.

I can still remember Ole Pop Saying to me.

"Son it's not the beginning or the end of his life that makes a man it's the journey he takes along the way."

Ole Pop and Jesse shaped me in ways words can never express with memories I will never forget. If it had not been for them I would not be in this place, at this time, remembering how this first started.

Chapter 1

My name is Andre Carl Wright I am sixteen years old and I am standing in front of a juvenile judge awaiting his decision. How I got here is a long story. However if the judge is not lenient I will serve ten years in an adult prison before I am eligible for parole.

The judge reads my sentence and to my relief I am put on probation for two years and given back to my mother one last time. I stand in front of the judge like his ruling doesn't affect me when I actually feel like passing out. The judge's last words to me are.

"If you do not obey your mother, and I see you in this courtroom again you will do every day of the ten year sentence I am setting aside today."

I said thank you to the judge but I really didn't mean it. Actually I really didn't care. I hadn't cared about my life since I was twelve. That's when my mother and father got a divorce and that's when I started walking the wrong road.

In the four years following their divorce I have gone from a promising student to America's most wanted. I have been in juvenile court only three times but this last one was the biggest of them all.

The court officer walks me back to my cell and in less than an hour I am a free man. I can't wait to get back to my boys and laugh with them about how the system had let me go again but momma had a different idea. When I get to the car there are several pieces of luggage in the back seat.

"You going somewhere momma?"

"No I'm not, but you are."

"What do you mean I'm going somewhere? I ain't going nowhere but home."

"You don't live with me anymore."

"Oh so you just gonna leave me on the street just like that huh? So you gonna walk out on me just like you walked out on dad? Go on then, I don't need your ass, hell I don't need nobody I can hustle and get what I . . . ."

Smack! My momma hit me with a right hand that spins my face to the side. This isn't a normal slap. This is a, "I'm gonna bring the pain all the way up from Louisiana, I'll knock you into the next century, I'm still your momma and I will bury your butt six feet deep before I let you disrespect me" slap.

She hit me so hard my knees buckle and even though it is daylight I see as many stars as there would be on a moonlit night. Mom had only hit me once before but that was a light touch compared to this. I've never been hit this hard in my life. Momma was mad and hurt and she wanted me to know it. But most of all she wanted me to wake up.

When I regain my senses, I am lying backward on the hood of the car, and mom has two handfuls of my shirt collar.

"Andre Carl Wright don't you ever talk to me like that again as long as you live! I have worked my life away so you can have a good home, and you will damn well respect me. Now you are going to your great uncles house . . . ."

I hadn't learned yet. "Aw hell naw!"

Smack! Smack! Smack! Momma hit me three more times and this time all I can do is duck and cover and even that doesn't help. I didn't know my mother could hit that hard. Damn, she hit me like a heavyweight fighter.

"Dammit Andre shut up and listen to me! Do you see that man standing over there?"

Mom has such a tight grip on my collar I can just barely breathe. And after being hit hard enough to buckle my knees several times she has convinced me it would be wise to just shut my mouth and do as I am told. Slowly I turn my head to the side and see a large man in a suit leaning against the courthouse wall. I nod my head yes to her.

"He's a parole officer."

Mom takes her left hand off me, reaches inside the car to the dashboard and pulls out a large brown envelope.

"And these papers I have in my hand."

She places the envelope directly in front of my eyes. "These papers are from the court and they say if you refuse to obey me all I have to do is sign them and this man will immediately pick you up and take you to jail. From there you will begin serving that ten year sentence the judge didn't give you this time."

Mom snatches me off the hood of the car then lets me go but she never takes her eyes off me. She still has that intense look in her eyes letting me know she would pop me again if I even blinked wrong. She looks at me for what seems like an hour then finally she drops her head, lets out an exasperated breath then looks back up at me.

"I'm about two seconds away from signing these papers. Once I sign them, I can't change my mind. You'll do all the time the judge set for you. Do you understand me?"

I nod my head yes again.

"Good, now get in the car you're going to Ole Pop and Uncle Jesse's house and you'll stay there until Old Pop says you can leave. If you run away, you had better make sure you stay lost forever. If he calls me and tells me you're gone I will sign these papers making you a wanted fugitive."

Mom looks extremely tired as she walks around to the driver's side of the car and gets in. I haven't gotten in yet so she leans over and looks out the window at me with that same killer look in her eyes.

"Well, what are you waiting for, get in the car."

I open the door, sit down and slam the door. Mom's reaction is quick because she expected me to act like a dumb teenager. She leans over until she's face to face with me and this time with a mean hiss she says, "Boy don't make me smack you again."

I don't say anything partially out of fear and partially because I'm pissed. Mom starts the car and we both are silent as she heads for the interstate.

Right about here I guess I should back up and explain how I got into this mess in the first place. It's not a long story and it's not a tragic one. It's just a story of a young man making some very dumb decisions in his early years. I have no excuses. I can't even say I was a victim of the system. I couldn't tell you anything about welfare because I have never been on welfare.

My mother has a master's degree in math, and teaches at Temple University, and my father has a master's degree in chemical engineering and works for a well-known plastic's firm. And even though he was an absent father he never missed his child support payments, so I never wanted for anything. Still there were things that bothered me, and I guess that's why I made some of the decisions I did.

Mom and dad separated when I was twelve. Mom caught dad with another woman in their bed and that was that. She filed for a legal separation then basically kicked him out of the house.

They were separated for a year and all during that time I just knew they were going to get back together but mom didn't see it the same way. She just couldn't forgive my father for cheating on her.

I found out later in life that she had been hurt before and even then she may have taken him back if he hadn't started drinking again. After that she just couldn't deal with him. She filed for a divorce a year later.

I stayed mad at her for three months. How could she divorce my old man? I know how bad he messed up but he was still my dad. I couldn't understand why if she loved him she couldn't forgive him. So for three months I wouldn't even speak to her, and everything positive in my life started to fall apart.

Before the divorce I was a straight A student. After the divorce I didn't care much about studying. My grades suffered, my attitude changed, and I settled into a mild depression. I missed my dad and all the things we used to do.

I got to see him on the weekends when he had his court appointed time with me but it wasn't the same. Most weekends he had to work his second job to pay my child support, and keep his own apartment. So I was left in his apartment alone. He never had time to play ball anymore, or wrestle around on the floor like he used to. When he came home at night he was always too tired.

The hardest part of this break up was watching my old man fall apart. For the first three months I didn't notice any difference in dad but little by little I started to see different changes in him.

After a month he started to bring home a couple of bottles of beer on the weekend. After another month and a half he was bringing home two six packs a week. By the fifth month he was drinking a six pack a night.

He would get home around ten o'clock P.M. from his second job and by eleven o'clock he had drank a six-pack. By twelve o'clock he was sleep in his chair. And when he wasn't sleep the only thing he talked about was how he messed things up with momma and how he wished he could get her back.

I was too young to know it then, but I was watching my old man slowly kill himself and as if that wasn't enough, when I went home I had to listen to momma crying in her bedroom behind her closed door. Of course every time I asked her why she was crying, she would just tell me that I didn't need to worry about it, and that she was doing just fine.

By my thirteenth birthday I had gotten to the point I was tired of both of them. I was too young to understand they were hurting as bad as I was. The only thing that mattered to me was all of a sudden neither of them had time for me and that's when the depression set in.

"Why me, why does all the bad stuff have to happen to me."

Now that I look back on it, I guess the pain and depression was necessary for me to get to the point I am today. But it sure hurt like hell when it was happening. I didn't think things could get any worse. The following year I found out they could.

The next school year after my folks broke up all hell broke lose in my life. It was November nineteenth I will never forget that day. That's when I met my worse nightmare.

His real name was Marcus Terry Jackson but he called himself "B nasT." It meant "Big Nasty and he was. The nasty part came from his attitude. He was so intimidating most people around school avoided him.

B nasT transferred in from the South side. His older brother had just recently purchased a house in a neighborhood three miles from ours. The neighborhood he moved to wasn't one of the best neighborhoods in Philadelphia, but it wasn't the worse one either. B nasT had come from the worse one in the city and he was a product of the neighborhood he had just left.

He was taller than me, as strong as an ox with a huge mean streak in his personality, in fact mean was his personality. That's because he was two years older and had been in juvenile detention for two years. He said all he had to do was eat and lift weights. All I know is that he was hard as a rock, and at the age of fourteen could bench press two hundred pounds.

I don't know why he decided I was the one he should mess with. I guess I was in the wrong place at the wrong time. He hadn't been there two days when I accidentally bumped into him. He grabbed me, hit me in the mouth and knocked me to the floor.

"Watch where the hell you're walking, I paid one hundred and ninety dollars for these shoes."

I got up, picked up my books and quickly walked away.

"That's right go on to class with yo punk ass before I bust your damn lip again."

When I got home, and momma saw my mouth, she made me tell her what happened. When she heard the full story, she drove me to the school the next day, and gave the principal a whole lot of grief. The principal told her that no one had reported an assault, so he wasn't aware that it happened. Then momma made him call B NasT to the office.

He walked in with that nasty look on his face and sit down in a chair facing me. All the time the principal was talking to him, he never took his eyes off me. I knew this wasn't over by a long shot.

After the principal got my story and his, he admitted that he hit me but he said it was because I hit him first. The principal suspended both of us for three days. Momma wasn't happy with that decision.

The next day she goes to B NasT's old school and finds out that he had been put out at least seven times for fighting the last time he was put out for good. She takes what she's learned back to the principal and tells him if B NasT assaults me again, she will sue the school, the school board, and any one else she feels is negligent.

The principal explains he would take care of me while I was in school but if anything happened off school grounds he couldn't be held responsible for it.

Later that night the phone rings and I answer it thinking it's my pops.

"Hello."

"Yeah lemme speak to Andre."

"This is Andre, Who's this?"

"You know who this is and you know I'm gonna kick yo ass everyday after school. I know you have to walk home cause yo ugly ass momma has to work. So every time I see yo ass I'm gonna put both of my feet in it."

I slammed the phone down and went upstairs to my room. Now I had real problems.

After I got back into school, I did the best I could to avoid B NasT and it worked for two days until Friday in algebra class when I asked to be excused to the bathroom.

I was standing next to the sink when B NasT and two of his partners walk in. They were skipping class and I just happened to be in the bathroom they chose to hide in. I knew instantly I was in for a lot of hurt.

B NasT walked up to me with the nastiest smile on his face.

"Whassup punk? Now what you gonna do? I guess you gonna start crying and call your momma. Yo punk ass is in trouble now."

He hit me in the mouth and I fell down.

"Yo momma can't help yo ass now. Get up punk?"

He kicked me in the side and rolled me over on my back. Then he walked over to me and tried to stomp me in the face. But I caught his foot and pushed him back.

He stumbled a little bit then caught his balance and smiled that evil smile of his.

"Well I'll be damned yo punk ass is trying to fight back. It don't matter though I'm still gonna to knock yo ass out."

By this time I'm back on my feet circling him trying to find a way out of the bathroom.

B NasT swings a hard right at me again and connects with my jaw but this time I don't even feel it. Something inside of me snaps.

The room goes dark, and all I can see is his face. It's as if a spotlight has been placed on him and the rest of the room has faded away.

The next thing I remember is our assistant principal screaming, "Let him go" as he a gym teacher and the school officer try to pull me away from B NasT. All three of them were grown men but they were having a hard time making me release the choke hold.

When I let BnasT go he fell to the floor like someone had cut his legs from under him. His eyes rolled up in the back of his head, drool fell from the corner of his mouth and he didn't appear to be breathing.

I was forced to the floor, handcuffed then pulled up and dragged to the office. After the officer filled out his report I was taken downtown to the police station. Later I found out I gave B NasT a concussion, two broken ribs, a black eye, and a broken nose which is why I was taken to the police station.After being booked for assault I am put in detention with the other two guys who were in the rest room when the fight started. They stay away from me but I can tell they are talking about me by the way they look at me. I guess they are afraid I will go off on them like I went off on B NasT and that works for me.

Four hours after I am taken to detention my mother gets me out. She is furious that the principal told the police to take me downtown. The next day she when she arrives at my school to have a conference with the principal he tells her I am being staffed out of the school. When mom gets home she is madder than I have ever seen her.

She immediately calls her lawyer. The next day he receives the police report. The report says the police have questioned the other two boys who were in the bathroom at the time. They both said B NasT started the fight.

Two weeks later mom and her lawyer meet with a representative of the school board, a social worker and a judge. The fight was ruled self-defense. After serving two weeks suspension I was free to go back to school but B NasT had to do three months in juvenile.

While I was out of school mom picked up my homework so I wouldn't fall behind then came home after work to check my assignments. She was determined that I was going to grow up to be an intelligent man but she knew I was going to be a hand full so she prayed every night for me.

I passed by her room one night and heard her talking. I didn't know who she was talking to until I heard her say the Lord's name. She was asking for his help as well as his protection for me. I was putting her through a lot but she loved me enough to put me in God's hands. Even then he was my protection but I didn't have enough sense to know it.

Chapter 2

When I got back to school, I was a hero. Nobody liked B NasT but everyone was afraid of him so all my friends were happy that I put him out of commission.

My life was getting much better even the thugs around school gave me respect. The best part is I was beginning to get conversation from some of the honeys in school who normally wouldn't even talk to me, so I was coming up.

From that point things began to go downhill in my life. I started hanging with the same thugs I used to be afraid of and that got me more respect from all the students who were afraid of them. It felt good to get this kind of respect.

The only bad thing about the new fame is all my old partners left me alone. They were afraid of the new people I hung around with. However that didn't matter to me at all, I was a thug now. I was a member of the bad boy set. I even started to miss classes to hang out. Things were going pretty good for me at least I thought they were.

Monday, after school let out for the day, I was walking home when a car pulled up beside me and three mean looking older guys got out. I kept walking because I didn't know them and I didn't want any trouble.

One of them caught up with me and started talking.

"So you're the one who kicked my brother's ass. Hell you don't look like you could kick your own ass but judging by my brother's face, I guess you can hold your own."

I knew he was talking about B NasT so I figured I was in for some serious pain, maybe even death.

I started to walk a little faster but he stepped in front of me and the other guys surrounded me.

"Hey slow down little brother. My name is Davon Jackson but my friends call me Trey and I just want to talk with you a minute. It ain't about the revenge thang if that's what you're worried about. You kicked Marcus ass, hell he needed that. I kept telling him that some of the people who walk away from him wasn't necessarily afraid of him. But he wouldn't listen. I hope this ass whoopin helps him understand. What's your name l'il man?"

"Andre Wright."

"Well Mr. Andre Wright I would like to make you a proposition. Do you like money and the finer things in life?"

"Yeah I guess so."

"Good then I want you to think about this."

He pulls a wad of bills out of his pocket that is as big as my fist.

"I need someone who knows the school and has a lot of connections to work with Marcus and I in a little business venture. I will provide the capital and the product you and Marcus will stake out a territory and sell my product."

Trey pulls a hundred dollar bill out of his roll of money and holds it up close to my face.

"If you do a good job I'll pay you twice this every time you sell out. If you sell more, I'll pay you more. Don't answer me now just think about it."

He puts the bill in my front pocket, and then gets back in the car.

"If you decide to join us, come by the old rail yard tonight at seven o'clock. Don't be late I don't work on CP time. If you don't show I'll take that to mean you don't want to join. Just remember this if you're not my friend you're my enemy."

Trey and his boys drive away leaving me standing there with a hundred dollar bill in my pocket, a taste for freedom, and scared thoughts of what that freedom may cost me.

When I get home my mother is waiting in the living room.

"Andre Carl Wright come here and sit down we need to have a talk."

Well I know when my mom uses my full name and that tone of voice it means I've done something wrong. I shake my head and walk into the den. I was about to get my ass chewed off about something.

"Andre I just got a call from your principal and he told me that you've been skipping classes. Is this true?"

"I didn't skip no class I was in another teacher's room finishing up a test I missed when I was out of school."

"Is that right? So you had to make up the same test three days in a row?"

"Why you ridin me about some classes? My grades are good so what's the problem?"

"Correction, your grades were good. According to your principle, you're making a D in every course but Geometry you're making an F in that. Andre I don't want to see you make a mistake that will follow you for the rest of your life. Today you skip one class tomorrow you skip two, pretty soon you're so far behind you can't catch up and in this day in time you need a good education to provide for yourself. Now since you decided to skip class and let your grades drop I'm grounding you for the next three weeks. If your grades don't improve I'm going to ground you until the end of the semester."

"You're grounding me just cause I missed a few classes. How you just gonna put me in jail just because of a few classes?"

"Andre I'm not going to argue with you about this. I've made up my mind, now go to your room, and start catching up your class work."

I turn around and walk away mumbling, "You're about to get on my damn nerves."

Unfortunately I forgot that just like all mothers my mom had those super sensitive ears and I didn't mumble quiet enough.

She grabbed me by the shoulder and spun me around. "What did you just say to me?"

"I didn't say nothing."

"Oh so now you're going to lie to me as well. Let me tell you one thing young man, I don't care if I'm getting on your nerves. I'm still your mother, and you will do what I tell you to do in this house. Oh and one other thing, if you ever cuss me again, I will knock your head into the front yard. Right now though you will go upstairs unplug your CD player and speakers, and put them in my room. You will get them back when I think you've learned some respect. Don't open your mouth again, or I will knock your teeth out."

Now I'm really pissed. I storm up the stairs into my room. Snatch the power cord to my CD player out of the wall, gather it and the speakers in my arms, walk into her room and dump them in a chair. Then I walk back to my room and slam the door.

I pace back and forth around in a circle in my room mumbling to myself.

"How is she going to take my shit just because I missed a few boring ass classes? Damn! She didn't even buy the shit, dad bought it. I'll be glad when I can leave this house, and I won't have to listen to her mouth."

After sitting down on the bed I take off my shirt and throw it across the room and right on cue the hundred dollar bill flies out of my pocket and falls to the floor. I forgot about Trey.

I pick up the bill, sit down on the bed, and looked at it. If I can make twice this much every week, I won't have to deal with her taking my stuff, I can buy my own. I'm about to make the biggest mistake of my life.

Hell, if I work hard enough Trey will probably make me a partner and I could move out of this damn house into my own. I could even have my own car. I'll be sixteen in another month and I know she ain't gonna let me have a car until my grades improve and even then I won't get it until she thinks I'm ready for it which means I probably won't get one until I'm seventeen or eighteen. It was right there that I made one of the dumbest decisions of my life.

Mom had a faculty meeting at the university at seven o'clock P.M. This meant that she would leave the house at six thirty. If I got on my bike and rode real hard, I could get to the rail yard by seven o'clock. I was gonna sell for Trey and get the hell out of my mom house so I could do what I wanted to do.

Of all the times for mom to leave late it had to be today. Usually she is out of the house by six twenty five, but today is her day to lead the faculty meeting, and she had some last minute papers to do on the computer so she was running late. She didn't leave the house until six forty so I had to hustle to get to the rail yard on time.

I jumped on my bike and rode as fast as I could. I ran a couple of lights, and almost got hit at the last one. When I finally got to the place Trey told me to meet him at, it was five minutes after seven o'clock.

"Didn't I tell you I don't work on CP time?"

"Couldn't help it I had to help my mom get ready to go to work before I could leave the house."

"Oh so your mom keeps check on you huh? Well maybe you ain't the right man for the job."

"Yeah I'm the right man for the job. I just had to take care of some business for her before I left."

"Okay so you want to work for me? Let me tell you what I expect. I expect you to bring me my money on time. I expect all of my cash to be there. I expect you to keep your mouth shut about our business. Don't tell anyone, and that includes your mom. I don't need anyone in my business. I expect you to inform me if someone is trying to sell product in my territory other than you and Marcus. I'll squash any beef anybody has with you. And lastly I expect you to keep your mouth shut if PoPo picks you up. I don't need any snitches in my organization. If you are picked up, just sit tight, keep your mouth shut, and my lawyer will come and get you."

"So you're saying that I might get arrested."

Trey and his boys start laughing. "Yeah little man, you might get arrested, but since it's your first offense, and you'll only be selling weed, you won't get anything but probation. But you won't have to worry about that if you and Marcus are smart, and careful. Make sure you never do business out in public. Pick somewhere around the school where you can do your business and get out quick if it gets hot. Set up your own loyal customers and don't try to grow too fast. When you grow too fast, you get police coming into your set and screwing it up. Just start slow, keep your customers satisfied, and let your business grow slowly. Never trust anyone you haven't seen around the school a lot and never deal with anyone who is new to the school. New kids are either PoPo or snitches."

Then Trey walked up to me and produced a gun from out of nowhere. He places it right between my eyes and grabs the back of my neck so I can't move. My knees get weak and I feel like I'm going to pass out right there.

Trey whispers to me, "Li'l man, if you screw me, I'll kill you and your mom too."

Then as quickly as the gun appeared, it disappears.

Trey hands me a cell phone, and a quarter pound of weed, already bagged up for resale.

"Sell this and bring my money back, and you'll get paid. If you sell it all before Saturday, call me on the phone, and I'll get you some more. The more you sell the more money you make. I'll see you Saturday right here at seven o'clock. Don't be late."

He gets in his car and he and his boys drive off.

I carry the bag home, hide it and try to go to sleep, but all I can think about is the gun Trey put to my head earlier. I was beginning to think this was a bad idea.

The next morning I get the sack, take out five quarter bags, put them in my pocket and put the rest back in my hiding place. When I get to school, I find one of the thugs I've been hanging with, and ask him if he wants to buy some weed and in a matter of seconds I sell two bags just like that.

By lunch time I had sold the other three to three different people. And by the end of school, the word had spread that I had that Killer weed, and fourteen kids had approached me to buy my product. Now I was in business.

When I returned to school the next day, I had five bags with me. By lunchtime I had sold all of them. I had another six at home, so I skipped math class, rode my bike home, got the other six, and sold all of them by the end of school. When I got home I called Trey.

"Hey Li'l man whuzzup? You can't be out of weed already?"

"Yeah man I sold it all. It was too easy. Yesterday all I did was sell a little to some of my friends and by the time school was out everybody wanted to buy some. Today I went in with half of what you gave me, and I sold that by lunchtime. I went back home and got the rest and sold it by the end of school. Every body is saying I got the Killer."

"I told you Li'l man, I don't have nothing but the best product. Now I tell you what you do. Meet me at the rail yard at seven o'clock with my money and I'll give you some more."

Trey hangs up the phone, and I begin working on my homework. The last thing I needed now was for the principal to call and tell mom that I wasn't doing my homework.

By seven o'clock I was sitting on some tires when Trey and his boys pull up.

"Well I see you got here on time this time. Where's my money?"

I give him a brown paper bag with five hundred dollars in it. He throws it in the back for one of his boys to count.

"Yeah Trey it's all here."

"Damn Li'l man you know how to take care of business. I knew you were the right one the minute I saw you. That's damn good work Li'l man. Here's some more." Trey hands me another quarter pound, and one hundred and thirty dollars. That's your cut little man.

"Thanks Trey. Look Trey I ain't trying to tell you how to run your business, but I can sell twice that if you trust me with it."

Trey looks at me then looks around the car at his boys, and they all bust out laughing.

"Look here Li'l man, don't think just because you sold some weed real quick that you a dope man now. Let me handle the quantity, and just sell what I give you."

"Trey I ain't trying to be no dope man, but listen to me for a minute, and if what I say doesn't make sense then just tell me to shut the hell up."

"Aeight Li'l man, I ain't one to pass on some money. You got one minute to impress me."

"Well this Thursday night is the senior trip to Sailors amusement park. They gonna want some weed. Friday is the homecoming game, everybody is gonna want some weed for that and Saturday is the big "Murderer's Row" concert at the Coliseum and you know everybody is gonna want some weed for that. Shit I bet I can sell a pound by this Sunday."

Trey looks at me for a few seconds then he laughs again.

"Damn little man, if you keep thinking like this, I'm going to have to make you a partner."

He takes back the first bag and hands me a bag with a pound in it.

"Go handle your business."

By two o'clock Tuesday afternoon I had sold all the weed Trey gave me. When I get home I call Trey.

"Trey I'm ready to settle up."

"Hey Li'l man, damn you mean to tell me you took care of all that already?"

"Yeah, I told you everybody needed to take care of they're business before the weekend hit."

"Well meet me at the usual place and we'll settle up."

At seven o'clock Trey and his boys drive up. I give Trey the paper bag, his boy counts the money and Trey tries to hand me another pound.

"Naw Trey I can't handle another pound right now. Everybody who's going to get some weed has already got it. And they're going to hold onto it until this weekend. The only people who will buy now will be the hard core smokers."

Trey looks and me for a minute then give me another bag with a quarter pound in it.

"I have to say one thing little man, you learned the game quicker than anyone I've ever seen. You gonna make some nice paper in this game. Now here's your cut."

Trey counts out five hundred and sixty dollars and hands it to me.

"That's four hundred and sixty dollars for your cut and one hundred for your bonus. Keep working it little man and I'll have to give you a bigger territory."

I get back to my room and count my money. There was the hundred dollar bill I got the first time I met Trey, One hundred thirty for my first sell, Five hundred sixty for this last sell, for a grand total of seven hundred ninety dollars. Seven hundred ninety dollars in three days, and all I had to do was stand in the right place and take the money. This shit was too easy, and momma wanted me to go to college. What the hell for? I could make more money on the street than I ever could with a damn college degree. Now I knew exactly what I was going to do with my life.

When B NasT came back to school he didn't come after me. Trey told him what was up and how I had learned the game so quick. Plus the fact I think he was a little afraid of me after I went off and tried to kill him. We were cool now and business really started booming. We handled Trey's product together I was the brains and B NasT was the muscle.

For the next three months I owned my high school. Trey ran all the other weed sellers away from the school so there was no competition.

B NasT and I had the school all to ourselves and since Trey had some of the best weed in town we started getting customers from the local technical college down the street from our school.

In money terms I was earning about five hundred dollars a week. Even then I was careful to keep my grades up so mom wouldn't give me any grief. As long as that report card was good, mom didn't question me about my friends, or where I was going on the weekend.

I begin going to the mall with Trey and his boys on Saturdays. I would buy the best, most expensive clothes, and leave them over to Trey's house. Then each morning I would leave home wearing what mom bought me and go to Trey's house, put on the stuff I bought, and ride to school. B NasT and me were the sharpest dressers in the school.

After school B NasT and I would go to the mall across the street from the school and hang with the rest of the kids. I would brag to my friends while I played video games. I told one guy I had just met.

"Shit I'm earning two G's a month and I don't even work hard."

"Aw nigga quit lying. You know you ain't making that kind of money."

"Nigga, look at my shoes, they cost two hundred dollars. They ain't even out in the stores around here yet. Look at my clothes. I spent three hundred dollars for the pants and shirt. Look at my wrist, my shit is real platinum not like that fake shit you got on your wrist. And when I'm ready Trey said he's going to make me his partner."

That one little mistake is the one that cost me my freedom. Loose lips sink ships, and my lips had just told a police informant who B NasT and I were working for. It wasn't long before I found myself face to face with a gun and a badge.

The undercover officer caught me with five-dime bags, and arrested me for having an illegal substance for the purpose of resell. An hour later I was in a room with two officers being questioned about my connections.

"C'mon Andre we know you can't bring the weed into town. Shit, you're just barely old enough to drive. But you're old enough to get your ass put away for a long time if you don't start cooperating with us."

"I want my phone call."

"Alright but this is going to get your ass sent up for a long time."

The officer puts a phone in front of him and walks out. I dialed the number Trey told me to call if I ever got caught by the police.

"Hello."

"Hey man I'm down here in jail, and if my mom finds out she's gonna freak. You need to get down here and get me out."

"Calm down Li'l man. My lawyer is already in the building. In fact you should be out in the next twenty minutes don't sweat it and keep your mouth shut."

Trey hangs up the phone and the officers come back in. They sat down in front of him and the one that was asking questions the first time sits down beside me.

"Look Andre I know you talked to your contact just now and he's probably sending someone to get you this time, but how many times do you think he's going to do that. The only reason he's coming to get you is because he doesn't want you to talk to us. As soon as he has no use for you or he gets himself in a bind he's going to let your ass rot in here and you can bet that."

"Excuse me officer but I think you should consider giving your advice to someone who needs it. My client doesn't need your help and if you don't mind we'll be leaving now."

I look up to see a man standing in the door with a briefcase. He motions for me to come to him, then takes me by the arm and leads me outside. We get into his car and drive off.

"Andre you didn't say anything to the police did you?"

"Naw, Trey told me not to say nothing and that he would handle any thing that came up."

"Good. Trey told me to tell you to call him tomorrow. You did good."

Two months later I'm arrested again. This time they catch me with the full pound of weed in my possession and this time they call my mother before they do anything else. When she gets to the police station and finds out what I've been charged with she goes ballistic.

"Andre what are you thinking about? Why are you purposely trying to ruin your life? How in the world did you manage to become a dope pusher?"

"Weed is not dope mom it's . . ."

"Shut up boy! Don't you say anything else until we've gotten out of this police station?"

We go before the judge and he sets a court date. After two hours I'm allowed to leave. Mom grabs me by the arm and drags me to the car and yells at me all the way home. When we finally get home mom drags me into the living room and slams me into a seat.

"I don't know what you call yourself doing but I do know this much, I'm not about to let you ruin your life over something stupid like this. From now until I say otherwise, you don't do anything but go to school and come back home. If you do anything else, I'll knock your head off your shoulders then I'll send you away to military school. Do you understand me?"

"Why you trippin? It ain't like I killed somebody, besides alcohol is worse than weed just look at daddy's drunk ass."

Right here is where mom loses it. She grabs me by the collar, and slaps me in the mouth. It shocks me, because she's never hit me before.

"Andre Wright don't you ever say anything like that about your father again. He's a sick man and he needs help with his addiction. Now I don't care what you think is wrong or right. You will not sell that stuff anymore, and you will come home right after school or so help me you will wish you had never disobeyed me ever in your life. Now go upstairs and do your home work."

I went upstairs. I was hurt, scared, and mad all at the same time, and I didn't know which one I was more of. Now I knew what it meant to have the taste slapped out of your mouth. Momma hits harder than B NasT did and how in the hell was she just going to hit me and then ground me for life. I hadn't done anything wrong. Weed wasn't harming anybody. Everybody likes weed and why is she still defending dad, she's the one who divorced him.

This was all confusing, but I didn't care, all I wanted to do was call Trey and get some more weed. Getting busted didn't mean anything to me. In fact getting busted will make my reputation that much better and the honeys will just keep coming after me.

I call Trey and tell him the situation. Trey tells me that he has decided to let me and B NasT lay low for a while until PoPo stopped patrolling so hard. We didn't sell any weed for the next month and a half until we were sure PoPo stopped showing up around campus. But as soon as we were sure they were gone it was business as usual.

I should have quit then but I was young and stupid and thought I was invincible. Yeah I thought no one could touch me and with Trey as my guardian and leader I was going to be big in the game. I didn't know the truth about the game but I was about to find out.

Chapter 3

During the month and a half of not selling, I went back to court. The judge put me on probation, and ordered me to do thirty hours of community service. I finished my community service and went right back to selling.

For the next three months my business was booming. What I didn't know was the police put a surveillance team on me. It was the same team that had been watching Trey for several months. The only difference was he knew about them and I didn't.

By this time four months had passed and as far as my mother knew I had stayed out of trouble. She still hadn't let me off probation but today was our final grade report day and my grades were good so I was hoping she would lighten up a little.

During the time mom had me on probation I came directly home everyday right after school. I also made sure she didn't find anything in my room when she searched it each week after I left for school.

I never kept any weed in the house after I got busted B NasT had the stuff with him. As far as mom could tell I had straightened out my life. She even started to laugh and joke with me again so I figured it was time to ask if I could get off probation. I finished my homework and walked downstairs to the kitchen.

"Hey mom, uh look, I've been doing pretty good in school and I've done everything you and the judge asks me to do. Do you think you could let me off grounding so I can go to the big end of school party at the skating rink Friday night?"

"I don't know Andre. I still don't know if I can trust you yet."

"Look mom I know I made a mistake but I took my punishment and I'm doing better can't you let me off at least for the party."

"What time does the party start?"

"Eight o'clock."

"What time does it end?"

"Eleven o'clock."

"And what time are you supposed to be home? With a big grin I say, "Two o'clock."

"See you just messed it up. You almost made it, but you had to get smart." I run over to her and hug her. She tries to push me away, but she's smiling.

"C'mon mom you know I was just playing. I'll be home by eleven thirty, I promise."

"Uh huh you'd better be. Don't make me have to come looking for you."

"I squeeze her, and kiss her on the jaw, "Thanks mom.""

Friday comes and I get dressed for the party. Mom comes upstairs to check on me. I smile when she walks in. "How do I look?"

"Like a boy who's trying to get a girl to notice him. Is someone special going to be at the party?"

"Naw, just all of my friends but you know a playa has to look good for all the honeys out there."

"Listen to you, calling your self a playa. You need a car and a job to be a playa."

"No you don't. You just have to know how to spit game."

"Uh huh just make sure your game doesn't include any babies. You're not ready for that kind of responsibility yet."

"Aw mom, I didn't say anything about no babies."

"Well I did and I'm serious."

"I know mom." I kiss her and walk out of the house. Just around the corner out of her eyesight I get in the car with B NasT.

"Whuzzup Nigga?"

"Whuzzup?"

"You ready for some wild ass shit tonight."

"Damn right. We gonna do some crazy shit and I know Trey's gonna have all the finest women at his house."

"Shit, the strippers from the club are already there. Two of em is already butt naked. When I left Trey was running them into the living room and letting them do their thing."

"No shit? Damn! Let's go."

We arrive at the party and it's jumping inside. Music's bumping, smoke is thick, women are butt naked everywhere you look, and people are engaged in different types of sex all over the house.

Trey meets me at the door.

"Whuzzup Li'l man, so you finally made it to your first party. Well let me introduce you around."

We walk all over the house while Trey introduces me to some of the major playas in town. After all the introductions Trey lights up a blunt, takes a hit and passes it to me. I look at it for a minute then take a puff. I immediately start coughing. Not a normal cough, but that special cough of a person who has never tried weed before.

"Well I'll be damned. You ain't never smoked any weed before have you?"

I couldn't answer because I was still coughing. Trey took me out on the porch for some fresh air and after I stop coughing Trey is still there laughing at me.

"Damn, Li'l man, why didn't you tell me you was a virgin. I would have started you off with some weak weed."

"I'm not a virgin. I've smoked before, but this is some different shit."

"You damn right it's some different shit. It came from my new connection, and it's the shit you and B NasT are going to sell from now on. Now take another hit, but don't hit it so hard."

I take another hit, but it doesn't seem like anything is happening and I'm about to tell Trey that this shit ain't no good then all of a sudden my head starts to feel real light, and I feel the effects of the blunt all over my body. My heart rate slows a slight bit, and I hear the music that's coming from inside, but I not only hear it, I feel it too. It's like I have become a part of the music and all that surrounds me, and knowing this makes me feel invincible. This is some of the best shit I've ever had.

"How do you feel now little man?"

"Damn Trey this is some good shit."

"I know it. Now come on inside and enjoy the party."

I go back to the party and continue to have a good time but fifteen minutes later I start feeling real dizzy. I try to walk out of the room but fall over the couch onto the floor. B NasT helps me up and leads me to a little room down the hall.

"Damn dog your ass is wasted. Lay down on the bed until you get yourself together."

"Thank you B NasT man you is a good friend."

I lay down on the bed and the room starts to spin. I close my eyes, the spinning stops and I fall asleep. It seems like only minutes after that when all of a sudden all hell breaks loose.

There are lights and men shouting and people running, and before I can fully focus on what's happening I'm on the floor with handcuffs on, while the undercover cops pull bag after bag of weed from under the bed I was just lying on.

Three weeks later I'm standing beside my mother, in front of another judge. Trey set me up and pleaded not guilty to his own charges. His lawyer told the judge that the marijuana actually belonged to me.

The prosecution argued that I was too young to have possession of that much Marijuana, but they couldn't prove otherwise. None of the bags had Trey's fingerprints on them, and they didn't have one witness who could put Trey anywhere near the room. They couldn't even prove the party was given by Trey. Besides this was the first time Trey had ever even been arrested for possession.

The only thing they had were some surveillance tapes of Trey handing me a couple of brown bags that may or may not have had weed in them. The judge dropped all charges against Trey and that was that.

I found out later that Trey had been informed by one of the officers he was paying off that a bust was coming so he decided to let me take the fall. He put a crushed up valium in the blunt he gave me, waited until I passed out and put me in the room with the marijuana. Since I had already been busted twice it wasn't a stretch to pin it on me.

However this time I had my own lawyer. The lawyer told me what Trey did to me but I was too stupid to believe him.

"Naw Trey wouldn't do nothing like that to me." Mom looked at me with you must be crazy look.

"Andre the man is a dope dealer he doesn't care about you."

"And I guess you do huh? Where were you and daddy when I needed you?"

Mom just held her head down and didn't say anything else. My lawyer instructs me to keep my mouth shut then tells me I need to cooperate with the District Attorney or I may have to go to jail then he leaves the room to try and work out a deal.

He asks the District Attorney to release me to my mother with certain stipulations but the District Attorney isn't buying it. He tells my attorney the police surveillance unit has picked up a conversation with Trey and Marcus about a large stash of dope. He then explains they know Marcus and I were friends so they are pretty sure I know where the stash is. If I could be persuaded to tell them what I know they would consider reducing the charges other wise they are going to try to get the maximum sentence for me.

My mother and my attorney take me to a conference room and try to get me to cooperate.

"Andre as your attorney I have to tell you to take this deal and save yourself because Trey has used you to avoid prosecution. He's not worth your loyalty now."

"I ain't makin no deals and I don't know nothin."

"Andre, baby, don't you understand that if you don't cooperate their going to send you to jail for a long time. Baby please cooperate with the court."

"Look mom, don't worry about it. I'm a juvenile they can't hold me for long."

"That's not true Andre. They've already caught you twice with marijuana for resale and under the three strike rule and given the amount of marijuana you were found with this time they can charge you as an adult and give you the maximum, which is fifteen years. Now before you say anything else let me show you something."

The attorney turns on a video monitor and images Trey and his attorney fill the screen. I sit there and watch as Trey's attorney tells the court that I was the one who had come to the party with the weed. He also tells them that Trey had only found out about the drug use after the police raid.

The lawyer's last statement is the one that pisses me off. He told the judge that I had come to the party uninvited and without his knowledge I sold weed to some of his friends. The bastard lied right there in court and left my ass out there to fry. I wasn't going to let him get away with that.

After looking at the tape I agreed to cooperate and told the district attorney what I knew. I told them how I got started in the business and who I sold with and then I laid the bombshell on them. Not even my attorney knew what I was about to say.

I told them I not only knew where the weed was I also knew where Trey kept his books and I would tell them for a reduced sentence.

I knew where Trey kept his books because I accidentally walked by Trey's study and saw him putting the books in a floor safe under his file cabinet. When I realized what he was doing I walked away real quick so he didn't know I saw him, but now I was going to nail his ass.

The district attorney said after I finished he had all he needed to bust Trey's organization and he would recommend probation for me. The day of the court appearance I stood in front of the judge with my lawyer.

"Mr. Wright you've been charged with possession of eight pounds of marijuana for the purpose of resale. How do you plead?"

"We plead guilty your honor and my client has fully cooperated with the district attorney's office in exchange for probation."

The judge reads over the documents from my lawyer for a minute, and then asks the lawyer for the District Attorneys office if his office agreed with this. The lawyer says yes. Then he asks my mom if she agrees, she says yes and the judge signs the papers.

The judge reads the sentence. "I'm once again putting you in your mother's custody. However I want you to know this young man. If you ever come into my courtroom again you will receive the maximum sentence."

He bangs his gavel and I get up and walk out of the courtroom with mom.

As I'm walking out of the courtroom a free man, Trey is walking in with handcuffs on. He slows his pace and say's to me as he passes.

"Remember what I told you about snitchin. Bet you see me again."

As I walk out I remember Trey telling me if I ever snitched on him he would kill me and my mom, and I remembered the gun, but instead of getting scared I got angry. I decided right then and there to get a gun of my own. Nobody was going to hurt mom without paying with their own life. I didn't know mom had other plans for me and they required that I leave Philadelphia.

Now we're in a car headed for Ole Pops house. Somewhere in the back woods down south, which brings us back to where, we started.

I sat in our speeding car as we head further and further away from the only home I have ever known. Finally we pass a sign that says "Welcome to Kentucky" and reality hits me. Momma is serious about this. I am really going to miss my home.

We drive for several hundred miles with neither of us talking. I've never known my mom to be this mad at me. She wouldn't even look at me but she also wouldn't let me out of her sight. The one time I was let out of the car was to use the bathroom, and she stood outside the door until I got through.

When we reach the Mississippi State line I muster up the courage to ask a question.

"How long I got to stay here."

"I already told you until Ole Pop and Uncle Jesse tell me you can come home."

"I don't even know them so why do I have to stay here?"

"Because I can no longer handle you and I need to know that you are safe and with someone that can make you do the right things."

"If you can't make me do nothing how do you think a stranger's gonna make me do anything?" Mom didn't bother to answer that question. She just kept her eyes on the road, and she never said another word.

Chapter 4

I sat back in my seat and make up my sixteen year old mind that no old man was going to tell me what to do. After she drops me off I'm going to run away. I know how to hustle and all I had to do was find a few connections and I could set myself up in business.

She could send who ever she wanted after me. I would kill anyone who got in my way. I didn't need Ole Pop, I didn't need my mom, Hell I didn't need anyone. I was going to become the biggest gangster this country had ever seen.

The next sign I saw read Oxford Mississippi thirty miles. At the next exit mom turns off the interstate onto a four-lane highway. After another thirty minutes she turns off that highway onto a two-lane highway. She keeps driving until we are a long way from the city.

A half hour goes by before she makes another turn. This time she turns onto a gravel road and there is no sign of civilization anywhere, no buildings, no cars, nothing. We stay on the gravel road and drive through cornfields for another half hour before mom makes another turn and the gravel disappears, and we're on dirt. After several more turns I am beginning to wonder if we are going to get to a house at all.

Mom just keeps driving and we ride through several dry creek beds. She makes a final left turn and heads for a creek with at least a foot of water in it. When I saw her turn the car toward it I looked at her.

"I know you're not going to run through that water are you?"

She didn't say anything she just kept driving. We hit the creek bed with a splash then moved on.

About fifteen minutes later she makes a turn around several tall trees and straight through another field with corn growing in it then stops the car and gets out.

After opening the trunk, taking my bags out and putting them on the ground she opens my door and tells me to get out. I take my time about getting out of the car and before I know it mom has grabbed me by the collar, snatched me out and pushed me toward my bags.

Without saying a word she shuts my door, walks back over to the driver's side and gets back in the car. With tears in her eyes she looks at me.

"Andre I love you but I can not handle you. Learn everything Ole Pop teaches you."

Then she puts the car in gear and drives off, leaving me standing in the middle of a corn field.

She just left me there just like that. I have no idea where I am, and no idea of which way to go to get back home. I'm about to panic when I hear this deep voice come from out of nowhere. Well deep isn't quite descriptive enough for this sound.

This was that kind of deep that seems to come from everywhere at once. The voice didn't just come to my ears it seemed to hit me all over my body at the same time like the kick of the bass speakers in Trey's Benz. It was a low rumble like the sound of thunder as it rumbles across the sky after a lightning flash.

"You just going to stand there, or are you going to pick up those bags and take them in the house?"

I turn to find out where the voice is coming from. At first it's hard to see because the sun is in my eyes, but as the man behind the deep voice moves closer his outline becomes clear.

Standing over me by at least a foot is the biggest man I've ever seen. He has to be all of six foot seven, and he has to weigh at least three hundred plus pounds.

He is so big it looks as if the sun is setting on his huge shoulders which in it's self is not special. However his shoulders are so wide he not only looks as if he can carry the sun but from my vantage point the sun actually appears to belong on his wide shoulders. As if God placed it there and said, "You will be the bearer of my light."

He notices me squinting in the sun and moves closer so that the sun is totally behind him and I can see his face clearly. He is as black as any man I have ever seen, a deep, dark, powerful, noble black with the posture and stance of someone born of royal lineage. Something about the way he stands seems to say, "Here is what your ancestors looked like in their native land."

He is a most impressive sight, standing there with sweat rolling down his chest and arms. He looks like someone has polished him to a high gloss and left him in the sun to harden as if he were a black diamond.

His arms are as big as my legs, and his legs are as big as a Mississippi tree. He is by far the biggest, strongest man I have ever seen in my life. The only thing bigger than his muscles is the smile on his face.

At first glance my eyes are locked into his. There is a fire in his eyes, a very intense tangible fire. He seems to be looking into my soul and finding all the things I don't want anyone to know.

I turn my head from him to stop him from reading my soul but I can still see his face. He has the kind of face that automatically makes you think he's someone's grandfather. It's a strong face with age lines in it like an older man who has been working in the sun all his life.

His head is covered with a mixture of gray and black hair. The gray hair almost looks white especially against his black skin. He has it cut in the short style old men wear, but it's still thick and wavy.

He is indeed an awesome sight. Even for a hard headed teenager like me his image is a lot to take in. The combination of his black skin, his height, his wide sun bearing shoulders, intense eyes, stern rumbling voice, and stark gray hair bring to mind images of my youth back when my family went to church.

My Sunday school teacher Mrs. Houston would read us stories from the bible. One of my favorite stories was about Moses and the Israelites. With their backs to the sea and Pharaoh's men coming after them Moses used the staff of God to part the water allowing the Israelites to escape.

Right here, right now, with this strong old black man standing in front of me, I feel as if I'm in the presence of Moses. The only thing missing is the staff of God. If he had been standing there with God's staff in his hands I would have expected to look to either side of us and see water standing high above our heads.

I stood there frozen to the spot trying to take in what I was looking at. I was truly amazed by the sight of this huge man but then he spoke and the moment was lost.

"Son, did you hear what I said?"

I snap out of my trance, and return to my stupid teenage attitude.

"Yeah I heard what the hell you said ole man."

As soon as the words leave my mouth, he leans down and places his right hand on my shoulder and squeezes it. His hand is so big it covers me from my neck to the end of my shoulder. I try to move from under his hand but he grips me tighter.

"Ole man you need to back up off me."

"Son let me explain . . ."

I put my elbow in his chest and try to push him away as hard as I can.

"Dammit ole man I said back the hell up off me."

Ole Pop doesn't budge. He doesn't even appear to notice the push. He tightens his grip on my shoulder and pushes down on me so hard that my butt hits the ground with a plop and I can't move an inch. Then Ole Pop leans down until his face is directly in front of mine. It is at this point that I realize saying anything else could get me hurt. So I shut up and listen as he talks.

"Now that I've got your attention let me explain something to you. My name is Buford Jefferson Anderson. You can call me Buford, or Jefferson, or BJ, or Ole Pop, or even Ole Man as long as it's done with respect. I will respect you and you will respect me. If you don't, I'll get one of these switches off one of these trees and whoop your butt with it and I don't care how old you are. Don't ever make the mistake of cussing me again. Do you understand me?"

I sit there and look at him the way I do my mother when she says something I don't like. He presses down a little harder which causes me to bend at the waist and let me know that he still hadn't put the pressure on me he could put on me if he wanted to. Then he speaks slowly as if I am either hard of hearing or a little slow.

"I-said-do-you-understand-me?"

With the little air I still have left in my body I answer him.

"Yes sir."

As soon as he hears that he lets me go and smiles.

"Ole Pop will do son. Now that we understand each other c'mon let me show you where you'll be staying."

I pick up two of my bags and expect the old man to help me with the rest of them but he's already heading toward the house. Right from the beginning he was teaching me that I was going to have to carry my own weight around here but I didn't understand this yet.

I figure it's my turn to talk bad to him.

"Hey ole man, you just gonna leave my bags out here like that."

He turns and looks at me then looks at the bags.

"You mean to tell me a strong boy like you can't carry four little bags at the same time. Shoot, the young boys around here would've already had those bags in the house by now. But I forget you're from the city. You spend most of your time chasing the girls. I guess that's what makes you soft like them."

I stand there and look at him with one of my most angry looks. What did he just say? Did he just say I was trying to be like a girl?

"Ole man I ain't trying to be like no girl."

"I'm sorry son I didn't mean to insult you, but you look like you might be a little soft for a boy."

Did this old man just call me a bitch? I stood there a minute and decided that he had indeed called me a bitch. I went back and picked up all four bags and started to drag them toward the house.

I heard him chuckle to himself and I thought he was laughing at me struggling with my bags. I didn't realize it then but this ole man had gotten me to do more in a minute than my mother could get me to do in two days. This old man is strong, smart, and sneaky and I am going to have to watch him every day or he will have me doing all kinds of stuff.

His long strides soon leave me far behind. He passed a row of tall corn stalks and rounded the corner. I lost sight of him and a slight panic went through me. What if I lost sight of him completely?

What if I get completely lost out here? Would he come back to get me or would he expect me to find my way?

Listen to that. Here I was planning on running away. I was going to live on my own and become the biggest gangster in America. But I couldn't even find my way through a corn field and not only that I'm scared to death.

I walk pass the last row of corn stalks, turn the corner and right there in front of me is the biggest, whitest, house ever made. It had two stories to it, and the biggest front porch I've ever seen which was going to be a problem since it had at least eight large steps and I was going to have to drag these heavy bags up every one of them.

An old dog lay at the bottom of the steps, which caused me some concern. I had never been in contact with too many dogs except for Trey's Pit Bulls, and they were so mean I didn't get close to them that often.

This dog was something different though. It was bigger than Trey's dogs in fact it looked like it could swallow two of Trey's dogs at the same time without any problem. I stood there and looked at it, but it didn't seem to concern it's self with me in fact it never even opened its eyes.

"Wut's da matta boy? Yuh ain't scared uh ole blue is ya?"

I look up to see another old man sitting on one of the chairs on the porch. He is older than Ole Pop. He looks to be at least fifty years old. I find out later he's fifty eight. He is as dark as Ole Pop but nowhere near as big. He is about three or four inches taller than me, about six foot one.

The skin around his arms and face is wrinkled but his arms have enough muscle on them to let you know he can still take care of himself. There is a light in his eyes that should have let me know his mind is still sharp but since I was an angry teenager I didn't notice it. I would soon find out my mistake.

It took me a minute to realize that I was staring at him. I look back at the dog and mumbled, "Ain't nothing around here that can scare me especially a old nasty looking dog."

"Be careful how yuh talk bout ole blue he might bite yuh."

"If he does I'm going to own this place cause I'm going to sue every body around here."

"Hoooweee Buford, this one's got a lot uh smart mouth and attitude. What yuh need tuh do right now is go git one of dem elm switches, take off all his clothes and converse wit him for uh while. Then maybe yuh can talk wit him later."

He starts to laugh and a brown substance comes out of his mouth. He reaches down beside him, picks up a cup, spits into it, and wipes his mouth then laughs again.

"Naw Jesse we got an understanding just a few minutes ago out there in the field. I don't think a hide stripping is going to be necessary right now."

Ole Pop turns to me, "Well son you gonna sleep at the bottom of those steps or are you gonna take those bags to your room?"

"Where is my room?"

"Through the door up the stairs to your right."

I drag my bags up the first set of steps, through the front door and then I have to set them down. By this time the whole front of my shirt is wet with sweat. It has to be at least ninety-five degrees outside and dragging these heavy bags was no easy matter.

I sit there on my bags and look at the stairs I have to climb next. There has to be at least sixteen steps before I get to my room. About this time the door opens, it's the older man from the porch.

"Look at ya boy. You ain't done uh lick uh work and ya sweatin like somebody done poured water on ya. What's da matter don't dey teach ya how to do a hard days work where you from. Shoot, if you can't walk up da steps without gittin tired, ya ain't never gonna earn ya keep round heah."

I start to laugh because he sounds like one of those cowboys on the old black and white movies I used to watch with my dad.

"You need to go head on wit that cowboy shit ole man."

You would think I would've learned my lesson with Ole Pop but I didn't. Something in the back of my head tries to warn me that I have said the wrong thing but it's too late.

Before I know it, this ole man has raised his hand and slapped me dead in the mouth and I didn't even see it coming. As old as he is I should have seen it coming but he moved so fast I didn't even have a chance to duck.

I end up on my back with my bags spread all over the floor and my lip slowly swelling. He leaned down, grabbed me by the arm, and dragged me to my feet. I tried to pull away but his grip was almost as strong as Ole Pops.

"Boy, don't you ever sass me like dat agin heah?"

I was a bit dazed, but I knew I had better answer in a hurry. This ole man didn't look like he had the same patience Ole Pop did.

"Yes sir."

"You ain't gotta call me sir, Jesse will do just fine."

Then his voice changed and in perfect English he said, "By the way, never underestimate someone you've just met. It may cost you in the long run."

Then he smiled and his southern drawl came back.

"Now lemme help ya wit dem bags."

He grabbed three of the bags and was up the steps before I could bend down and pick mine up. By the time I made it to the top of the steps he was coming back down.

"Dats yo room over yonder."

He pointed to the open door and went on back down the steps. I carried my bag into the room and put it down. This room was much bigger than my bedroom at home, but the only things it had in it were a bed and a small dresser. It was hot in there too. The sun was coming through the opened window which made the room hotter than normal. It had to be a hundred degrees in there and even though the window was open there wasn't a breeze so that didn't help.

I sit down on the bed, feel my lip, look around the room and almost started crying. How could mom leave me here with these mean old men? All she had to do was let me come home I would have done what she told me to do. As I sat there I began to wonder if I would ever see her again.

"Son you need to start unpacking your things. Dinner will be ready in a while."

I looked up at the door and it was Ole Pop. I just stared at him. He was even bigger than I thought he was at first. He filled the whole doorway with his body. His shoulders were only a half an inch from touching both sides of the door. He walked into the room, and sat down on the dresser.

"What happened to your lip?"

"Nothing."

"Uh huh, just decided to swell up on its own huh?"

I looked at the floor and didn't say anything and he got up to leave the room.

"Well just put your things away and if you need some more space you can get the dresser out of the storage shed in the back."

He starts to walk out but before he leaves, over his shoulder he says, "Ole Jesse's pretty fast and hit's pretty hard for an old man don't he?" Then he heads back down the steps.

I sit there for a few more minutes then I start to unpack. I've made up my mind that as soon as I find out where I was, I was out of here. But as long as I was here I might as well make myself comfortable. The first thing I need is my CD player. I'll put the headphones on, turn the CD player up, and not listen to anything either one of them has to say.

I open the first bag, then the second, then the third, and then the fourth. No CD player in any of them. Mom forgot to pack my CD player. How was I going to survive without my music?

Twenty minutes later Ole Pop walks back into my room.

"Son, dinner is ready, and by the way if you're looking for your CD player, I told your mom not to pack it. When I talk I want to make sure you hear every word I say."

As soon as he says this he turns back around and before I can say anything he's headed back down the steps.

"How the hell is he gonna tell my mom not to pack my CD player. Who the hell does he think he is? He ain't my daddy, and he ain't gonna run my life. As soon as I can I'll be out of this damn house."

I sit back down on the bed mad as hell. I ain't gonna listen to what he has to say, I ain't gonna do nothing around here, and I sure as hell ain't going down those steps to eat with a man I can't stand. I'll just sit up here and wait until it cools down so I can go to sleep.

Chapter 5

Thirty minutes pass and I lay back on the bed to think of how I was going to make my escape. I was still mad and determined that I wasn't going downstairs but my stomach was starting to betray me.

I lay there for another fifteen minutes until an aroma I had never smelled before came up the stairs to get me. It was a faint scent at first, but it kept getting stronger and stronger. It was a sweet smell like cake, but not quite cake. It came up the stairs, into my room, and surrounded me. It was warm and friendly and it settled in my nose and made my stomach pay attention to it.

What is that wonderful smell my stomach kept saying, but I was determined not to go down the stairs. As determined as I was though, my stomach was even more determined. At first it just rumbled but soon the rumble got louder and louder and then as if to tell me I wasn't listening my stomach started to hurt. After about twenty more minutes of this I could ignore it no longer I slowly made my way down the stairs to the kitchen.

When I get to the kitchen I see Ole Pop standing by the sink washing dishes. There is no food anywhere in the kitchen. Sitting at the table was Jesse with that crooked smile on his face eating what was left of his food.

"Well look who decided to come downstairs? Boy you're a little late. We're through eating now."

I sit down in a chair beside the table and my stomach growls again. Ole Pop speaks to me with his back turned.

"Son I told you dinner was ready about an hour ago. We eat dinner together and on time around here."

Now I'm mad cause I came down and mad cause there wasn't anything to eat. Ole Pop finishes washing the dishes then slides a plate full of food in front of me and walks away. However once again, over his shoulder as he walks away, he says.

"Don't miss dinner time again. I won't hold a plate for you next time. Before you eat don't forget to say grace and wash that plate before you leave the kitchen."

He walks out the door and I turn back around, pick up a chicken leg, and just before I can put it to my lips, Jesse puts his hand gently on my arm.

"Boy, always give thanks to the Lord. He provides everything you'll ever need."

I don't argue. I bow my head and say grace. Jesse gets up from the table, washes his plate and fork then leaves me alone to eat in peace.

I sat there eating the chicken and the bread. I don't know which I liked the best, the chicken or the bread? The chicken tasted better than any thing we ever got from any of the chicken places back home and they were bigger pieces too and the bread was the best bread I've ever put in my mouth.

It is sweet and so smooth it almost melts in your mouth. This must be what I smelled when I was up in the room. I finished the bread and chicken, but I didn't eat any of the vegetables on the plate.

After I finished, I walked over to the trash can, opened the lid and started to pour the rest of the contents of the plate in the trash when I heard Jesse's voice.

"What you doing boy?"

I turn to face him, "I'm cleaning my plate like the ole man told me to do."

"Why you throwing that good food away?"

"I didn't want it, and nobodies going to eat after me."

"Uh huh. Is that what they teach you in the city boy? If you don't like it just throw it away. No wonder ya'll always buying stuff and staying in debt up there. You're always wasting things. Ain't no call for you to dump that food in the trash can when there's a slop can out back you can put it in so it can be fed to the hogs."

"A slop can? What's a slop can?"

Jesse starts laughing again and spits that brown stuff out of his mouth. After he stops laughing he wipes his mouth.

"I just told you what it is. It's the place you put food you don't want so it won't go to waste cause it can be fed to the hogs."

"What is a hog?"

Evidently that was more than Jesse could take. He starts laughing, and spitting until he has to sit down. By that time Ole Pop has joined us in the kitchen.

"What's going on in here? Jesse, what's got you laughing so hard?"

It took Jesse a minute to answer because he was trying to talk, and laugh, and spit at the same time. When he finally calmed down and wiped his chin, Ole Pop was sitting down at the kitchen table.

"Buford the boy don't even know what a hog is."

Ole Pop let out a deep little chuckle, "Son is that right? You don't know what a hog is."

"Why would I need to know what a hog is? I ain't never seen one where I live. That's just one of those country things you old folks down here have."

"Is that right? Well let me ask you another question. Do you like bacon, pork chops, ham, or hot dogs?"

"Yeah I do, so what?"

"Do you know where those things come from?"

"Yeah, they come from a pig?"

"Well, well, well Jesse at least he knows that much. Well son a hog is a bigger version of a pig."

"In other words hog is the country word for pig."

"No. A hog is just what I said it is. It's a bigger version of a pig."

Jesse gets up walks over to the kitchen window that overlooks the back yard then motions for me to come over where he is. I walk over there and stand beside him.

"You see that little bitty brown thing over there by the barn."

It took a few seconds because the animal was so little and its color almost matched the barn, but I finally saw it.

"Yeah I see it that's a pig."

"Well Jesse he got that one right."

They both laugh then he points toward another direction and when I turn all I see at first is mud. After a few seconds something big rises up out of the mud. It had to be three times as big as any dog

I had ever seen and it was wide too. The little pig ran over and got up under it.

Ole Pop smiles, "That there is a hog."

I watch as the pig takes something in its mouth and holds onto to it.

"What's the pig doing to it?" Jesse spoke up, "It's suckin teat."

"It's what."

"It's suckin milk from its momma's teat?"

"Ughhhh! That's just nasty."

Jesse laughed and said, "You didn't say that when you was suckin teat?"

"Don't play Ole man I never sucked nobodies teat."

Ole Pop let out a booming laugh. These old men were having quite a laugh at my expense.

I turned and looked at him, "What you laughing at ole man?"

"Right after you were born I went into your mother's room. When I asked her how she was doing she said she was alright but her breast felt a little funny cause she had just breast fed you for the first time."

Right about there Jesse lost it again. He spit that brown stuff all over the floor in front of him.

"See there I told ya. I knew you had sucked some teat."

He fell out laughing again. I just looked at him until he got himself composed. Then I ask him a question,

"Ole man what is that brown stuff you keep spitting all over the floor?"

He pulls out a tin can with a label on it that said "Snuff" and puts it on the table. "It's called snuff. You want to try a little bit."

"Naw that stuff looks nasty. How do you put that stuff in your mouth?"

"The same way you inhale that stuff that makes you silly, into your lungs." I turn and walk away, "I don't know what you're talking about ole man."

"Yeah you do. You know what I mean. What do they call that stuff? They call it weed don't they? Well boy if it's really weed, why is it illegal?"

"Cause the white man don't want to see a Nigga make some money and come up in the world."

Ole Pop looks me dead in the eyes. "Son that's a word we don't use around here."

"What word?"

"That ignorant term you just used for your own race."

"You mean nigga."

"Once again son we don't use that word in this house."

"Why Ole man? What's wrong with the word nigga?"

"It's a word invented by ignorant people, to deny another race of people their dignity."

"Naw it ain't ole man. I know that's what it used to be, but we flipped the script on the white man. When we use it, it's a positive thang. Like when I call my boy my nigga that means he's my friend."

"I see. So what you're saying is since you young boys use it on each other that makes it all right. It becomes a good thing. Then why did you get offended back there in the corn field when I told you, you were soft like a girl? I mean after all you are my nephew and I meant it in the best of terms."

"I ain't tryin to be no girl."

"What's the matter son does it bother you that I used a negative term toward you? I thought you said since it was used by some one you knew it was alright."

"I don't know you and we wasn't talking about me we was talking about the word nigga."

"Right, the word nigga is a negative term. Just like the words I used that you took offense to. Words are very powerful. And negative words should never be used especially to describe a race of people. You need to understand something son. If something smells like shit when it's in your hands no matter how you try to change it, even if you add perfume to it, it's still gonna smell like shit when you pass it to me. So if you and your friends think using the word nigga to describe each other makes it right then all you're doing is spreading shit all over the place and I prefer that you don't spread it in my house."

Ole Pop gets up and walks out of the room followed by Jesse who is still laughing at me as he walks out. Both these old men are about on my last nerve. I'll be glad when I find out where I am so I can leave this place.

I walk back into my room and sit down. Ole Pop has put a fan in my window, and a lamp on my dressing table. That's when I realize there is no light-switch on the wall and no ceiling light, and the lamp is a little thing with a forty-watt bulb in it. Right now that doesn't mean anything but I will find out how much it really means later on tonight.

It's still hot, but the sun has just about set and the fan is circulating air through the room so it's cooling off slowly. It won't be long before it will be cool enough for me to go to sleep. And after that long ride from Philadelphia I was wore out any way.

At nine o'clock, Ole Pop turns off the television and heads for bed. The house grows dark and silent. I shut my door and get in the bed. That little bitty lamp Ole Pop put in the room is on the opposite end of the room and the little light it gives off is barely enough to light the whole room properly.

As I lie there I start to notice things about the country. First of all it's too quiet here. I don't mean kinda quiet like in Philadelphia. I mean grave yard quiet.

In Philadelphia even when it's two o'clock in the morning you can still hear all kinds of sounds coming from the street. Someone is always driving through, or you can hear the trucks driving across the interstate, or someone's stereo system is blasting. Something is always making noise in the night.

In the country none of those sounds are heard. Just a total quiet that is unnerving. You would think that with all the animals around a farm there would be a lot of noise at night, but I guess they go to sleep too. After a few minutes I realize there are sounds outside, they're just different. I start to focus in on the sounds around me. I have never heard any of these sounds in Philadelphia.

The first one I remember is the sound of crickets. They sound like they are in the room with me. Then way off in the distance I hear a wolf howl. If you've never heard a wolf howl on a country night in a quiet house then you've never really had goose bumps rise up on your back. That has got to be one of the most eerie sounds I have ever heard. I half expect some crazy person to start chopping on my door with an axe.

While my imagination runs wild I hear a rumbling sound and it sounds as if it were getting closer. After a few moments I realized it is a train. Way off in the distance you can hear it rumbling across the tracks.

That rumbling sound actually was kind of soothing but the effect didn't last long. From out of nowhere came the train whistle. I don't know why they call it a whistle. From a distance it sounds more like a woman moaning in pain and in the dark and quiet of the country it is a very scary sound.

I sat up in bed and the trained whistles again. This time it sounds like a woman crying in the night. It makes me think of my mother. I start to cry I missed her so much. I didn't want to admit to myself I was scared, but I was. I wasn't used to this and I was absolutely sure I wouldn't be staying here very long.

The breeze coming through the window picked up causing the limbs on the tree beside the house to move. Every once in a while one of those limbs would scrape the side of the house causing me to stiffen and look around as if someone or something was trying to enter the room. I laid there with the covers up around my chin for about an hour before I drifted off to sleep.

At two o'clock in the morning I awake to the sound of someone coming up the stairs. At first I am disoriented and don't realize where I am, then as I become aware of where I am I realize that someone has cut off my light. It is pitch black in my room. I also have a blanket on me that wasn't on me at first. And then it hits me. I'm shaking and it is cold in the room.

It has to be at least seventy-five degrees in here. And while seventy five degrees isn't really cold, it feels cold since it had been one hundred degrees just a few hours ago. I pull the blanket under my chin and wait for whoever it is coming up the stairs to walk into my room but they never do.

There is a full moon outside my window my eyes start to focus and after a while I'm able to see everything in the room. There are shadows all over the place and they seem to be moving around. It's just my imagination but one of the shadows outside appears to be a man standing beside my window.

I'm on the second floor at least fifteen feet off the ground. My mind knows this isn't possible but my heart doesn't agree, I get up, turn the light back on, get back in bed but find it hard to go back to sleep.

It's four o'clock before I fall asleep again and just when I'm about to turn over and get that good sleep, Ole Pop comes in and shakes me.

"Son it's five o'clock time to get up and go to work."

I roll over, look at him like he's crazy and roll back over. He shakes me again.

"I said its five o'clock time to go to work."

I mumble something and cover my head. The next thing I know the blanket and sheet are off me and I'm on the floor.

"Son, I'm not about to argue with you every morning about getting up. At five o'clock you will get up and get ready to go to work. Everyone around here works or they don't eat."

I get up off the floor, "Ole man I ain't about to do no work around here. I didn't ask to come here in the first place."

"That's fine son. But you won't stay in the bed all day either. Now go wash up. There are rags and towels in the hall closet. Then get dressed and make up your bed. Oh and if you don't plan on doing any work, don't bother coming down to breakfast."

He turns and heads back down stairs.

I wash up, get dressed, make up my bed, and sit down on it. I'm lost in my plans to run away when Ole Pop interrupts my thoughts.

"By the way did I tell you that you were free to leave here anytime you wanted?"

"That's not what mom said. She said I couldn't leave here until you said I could."

Ole Pop drops his head to the side and stares into my eyes with a look that screamed, "Are you really as stupid as you sound?"

"Son you don't listen very well do you? Didn't I just get through saying you could leave here anytime you want to?"

I look at him for a minute not comprehending what he's just said. Why would mom bring me all the way down here just so he could let me go the next day? Ole Pop interrupts my thoughts again.

"Are you still with me son?"

"Yeah I hear you ole man and I'm outta here."

"Well before you go, you might want to take a look out this window."

I walk over to the window and he shows me the farm.

"Son, Jesse and I own fifty five hundred acres of land. That's a lot more than a city block. Most of it is still undeveloped. Beyond my land is fifteen miles of woods. Now I know you can take care of yourself, but before you go let me give you some advice. Look over to your left."

I look over and see a huge bull roaming around in a large pinned in area.

"That's Buster. He's the biggest meanest bull in Mississippi. I bought him for breeding purposes but I also got him so he can patrol that part of the farm where the cows are, and keep the bobcats, and wolves and bears away from the herd. If you decide to leave, you need to know that you won't get to another house for twenty five miles in any direction. You won't get to a highway for thirty miles in any direction, and I don't think you can hike twenty or thirty miles while the sun is up especially since you don't know where you're going. Which means you will have to travel at night and there are animals out there that will kill and eat you. And there are also animals out there you've been taught are timid like deer that will kill you to protect their turf. If you don't believe me take these field glasses and look for yourself."

Ole Pop hands me the binoculars and look through them at the woods he's pointing at. I see five or six full-grown wolves circling a deer. I'm fascinated because the only time I've ever seen this is on cable television.

I watch as the wolves attack the deer. The deer fights them off for a long time but eventually the wolves win. After they get the deer down they began tearing him apart. I stop looking after that.

Ole Pop takes the glasses. "Now son you're free to go. I ain't gonna try and stop you, but I also ain't gonna come looking for you. I'll call your momma and tell her you decided to leave and if you make it home that'll be just fine with me. Then he turned around and walked out the door leaving me to think about my plans to leave.

Chapter 6

So he thinks that a few wild animals are going to keep me here. I ain't scared of no animals. I survived the streets can't nothing be harder than that. But still I couldn't get the sight of those wolves tearing at the flesh off that deer out of my mind. The more I thought about it, the more I figured I would just stay here until I could find some transportation.

I sat there by the window and watched Ole Pop and Jesse get the tractor out of the barn and head out to the fields. I waited until they were out of sight and decided I would go and look for the transportation I needed.

I walked out onto the porch and there at the bottom of the steps was that big ole dog again, but this time I wasn't too much worried about him. I did however walk as far to the other side of the steps as possible. I still didn't want to get too close.

I looked around and decided to start with the barn. As I crossed the yard I noticed what looked like a big chicken coming toward me. It wasn't until I had been pecked twice that I realized this big chicken was after me.

I sprinted to the barn and with it running close behind me opened the door, ran in, and shut the door. I stopped there for a second and heard a noise behind me. When I turned around the biggest, meanest, foul smelling mule I have ever seen confronted me. He made a loud noise like a car horn and I was off again.

I ran out the door leaving it opened and ran back toward the porch. The big chicken spotted me, spread its wings, and started running after me. I stumbled, and fell and before I knew it the big chicken was on me. I covered my head to keep from getting pecked in the eyes then all of a sudden I heard this loud bark and the big chicken was gone. I looked up just in time to see the ole dog that had been sitting by the porch chasing the big chicken back toward the barn. I didn't know it yet but ole blue was going to be my best friend.

After my experience in the yard, I went back into the house and sat down on the living room couch. My back and neck were hurting and I still didn't find what I was looking for and as far as I was concerned if the rest of the animals in the yard were like that big chicken then it was going to be a long time before I found transportation. I was still sitting there at twelve looking at television when Ole Pop and Jesse came back.

Ole Pop walked into the house right pass me without saying a word. Jesse came in behind him and looked at me.

"Boy, what happened to your neck?"

"Nothing."

"Nothing huh? Looks to me like you been bit or something."

Ole Pop walked back into the room, put his hand on the side of my face, and tilted it a little so he could see the peck marks.

"Son, what happened?"

"I said nothing."

"It had to be something. You're bleeding."

He let my face go, walked back into the kitchen, and got some alcohol and cotton. He returns, sits down beside me, pours some alcohol on the cotton, and presses it to my wound. I grimace because it burns.

"Now, you want to tell me what happened."

"I went out in the yard and that big chicken chased me. I fell down and he jumped me and pecked me."

Jesse let out a laugh that was so loud ole blue started barking.

"Chicken, Buford he called it a chicken."

"That's what it is ole man a chicken. I know what a chicken looks like."

"Son, that's not a chicken it's a Tom turkey."

"A what?"

"A male turkey, you know the bird your mother cooks every Christmas."

"That's a turkey? Why did it attack me?"

"He was protecting his territory. Anything between here and the barn is his territory and you're lucky, it could have been worse. He not only pecked you but he spurred you as well. If he had got to your eyes you would have been in trouble. How did you get him off of you?"

"The dog ran him away."

Jesse laughed again. "So ole blue likes ya huh? Well you must be somethin special cause ole blue don't just take up with everybody."

Ole Pop finished putting the band-aid on my neck, got up and went back into the kitchen. After about thirty minutes I smelled that wonderful smell coming from the kitchen again so I walked in. Ole Pop and Jesse were eating and on the table was ham and those wonderful rolls. I walked over to the cabinet and got a plate and a fork. I sit down and was about to pick up a roll when Ole Pop said, "What are you doing?"

"I'm getting something to eat."

"Son I told you this morning, around here, if you don't work, you don't eat and I meant that."

"Oh so you're going to let me go hungry just to prove a point. Wait until mom hears about this."

"Will you listen to that Jesse? Fifteen years old, been to court more times than I have and I'm fifty two, trying to act tough like a man, and the first thing he does when his butt gets in trouble is call his momma."

I sat there and looked at him. I can't believe it. Now this old man is calling me a momma's boy which to a young man like me is the same thing as a bitch. This old man has called me a bitch twice and gotten away with it. I'm really starting to get tired of his ass.

He turns around and looks me square in the eyes.

"Well you go ahead and call her, but I can guarantee she won't be coming for you. She brought you down here so you could learn about responsibility and being a man and the first thing you're going to learn around here is to take responsibility for your own actions. I'm not the one who's causing you to be hungry, you are. The rules around here are simple. If you work you eat, if you don't work you don't eat. You are the one who determines if you eat or not. All you have to do is go by the rules."

"I'm not going to be a slave for nobody ole man."

Ole Pop gives me that same "Are you stupid" look he gave me this morning. Then he proceeds to cut me to shreds and teach me some history at the same time.

"You don't know what it is to be a slave. You wouldn't have survived if you had been a slave. It takes a strong person to survive under bondage and you're too busy feeling sorry for yourself to be one of them. Besides I haven't shackled you, beat you, sold you to, or bought you from anyone. So stop acting like I'm trying to take advantage of you. You want to act like a grown man with all the privileges but you don't want any of the responsibility. Well around here that ain't gonna cut it. If you work you eat, if you go to school you get an education, if you get an education you get a good job. I hope you noticed that all these things can be accomplished only if you do what you're supposed to do. Nothing positive will ever happen in your life as long as you don't take control of it. Now if you want something to eat go up to your room and put your clothes away like I told you to do yesterday. Then you can come back down and eat but you had better make it fast, lunch is over in thirty minutes."

What could I do? I was stuck out in the wilderness, I didn't have a clue where I was, I didn't have any transportation, and I had just been attacked and beaten by a turkey. I didn't really have much of a choice. I went upstairs, rolled my clothes up into individual balls and stuffed them in the drawers the best I could then I went downstairs to eat.

Once again the ole man had gotten me to do in five minutes what my mother couldn't get me to do in a week. I had only been here two days but now I wish I had just gone to jail. This was going to be worse than any jail time I could've done. I had to find a way out of here.

After lunch Ole Pop asked me if I was ready to earn my way. I looked at him and asked him if I had any choice. He said no and that was that. He handed me a straw hat and I got on the back of the tractor and headed out to the fields with him.

When we got there Ole Pop led me out to a field of beans. He handed me a funny looking rake and told me it was a hoe. This time it was my turn to laugh. He asked me what I was laughing at and I told him the only time I had ever heard that word was when someone was talking about a woman.

He gave me that look of disapproval then told me he didn't think it was funny to belittle our women like that. He said women are truly a wondrous gift from God. However right after that he said at least I was showing signs of having a sense of humor even if it was the wrong kind.

He took me out to the middle of a cornfield, showed me how to use a hoe, told me to put my hat on, and left me out there in the hot sun to work. I wasn't about to put that hat on. I wasn't going to look like a dumb ass country boys and since I didn't want to be there anyway and it was hot, I took my time doing the work.

I'd been out there about an hour when I felt a bug crawling on my arm and I smacked it without looking. Three seconds later my arm felt like it was on fire. I had never felt anything that hurt as bad as that. I screamed and started running toward the tractor. Half way there Jesse caught me.

"What's wrong boy?"

I pointed to the spot on my arm, "Something bit me."

"Here let me see that."

He took my arm and looked at it. By that time Ole Pop had found us.

"What's wrong Jesse?"

"He just got hisself stung by a yellow jacket that's all."

"Son are you allergic to stings?"

"I don't know but this hurts bad."

"Well Jesse is going to take care of you."

Jesse took out a pouch, opened it up and pulled out some stuff that could have been mistaken for weed. He put a small amount in his mouth and chewed it then pulled it out was about to put it on my arm. I pulled my arm back.

"What you getting ready to do with that?"

"I'm gonna to put it on your arm so it can pull the stinger out and reduce the swelling."

"Naw you ain't. I ain't gonna let you take something out of your mouth and put it on my arm."

"Okay, suit yourself. When you want that sting to stop hurting let me know."

He turns to walk away. Was he joking or was he for real? I decided that it hurt bad enough to at least let him try it.

"Jesse are you serious about that stuff. You ain't trying to play another joke on me are you?"

"Boy I don't play when it comes to bites and stings. I've seen people almost die from a sting or a bite. Now if you want my help I'll help you."

I stuck my arm out, turned my head and closed my eyes. He put the stuff on me and wrapped a rag around it and almost immediately it stopped hurting.

"Hey it stopped hurting. What is that stuff?"

"It's tobacco and like I told ya it draws the stinger out so the wound can heal."

"How did you find that out Jesse?"

"Boy there are a lot of things old black folks know that will help when it comes to healing. Some were brought with us from Africa and others were discovered out of necessity. We didn't always have money for doctors. We had to find ways of healing our selves without the benefit of hospitals. We tried lots of things and those things that worked have been passed down from generation to generation."

Jesse pronounced me cured and Ole Pop put me back to work. But this time he didn't put me where I could stand in the middle of the field, half doing the work he put me in the cornfield pulling and shucking corn. My instructions were to have six-bushel baskets filled with shucked corn before dinner. But before he could leave he had to show me what shucking meant.

"Son, you really don't know anything about farm work do you? All shucking means is to take the green leafy cover off the corn so you can see the corn kernels."

He pulled an ear of corn off the stalk and shucked it so I could see what he meant then he turned to walk away and said over his shoulder, "And you better hurry up, dinner is in three hours."

Now I had to work. The old man was smart. I couldn't get away with nothing around here.

Every once in a while Ole Pop would come and check on me and joke about how little work I was getting done, and make me take ten minutes in the shade. He said I needed time to get use to work in the sun. Whatever the reason for the ten minute breaks I was glad he was letting me take them.

In about an hour's time I had done two bushels of corn. I thought I was getting the hang of it. In fact I thought I was probably as good and fast as Ole Pop and Jesse. Of course that thought only lasted a little while until Jesse turned the corner on the row beside me.

I was half way finished with my row when he turned the corner but by the time I had gotten to the three quarter point he was almost even with me. I tried to go faster just to show him I could work as hard as he could but there was no way to keep up with him. He was moving so fast that I began to have doubts about his age. There ain't no way he could be sixty something years old. No one that's as old as he claims to be could move that fast. In thirty minutes he had two bushel baskets filled and was working on his third. I stopped to look at him and he saw me.

"What you looking at boy? You didn't think ole Jesse could move as fast as he does did ya? Well boy I can keep up with young'ns half my age and I been doing this for a long time. Now hustle up it's almost time to go home."

I didn't say anything I just turned around and tried to improve my speed.

These old men were making me look bad at every turn and there wasn't a thing I could do to stop them. All I could do was the best I could and hope that I finally get to go back to the house cause the heat was terrible and the sun just beamed down on my head but even that would be alright if I could keep it out of my eyes so I could see better. Right about this time Ole Pop walked up to me and put that big ole straw hat on my head.

"Son I don't care if you think the hat is country, I do care if you suffer heat stroke out here because you didn't wear it. Besides it will keep the sun out of your eyes and help you see better. And oh yeah, every straw boss has to wear his hat."

"What's a straw boss?"

Ole Pop looked at me and let out that low rumbling laugh.

"The straw boss is the head slave." Then he turned around and walked away.

Now I was mad. He was making fun of me again. This old man is getting on my nerves and how the hell does he come around at the right time every time? It seems like every time I get a thought in my head he comes by and reads it and has a solution for it.

This was getting scary. He hadn't known me but two days and already he seemed to know more about me than I wanted him to know. I'm going to have to be careful what I think around him. What did I just say? Now I'm acting like I actually think he can read minds. I think the sun is getting to me.

At six o'clock Ole Pop came and told me it was quitting time. By that time I had done five and a half bushels of corn. Ole Pop looked at the basket then told me that I did a pretty good job for a city boy and I actually smiled. After I got my baskets on the trailer we headed for home.

We pulled the trailer into the barn, unloaded the vegetables and put them in the storage room inside the barn and headed for the house. I went upstairs to wash up and Ole Pop started dinner. Forty-five minutes later Ole Pop called me down to dinner we said grace and started to eat. Jesse started right in on me,

"Buford did you see the boy running through the field? You'd uh thought buster was afta him he was running so fast."

"Yeah and he can holler real loud too."

"Whoowee, sounded like a freight train coming through the field."

They both broke up laughing and continued to eat. I didn't see nothing funny about it. That wasp sting hurt like hell and I had never seen a wasp like that before.

We finished eating and washed the dishes and I went into the living room to watch television. Jesse and Ole Pop walked past me. Jesse had a guitar in his hand and I wondered what he was going to do with that. I hoped he wasn't going to play any of that country stuff.

After about five minutes I hear guitar music coming through the window from the porch but it's not country its blues and it has a good beat to it. I moved over by the door and listened.

Jesse was playing the guitar and Ole Pop was playing the harmonica. He put it up to his mouth and blew and it sounded a little like the organ we had at our church. They played for a while and I was beginning to like what I heard.

Jesse asked Ole Pop if he remembered the apple wine blues. Ole Pop said yeah and Jesse started to play and to my surprise Ole Pop started to sing in that deep bass voice and he sounded good.

Twang twang twang twang twang, "Well my woman done left me."
Twang twang twang twang twang, "Left me wit my ole dog blue."
Twang twang twang twang twang, "And he done sit up and told me."
Twang twang twang twang twang, "Son I'm gonna leave you too."
Twang twang twang twang twang, "The crops done burned up."
Twang twang twang twang twang, "The tractor broke down."
Twang twang twang twang twang, "I ain't got nothin left but this bottle of apple wine."

Jesse joined in on the chorus, "Apple wine, apple wine let's get drunk off this good ole apple wine. Apple wine apple wine another drink and everything will be fine."

I sat there and listened to Jesse and Ole Pop sing the song and didn't realize I was tapping my feet to the rhythm. This was pretty good music, not as good as my rap but it was pretty good just the same.

At nine o'clock Ole Pop told me it was time for bed. My first thought was, "How you gonna tell a grown man what time he had to go to bed?" I thought it but I didn't say it. I didn't feel like listening to another lecture by Ole Pop besides I was too damn tired to argue.

I have never been this tired in all my life. He didn't have to tell me twice. I was so tired I didn't think I could get up the stairs to my room. I was asleep before I had settled down in the bed good. I didn't have to worry about being afraid tonight the fan was blowing a nice cool breeze across my bed and sleep was the only thing on my mind.

Chapter 7

Five o'clock the next morning Ole Pop woke me up.

"C'mon son it's time to get up."

"Aw mom, I ain't gotta go to school today." Ole Pop laughed, "I know you don't but you do have to go to work."

I open my eyes and focus on Ole Pop's back as he walks out the door and remember I'm not at home and mom wasn't the one waking me up. I've been here four days and I miss her so much. Tears fill my eyes and I don't notice that Ole Pop has walked back into the room.

"You're beginning to miss your mom aren't you son?"

I immediately wipe my eyes and put that tough teenage attitude back on.

"What's it to you old man? It ain't like you're going to let me go home any time soon."

"Son like I told you at first, you can leave any time you feel you're ready."

"Do I look like an idiot? I don't know where I am and according to you I gotta walk for two or three days just to get to the nearest house. And to top that there are wild animals out in the woods I have to walk through. The only way I'm going to get back home is to wait on somebody around here to take me and that ain't going to happen too soon. So you know I don't have any choice but to stay here."

"Well son I think I'll start with your first question. Do you look like an idiot? Yes you do but it's not for the reasons you just gave. You look like an idiot because you're the one who got your butt sent down here in the first place. If you had taken the time to obey

61

the mother that you're sitting here missing right now you wouldn't even be here. Once again you want to blame every one else for the mistakes you made. Now son I'm going to say this again and I'll keep saying it until you hear me. I'm not keeping you here. I would like for you to stay and enjoy yourself, but I don't beg anybody to stay in my house. In life there are always choices and you're the one who controls that part of your life. Right now you have a choice to make, stay or go. If you go that's your concern, but if you stay you will take responsibility for your own actions and you will work just like every one else. Oh, and if you decide to stay you need get dressed and come downstairs, breakfast is ready."

Ole Pop turns and walks out of my room. I stand there staring at his back with pure hatred in my eyes. Who the hell does he think he is? He ain't nothing but an old man with a broke down ass farm. There ain't no way I am going to let his country ass tell me what to do.

I decide right then and there I'm not going to work today and as soon as they leave I'm out of here. These two old men have seen the last of me. I ain't about to stay in this country ass place for the rest of my life. I'm gonna make it back home and when I do I'm going to hustle so hard that in three years I can retire and live the good life.

Thirty minutes later Ole Pop walks back into my room.

"It's time to go son."

"I ain't going."

Ole Pop looks at me with that same look he gave me in the field when we first met and I look away. He turns to walk away and says over his shoulder, "Be careful out there in the woods and if you get into trouble you know where the house is."

Then he walks out of my room down the steps, through the front door and gets on his tractor.

I wait until I see the tractor with Ole Pop and Jesse on it turn the corner around the corn field then I get some clothes and my back pack, go into the kitchen and get some food put it all in my backpack get the baseball bat from Ole Pops hall closet and leave the house.

First thing I had to decide was which way I was going to go. Actually that was the easiest decision. I couldn't go in the direction Ole Pop did, that would mean I would have to listen to Jesse laugh at me as I passed them in the field so I went in the opposite direction.

As I walked I noticed that everything looked alike. There wasn't anything in these woods that I could mark to tell me which way to go. Every tree looked the same.

After two hours of walking and seeing the same trees I had just about decided I was walking in circles so I sat down to rest. That was when I noticed the dog way off in the distance. He was just standing there looking at me. He wasn't a big dog in fact he was rather thin so it didn't bother me that he was there.

After I took a drink of water and ate a piece of chicken, I got up and started walking again. I heard a rustling sound behind me and I turned to see the same dog. He had gotten a little closer and I could see that he had a gray color, which I thought was unusual, I had never seen a dog with that kind of color to him.

As I walked I would look back every once in a while to see if my visitor was still there and every time I looked around he was there. I decided I would try to make friends with him after all I could use the company but every time I would stop and try to get close or call him he would stop or back off so I decided to try to get closer by throwing him a piece of chicken.

He picked up the chicken and watched me while he backed off and ate it. I soon realized he wasn't going to make friends he was just going to follow me in hopes of getting more food out of me so I turned around and kept walking. After another hour I got tired and decided to rest.

I found a dead tree lying on the ground and sat down on it, that's when I heard the growling. I turned around expecting to see the gray dog standing in the distance like he had been and instead was confronted by him and three others, and they weren't dogs, they were wolves and they were just a few yards from me. I got up and turned to run and froze in my tracks. Just five yards in front of me was another wolf but this one was bigger than the others.

They all started walking toward me and I dropped the backpack and grabbed the baseball bat in both hands. All of a sudden I heard this barking and I looked around and saw ole blue coming to my rescue. He jumped the biggest wolf and they rolled over on the ground.

The other wolves ran toward me and I started swinging. I hit the first one in the head and caught him good. He tumbled over the tree and laid still. One of the other three ran toward me and bit me on my thigh. I caught him under the chin and broke the bat when I hit him but he went down and didn't get back up.

Now I was standing with a three-inch piece of wood and two wolves in front of me. They both attacked at the same time but before they could reach me ole blue jumped them. He leaped on one of them and pushed him into the other and they tumbled to the ground. I ran back to the tree and found a lose limb and ran back over to help ole blue but the fight was over and the wolves were running away.

I didn't know at the time that Ole Pop and Jesse had been watching the whole thing from about a hundred yards away on the other side of the tree line. They had sent old blue after me. Both of them had their rifles with them and both of them were great shots. If old blue and I hadn't beaten the wolves Ole Pop and Jesse would have killed them.

Ole blue sat down and started to lick his wounds and I sat down beside him and rubbed his head. Considering we had just fought off five wolves we didn't look so bad. But it was right there and then I decided I was going back to the farm if I could find my way back and I would just have to deal with those two old men until my time was up. Now how would I find my way back to the house?

As if ole blue knew what I was thinking he got up and gave me that, "C'mon lets go home" look. We walked for about two hours and then we rested for a while and I gave him some of my water then we got up and started walking again. It was almost dark when we arrived back at the farm.

Ole Pop and Jesse were sitting on the porch watching us as we walked up the path to the house.

"Well, well, well, Jesse would you look who decided to come back to the house."

"Yeah but he's kinda raggedy Buford. He looks like he was in a bear fight and every body had a bear but him. What happened to ya boy?"

"I got attacked by some wolves and they would have got me if it hadn't been for ole blue."

"Well like Jesse said when you fought Ceasar. You must be something special cause ole blue don't just take up with anybody. Jesse, see bout ole blue while I take this one inside and fix him up."

Ole Pop gets up, opens the door and lets me in then walks in behind me.

"Son let me ask you a question? Have you always done things this dumb or is it just me that makes you do them?"

"Look ole man I don't like it here but I guess I'm stuck here and if I'm gonna be here I guess I'll have to do what you say. Is that what you wanted to hear?"

"What I want or don't want to hear is irrelevant to your life. You can't be a man if you continue to do things just to make people happy or make your life easier. You have to decide on some positive goals for your life and pursue them then you will become the type of positive Black man our race can anchor itself too. And make no mistake we need positive, young, strong, Black men in this country. Now all you have to do is decide if you have the determination, courage, and discipline to master the world and not let the world master you. And don't bother telling me that life ain't fair. It never has been and it never will be but you have to go on anyway."

Ole Pop leans down until his face is close to mine and lowers his voice.

"If you don't remember anything else I tell you, remember this. Life is going to kick your butt and there's absolutely nothing you can do about it. But the secret is to never let the negative people or circumstances life brings to you knock you down. If you do life's going to stomp you, but if you keep standing while life kicks your butt it will always have to kick up at you, and as long as life is kicking up at you, the harder life kicks you the higher you're going to climb."

Ole Pop finished wrapping my leg and walked out of the room leaving me to think about what he said. I had been in my own little world every since my mom and pop had divorced and had just about decided that life sucked and here was this old man telling that I had just laid down and let the world stomp me and he was right. Now I had to make some decisions in my life and I needed to start right now.

Later that night I went to bed but didn't fall asleep right away.
I kept thinking about what Ole Pop had said and things started to
make sense. Why should I hustle on the street when I could get my
grades up, go to any college I choose, get a good job like my mom has
and live the good life legally.

I hustled for Trey for a year and made more money than even
my mom made but I had also been to jail twice, been betrayed by
someone I trusted, and almost lost my freedom for the next fifteen
years. Yeah I made the cash but the price was too high. The last
thought I had before I went to sleep was, "Andre you've been a damn
fool but not any more."

The next morning when Ole Pop came to wake me up he was
surprised to see that I was up, dressed and ready for breakfast.

"Well son I'm surprised to see you up this early."

"Old man I thought about what you said last night and it made
sense. If you don't mind I think I'll stick around here for a while and
see what turns up."

"Son you're always welcome around here but you know . . ."

"I know. I have to work to eat. You sure you ain't a slave driver?"

"No, but if I was, I bet you'd fetch a fair price at auction."

We both went down the steps laughing.

When we got down to the kitchen Jesse looked at us.

"Buford why is he so happy today and why is he up so early?"

"Well Jesse let's just say there's a little day light entering his
brain."

"You mean to tell me that he's finally getting rid of that city smog
that's been cloggin his brain cells."

"See you two old men need to be on BET with all the jokes."

Jesse looked at me, "On what?"

Now it was my turn to laugh, "BET is a television station for
Black people, it comes on cable television."

"What kinda shows do they show on there?"

"Mostly music videos."

"Music videos? That's them things where all the women are
showing their butts and shaking all over the place so you young boys
will buy the records and believe that stuff about being a gangster."

"It ain't always about the gangster thang. Some of our music is
pretty good."

"Ta hell you say! Most of it is about guns, drugs, and sex. Ya'll don't have anybody in your music I want to hear except that girl, you know the one that sings so pretty. You know the one I'm talking about. The pretty girl who was on that show with that smart talking English man on it."

I look at Ole Pop with a puzzled look and he gives me the same look. Jesse ignores us and keeps on talking.

"You know the one who won that award for singing with that other girl. You know she was in that movie about that girl singing group. Her name was Glenda or was it Jenny or some'tn like that."

"You mean Jennifer Hudson."

"Yeah that's the one. Whoooooweeee that girl can sang her face off."

"Yeah she can sing but hold up Jesse let's talk about your music. Who knows anything about blues these days? And talk about bad lyrics, all your music is about the woman that left you or the bills you can't pay, or the wine you drink. What's up wit that?"

Ole Pop started laughing, "He got you there Jesse. We do talk about wine, women, and bills."

"Yeah but at least when our song is over every body is still alive. Have you ever listened to their music or watched one of dem videos? They go like this, "Boom, boom, boom, boom then someone says something nobody understands, Boom, boom, boom and some little gal is shaking her butt, Boom, boom, boom, then someone comes up the street screeching tires and shooting into the crowd and after the music is over there are bodies all over the street, and they call this having a good time."

Even I had to laugh at that one, "Dang Jesse you make it sound like every time rap music is played somebody has to die. It ain't that crucial. We can listen to our music, and have a good time without the conflict and we have a lot of good singers."

"Well the next time you get one of those CB's-

"Those what?"

"You know those little album things you play on that tape player with the head phones."

"Oh you mean CD."

"CD, CB what ever it's called. The next time you get one that has some good singing on it let me hear it.

We sit down at the table, say grace and eat then get on the tractor and head for the fields. As we ride I find myself opening up to this country life. I smell the fresh air and see all the greenery, and hear the birds chirping and for the first time I start to feel comfortable here. I don't know how long I'm going to stay but I do know I think I'm beginning to like it here. Now if I can get used to the hard work and the hot days this just might work.

However just because I decided to stay and do what I was told didn't mean Ole Pop took it easy on me. He gave me the hardest jobs on the farm. Every morning I had to slop the hogs, feed the chickens, let the cows out so they could go graze and feed those mean ass turkeys. But before I could take over the job of feeding the turkeys I had to conquer the one they called Caesar.

The first day I went into the barnyard he was waiting. As soon as he spotted me he came running at me with his wings spread gobbling real loud but this time he was in for a surprise.

Jesse had told me what to do when he attacked so I waited until he was right on top of me then I back handed him with a left and caught him square in the face. I hit him so hard he flipped over.

He landed on his back and got up looking like he wanted to run at me again but he stopped, turned around and went back where he came from. From then on I didn't have to worry about him, he stayed away from me and I came and went as I pleased.

After doing my morning chores I had to get on the tractor and head out with Ole Pop and Jesse to the fields where I learned to shuck corn, pick pole beans, pick tomatoes, and black berries. The latter one was dangerous because of one simple fact. Snakes like black berries too and if you didn't watch what you were doing you could reach into a bush and pull out one of them. I never pulled one out but I saw several of them and I was extremely careful about the berries I reached for.

I was a quick learner and by the end of the month I had become a pretty good farmer. Ole Pop gave me my own piece of land to farm and anything I grew on my piece of land I could sell at the market and make my own money.

Just before school started we went to market and I sold what I raised for three hundred dollars. I know that doesn't seem like a lot compared to the thousands of dollars I made selling weed but this was something I did from beginning to end. I planted it, kept the weeds out of it, picked it and sold it all by myself and I was proud of that fact and so was Ole Pop. I was beginning to grow up and take responsibility for my life and that's all Ole Pop wanted me to do.

Chapter 8

After a month on the farm there were still a few things Ole Pop and I didn't see eye to eye on. One of those things was religion. I told him I didn't believe in organized religion. I explained that organized religion was only good for making the preachers richer besides going to church was dull and boring.

He stopped me right there and said. "Son you're not going to church to be entertained you're going to learn the word of God."

"I can do that at home by myself."

"Is that right? Well answer this question for me? What does John 3:16 say?"

I look at Ole Pop for a minute then drop my head. "I don't know."

"Son Before you disagree with a subject or idea you need to at least understand what you're disagreeing about. A lot of people think they can study their bible at home and learn all they need to know about God but it's the gathering together of the children of God that helps strengthen your knowledge and love of the Lord. Matthew 18:20 says, "For where two or three are gathered together in my name, there am I in the midst of them." And by the way John 3:16 says "For God so loved the world that he gave his only begotten son, that whoever believeth in him shall not perish but have everlasting life."

After quoting that scripture Ole Pop smiled, turned around and walked out of the room. Once again he had left me something to think about.

For his part Ole Pop was patient with me on the subject. He never tried to force his religious beliefs on me but he did make me go to church every Sunday. We even visited several different religious services so I could see several different types of worship. He said even though he wanted me to find my own path I still needed to study the word so I could make an intelligent informed decision about the path I wanted to take.

I hadn't been to church in a couple of years. While I was in Philadelphia mom and I argued back and forth every Sunday about my going to church.

I would do all the things a typical teenager does when they don't go to church.

I would try to stay in the bed until the last minute then take my time getting ready to make mom late. Or I would wait until the last minute to tell mom I didn't have anything to wear because none of my clothes had been washed yet. I was supposed to wash my clothes every Saturday night but on several occasions I didn't wash them just so I didn't have to go to church.

The first Sunday morning I got up to go to church with Ole Pop I tried the "I don't have anything to wear" trick on him.

He smiled that all knowing smile and told me to put on whatever was the cleanest and come on. I looked at him like he was crazy.

"I don't want to go into church in some dirty clothes."

"Son it doesn't matter what you look like. What matters is your soul. Your soul doesn't have clothes on. To God you are as naked as you were when you came into this world. Oh and by the way, just so you know. You will be going to church no matter how many times you don't wash your clothes. And another thing, don't try to be make us late hoping you won't have to go because if you do the next Sunday I'm going to wake you up at four in the morning and stay in your room until you are dressed."

Ole Pop walked out of the room leaving me to wonder how he knows everything I'm about to do before I do it. He's really going to take some getting use to. I get dressed in my cleanest clothes and head downstairs.

The first time I saw Mount Zion Primitive Baptist church I am amazed at how old it looks. It is a large white building with two large doors in the front and the same tall steps and porch Ole Pop has in front of his house.

Inside the church the long brown pews look like an older version of the ones in mom's church. The only difference is the pews aren't secured to the floor so they rock back and forth when the people sitting on the pews are clapping and moving to the beat.

The next thing I notice about Mount Zion is the fact that there are four window air conditioners in the church and even though they all work well. It isn't enough to handle ninety to a hundred plus degree heat and a church full of spirit filled worshipers.

To compensate there are church fans on each pew and after a good song and a spirit filled prayer by one of the deacons the church will begin to heat up. People will start fanning themselves and if you look around the church there always seems to be a sea of fans moving in unison.

From the time the service starts I am captivated by it. This is a real old time worship service. If you've never been to a Primitive Baptist Church it is an experience I recommend. It is the closest thing to old style worship I've ever been a part of.

First of all the ladies of the mother board always wear white and sit in their own corner. A lot of these women can sing real well and they are always humming throughout the service.

The first time I sat through the service I was amazed at how much spirit was in the church. This was nothing like the church mom went to in Philadelphia. Her church was filled with upper middle class people who didn't believe in loud singing and shouting. They held what they called a dignified service which meant there wasn't a whole lot of emotion in the church.

After my first service at Mount Zion I asked Ole Pop about the difference between the two churches.

"Son every one has to seek their own level of comfort when talking to Jesus. If emotion isn't the way you worship then worship God in your way but make sure you study the word and know of what you speak when you speak and Jesus will understand."

"Well I liked this service a lot."

"And that's a good thing. There's nothing wrong with enjoying the worship service."

As I said, Mount Zion is filled with emotion, spirit, song, praise, and preaching. The service always starts with Ole Pop who is a deacon and song leader opening up the praise part of the service with a Dr. Watts.

A Dr. Watts is a song, sung by the congregation that has no music or set pattern to it. It goes all the way back to slave times when we didn't have money for instruments.

Ole Pop stands in front of the church with his deep baritone voice and sings, "I love the Lord he heard my cry."

After that the whole church joins in, "Aaii Aaay oh oh oh Aaii Aaaaay."

The song is sort of like a long moan with a melody to it.

There is something about this moaning song that fills the church up with music. Every one in the church moans and hums. If you've had a bad week a Dr. Watts will some how cleanse you of it. If you have a problem you just can't figure out a Dr. Watts will clear your mind and let you think better or if you simply want to tell the Lord that you love him a Dr. Watts will lift your voice until you are sure the Lord hears you.

The song usually last five or six minutes depending on if one of the mothers of the mother board is feeling the spirit really good that day then just about the time the song is going to end she will start another chorus and the song will go on a little longer.

After we finish the song Ole Pop or one of the other Deacons will get down on one knee beside a chair in front of the alter and put his face in the chair and start his prayer. Ole Pop's prayer always starts with him saying.

"This morning most Holy and wonderful Father. You are The Prince of Peace, The bread of life, Alpha and Omega, The bright and morning star, The lily of the valley, The great I am, The Rose of Sharon. I come to you today Lord realizing that all I do is as of filthy rags in your sight."

All the time Ole Pop, Jesse or any other Deacon is praying the rest of the Deacon board is talking from the deacon's bench behind him, pushing him on, saying things like, "Say it," Make it plain son," or "Tell it," or "Speak on it" or "Talk to him son."

And while the deacon is praying and the deacon board is pushing him on the mother board is still humming that same Dr. Watts.

Sometimes by the time the singing and prayer is over the spirit is so high in the church the preacher really doesn't have to preach. I told Ole Pop what I thought about the service one day and he said,

"Son, man can't live on emotion alone he needs the word of God to feed his soul. John 1:1 says "In the beginning was the word and the word was with God and the word was God." The sermon delivers the word and the word is the most important part of the service. Without the sermon there is no worship."

Of course he was right, besides we had a very dynamic preacher named Pastor Charles Fitzgerald Nance Jr. This man could bring the fire into your soul with his sermons.

I remember the first time I saw Pastor Nance. He was a dark skinned man with gray hair. He was about the same age as Jesse. He had fire in his eyes and his voice was deep and powerful like Ole Pops. He had a physical handicap though. His legs were arthritic and he had to walk with two canes.

Both of his legs kinda bent toward each other when he stood and he sort of wobbled when he walked. The first time I saw him preach I remember thinking this man isn't going to be able to stand up, how is he going to preach? But when it came time for the sermon he picked up his canes and walked to the pulpit.

His sermon that day was on prayer and the importance of it and as he moved into the middle of his sermon you could see his back straighten and his legs straighten. His voice got a little louder and clearer and finally he dropped both canes and was standing beside the pulpit without them. Then he stepped down the steps in front of the pulpit and walked into the congregation. He came right to the pew I was sitting on and rested his hand on the back of it. His voice was really powerful and he had my full attention.

Right then is when I realized this man didn't just read scripture he seemed to call the Apostles like they were in the church right there with us and as if he had known them all his life.

He stopped beside me and in a booming voice said, "Every body needs to pray and if you don't know how to pray let me tell you what Jesus said to do."

That's when he called Matthew. His voice rose and echoed around the old church building as he said, "Come here Matthew six, five through thirteen."

He said it with such conviction I actually looked up expecting to see Matthew walking down the aisles to talk to him. Reverend Nance's sermon was dynamic, informative and spirit filled. After that I didn't mind going to church and after going to church for two months I accepted the Lord and was baptized.

Mom came down to see me and after the service she didn't seem to be able to stop crying. She kept telling me how proud she was of me and how much she loved me. I didn't realize that this would make her so happy but I was glad I was able to do something other than cause her grief.

Before she left I asked if I could come back home. She looked at me and said she loved me very much but she wanted me to stay with Ole Pop because she was afraid that if I came back home I would fall back into my old ways.

The day she left she kissed me on the jaw and with tears in her eyes she got in her car and drove off. I was going to miss her but this time I understood that she was doing the right thing for my sake.

Chapter 9

Actually I wanted to stay with Ole Pop. I enjoyed listening to them speak about our history. Of course it didn't hurt that they had some funny jokes too. A lot of the jokes were about me but now that I felt at home with them I didn't take them to heart, besides I had my share of jokes for them too. One of the things Ole Pop and Jesse joked about was something called the "Poko Doblins."

One night just before bed time I warmed up some chitlins and ate them. Ole Pop told me not to eat chitlins and hot sauce so late at night but I was hungry and besides it was his fault I liked chitlins in the first place.

After I finished eating Jesse told me the "Poko Doblins" were going to come and get me when I went to sleep. When I asked him what the Poko Doblins were he said, "Just wait until you go to sleep you'll find out" and he and Ole Pop laughed liked they usually did.

Well I decided Jesse and Ole Pop were again having fun at my expense and I went to bed. Around two o'clock in the morning I began having a nightmare. Someone was chasing me with a really big butcher's knife and I couldn't see who it was. I tried to get away but the harder I ran the closer they got.

I woke up with my heart racing and sweat rolling down my forehead and chest. I lie in bed realizing it was just a dream but dealing with the fact that it seemed so real. Finally I shook the spooks off and went back to sleep and as soon as I did they started chasing me again.

The nightmare kept coming back for the rest of the night. Every time I attempted to go back to sleep the nightmare would start right where it ended. This went on until five o'clock in the morning I finally gave up on sleeping and got up.

As soon as I walked downstairs I told Ole Pop and Jesse about the dreams while we ate breakfast and they both laughed their butts off.

Then Jesse said, "I told ya when ya ate those chitlins the Poko Doblins would get ya."

Now I knew what the Poko Doblins were and I've never again eaten chitlins or anything spicey when it's close to bedtime.

I learned a lot of lessons about life from those old men and being on the farm had turned out to be a good experience for me. The best thing about it was just about the time I thought I knew everything about Ole Pop and Jesse I would find out something new.

One of the early things I found out about him and Jesse was they both had girlfriends. I didn't think men their age needed the companionship of a woman but I found out differently when Mrs. Delia Sue Boleyjack came to see Ole Pop one evening.

Mrs. Boleyjack came to ask Ole Pop about her car but she was dressed up and smelling good like she was headed for church. However it was Tuesday and there wasn't anything going on at the church that evening.

Ole Pop invited her up on the porch and looked at me and Jesse. Jesse touched me on the arm and told me to come inside with him. I wanted to stay out on the porch, enjoy the breeze and listen to their conversation but Jesse insisted that we go in the house.

I was puzzled about the whole thing and asked Jesse why we had to leave the porch. Jesse smiled and said, "Yo uncle and Mrs. Boleyjack have been sparking for near two years now."

Jesse quietly laughed when he saw my face and it only got worse when I asked him, "What does sparking mean?"

He almost spit snuff down the front of his shirt. When he was finally able to stop laughing he looked at me and said, "You know, girlfrining and boyfrining."

I couldn't believe my ears. I started to laugh out loud but Jesse put his hand over my mouth.

"Shhh boy do you want them to hear us. Follow me into the kitchen."

I followed him to the kitchen and as soon as he shut the door and sat down I was on him with questions.

"Why haven't I seen her before?"

"Cause your uncle is very quiet about his relationship with her."

"Why is that?"

"Buford is just that way, besides a lot of people in this community like to get all up in ya business and Buford don't like to answer questions."

"So why haven't they gotten married?"

"Buford has been single every since yo aunt Thelma died when they were both in their twenties. Delia Sue has been a widow for going on fifteen years now. They are both set in their ways but they like being around each other. They both decided a while back they have been single for so long they just didn't want to get married they just wanted to enjoy each other's company."

I look at Jesse and grin because something has just come together in my head. On Wednesdays Jesse gets real clean and leaves the house about seven. I've asked him several times where he is going but all he ever tells me is "I gots some business to handle." Now it's my turn to make some jokes.

"Uh huh and what about you? Which one of the women in the community do you go see on Wednesdays when you get sharp and leave the house?"

Jesse leans over and pops me on the top of the head.

"Nephew stay out my business."

Then he smiles, gets up and walks away from the table. I found out later that Jesse was sparking with Miss Gladys Peppers.

Things like that just kept popping up when I least expected them. One of the most amazing things I found out was the fact that after being discharged from the army they attended Tennessee State University and earned engineering degrees. And that's why Jesse told me when I first got there never to underestimate someone I just met.

I also found out they both worked for a large computer engineering firm that made parts for some of the earliest computers back in the early seventies.

While working for the company they took out stock options that paid off well later on. That is why they had the money to buy the farm and the other parcels of land around it.

These old men were smart, strong Black men, the kind of Black men a lot of young men could learn something from and by now I was bound and determined to learn everything from them I could.

I learned a lot about the men who's charge it was to make sure I grew up and became a God fearing, strong, intelligent man that not only our race needed but that our community as well as our nation needed.

Ole Pop explained to me that this country needed men who were willing to stand up for what they believed. It didn't matter their culture or skin tone. This country needed real men with real convictions or this country wouldn't survive.

They taught me a real man will do anything to protect his family, his community and those less fortunate. Even if it appears to be a lost cause which was the case with Corinna Jean Postly.

Corinna was the daughter of one of our church members. She was three years older than me. When I first met her she was buck wild and she hated living in the country. She lived alone with her mother because her father had left them long ago. She blamed her mother for the breakup and they fought constantly.

She was a very pretty girl with a good figure. Ole Pop told me while she was in high school her grades were real good but after she graduated she hooked up with a young man named Darious Jenkins. He was from Corinth Mississippi and about as trifling as they come.

When I first met Corinna she was pregnant with Darious baby and after meeting him I knew exactly what Ole Pop was talking about when he said he was "Too lazy to swat a mosquito off his own arm."

He reminded me of Trey. He had the same attitude toward life. He acted like everybody owed him something. He walked and looked like he was better than every body on the planet. He had a little sneer on his face that made you want to walk up to him and knock his teeth out. But I knew it wouldn't have done any good because I knew his kind. There was a time when I used to be his kind.

Corinna's mother tried to get her to leave him especially after he got sent to prison for a year but she loved him and that's why she and her mother had most of their arguments and that's also how she came to stay in one of the houses on Ole Pop's property.

After a particularly nasty argument between Corinna and her mother about Darious she slapped her mother and her mother put her out right then and there. She made her pack her bags and get out. Corinna began walking toward town and it didn't take long for her to figure out she had made a mistake.

Ole Pop was driving to town and spotted her walking on the side of the road. She was crying, with her baby in one hand and her bag in the other hand dragging it behind her.

Ole Pop picked her up, convinced her to go back to her mother's house then acted as a mediator between her and her mother. After two hours of talking it was decided that she couldn't stay with her mother anymore but Ole Pop would allow her to stay in one of his houses until she could get a job and move to the city.

For a while every thing was fine. Corinna kept the house clean and she found a job working in the bank down town. Things were beginning to look up for her until Darious got out of jail then things went bad in a hurry.

As soon as Darious got out of jail he moved in with Corinna. Corinna tried to keep it a secret from Ole Pop because one of the stipulations of her living in his house was that Darious couldn't live with her.

It wasn't long before Darious was manufacturing and selling Meth in Ole Pop's house. And it also wasn't long after that Ole Pop received a call from the Sheriff.

The Sheriff, Ole Pop and Jesse had been friends for a long time so when the Sheriff got the arrest warrant he immediately called Ole Pop to tell him he needed to get them out of his house. If Darious was caught in Ole Pop's house with a Meth lab Ole Pop and Jesse could lose everything they had worked so hard for.

Ole Pop and Jesse immediately left the house. Jesse took his shot gun with him just in case. They told me later that Ole Pop let Jesse out of the truck a couple hundred yards from the house and just like they thought Darious came out of the house with a gun when he saw Ole Pop pull up in front of the house.

He told Ole Pop to leave before he shot his old ass and that's when Jesse walked up behind him and tapped him on the back of the head with the butt of the shot gun knocking him out.

Corinna screamed and started cussing Ole Pop. Jesse said that Ole Pop got a kind of sorry look on his face. He told Corinna he knew about the meth lab and he was going to call the police. Then he told her she had twenty minutes to pack her things and get out of his house.

Corinna ran back to the house, put a few clothes in her bag, brought the bag and her daughter out of the house and put them in Darious car. She tried to walk over to Darious and wake him but Ole Pop told her to leave him where he was or he would call the police on both of them. She cussed Ole Pop again then got in the car and drove off.

Ole Pop and Jesse waited at the house until the Sheriff and a deputy got there. They found enough Meth on Darious to be used for resale and arrested him. They didn't even go into the house they just cuffed Darious and put him in one of their cars. The next day Ole Pop and Jesse got rid of all the chemicals they found in the house then tore it down.

For several days after that Ole Pop wasn't himself. He was real quiet and sad. I asked him what was wrong but he just kinda side stepped the question. Finally when he felt like talking the only thing he said was "I hate to lose children to bad decisions."

Ole Pop was rough around the edges but he had a big ole heart of gold and the heart led to what I can only describe as a miracle. It was a hot July night and Ole Pop did something that shouldn't have been humanly possible. It would later become a legend people still talk about.

We were riding to town with nothing on our minds but getting some supplies for the farm and singing the blues. Yeah I know I said blues was just alright but over the last few months Ole Pop and Jesse had suckered me in.

Ole Pop was driving, Jesse was playing the guitar and I was sitting in the back of the truck singing in my usual non key. Ole Pop once told me that my voice was so bad all the animals on the farm went to sleep just to keep from hearing me sing. Jesse said I sounded like the old steam engine train that ran early in the morning blowing its whistle as it passed by.

That was alright with me I didn't care if I couldn't sing I liked to try anyway. So we were having a good time when Ole Pop suddenly braked to a stop at "Bristle's swamp."

Bristle's swamp is a large area that at one time had been a field with trees and bushes and wild life. Until it was flooded to lower the level of the nearby lake so a road could be built to the interstate.

Now it looked like a dead swamp with the tops of several trees rising just above the surface of the water like sharp spikes. It was a very dangerous place to be. However some of our neighbors fished the area because it was full of bass, stripe and catfish.

I look over the cab of our truck and I could see the tires of another truck sticking out of the water. I looked down the road and I could see the skid marks leading from the road to the swamp.

The truck had skidded out of control into the swamp and flipped over. It had come to rest upside down and the only thing keeping it from sinking completely in the water was the fact that it had landed on top of one of the trees sticking out of the water.

There were several other cars stopped on the side of the road and several of the men driving them had jumped into the swamp to see if they could help the people inside.

We got out and ran down to see if we could help and that's when we saw the baby girl with her head hanging out the passenger side window. She was gasping for air and crying. She couldn't have been more than five or six years old. Her red hair was matted to her forehead and her father was trying to hold her head above water.

We were told later that several men had tried to pull the truck up so they could get to the child. However every time they tried the truck would rise up then sink back in as their strength gave out.

Finally all they could do was keep the truck from sinking further into the water. But slowly the tree helping them hold the truck up was giving way.

Each time the tree made a creaking sound the truck would lower just a few inches deeper into the water. Each time the truck lowered the child's head would dip below the water and her father would pull her head back up. But he was beginning to put strain on her neck. Eventually she was going to drown.

Ole Pop took one look at the situation, walked into the water and made his way to the front end of the truck. He found two tree stumps just below the water to stand on then told all of us to try and steady the truck as much as we could while he ducked under the water.

Seconds later the truck began to rise out of the water then Ole Pop's head came up. With all of us pulling with him Ole Pop was able to pull the truck up until the little girl was almost completely visible and the truck was still rising.

Ole Pop's eyes were closed and he looked like he was in a trance. The muscles in his neck were straining as well as the muscles in his arms but somehow he held his position.

Slowly the water inside the truck spilled out as it rose out of the water until it was up far enough for the little girl's father to see that she was trapped under the seat. He took his knife out of his pocket, cut the seat belt then with his bare hands pulled the metal away from her legs and pulled her out of the water.

As soon as the baby was out of the water Jesse looked at Ole Pop as if he had seen him do this before and said very quietly. "Buford the child is safe." And without opening his eyes Ole Pop said in a very calm voice "Every body step back from the truck."

No one moved for fear of the truck drowning Ole Pop. Jesse spoke in that quiet voice again.

"Buford if we move from this truck it's liable to take you down with it."

"Don't worry about me Jesse. According to the boy I'm too mean to die. Now yall back up."

We did like he asked us to do leaving him the only one holding the truck up. Ole Pop exhaled then took in a deep breath and pushed himself away from the truck.

It sank like a rock and so did Ole Pop. We just knew he was gone but after a few seconds his head came up as he waded through the water until he made it to dry land.

The men begin applauding and the little girl's mother kissed Ole Pop on the cheek. Of course Jesse had to make a joke about it.

"Well superman I guess what ya need ta do now is git a needle and some thread and sew a big red S on ya chest. By the way does you fly too?"

Ole Pop laughed, "Jesse Ustes Anderson, leave me alone before I bust you in tha eye."

Now it was my turn. "Careful Ole Pop Jesse might have some kryptonite in his pocket."

Jesse started laughing, "Dats right tell em nephew I just might have a chunk of it hid away somewhere."

Everybody standing with us start to laugh including Ole Pop then he turns around and heads for the truck. We get back in our truck and begin singing the blues again as we head for town.

The next day several reporters came out to Ole Pop's House and tried to interview him but he wouldn't have anything to do with them.

I told him he should do the interview since he had done a good thing. He turned and looked at me and said, "There is none good but the Lord" then he walked away and that was that.

Chapter 10

It's been three months since I decided to stay with Ole Pop and the work has been hard but I find myself enjoying it. Besides the work has put me in shape and I am beginning to come into my own as a young man.

I have put on thirty pounds of muscle, grown from five foot seven to six foot one and a half and my skin has cleared up. Ole Pop said it's because I stopped drinking pops and smoking that stuff and started eating vegetables and drinking water so the poison has been cleaned out of my system. I don't know about all that but I listened to him just the same.

Through the summer I worked harder than I had worked my whole life and I also decided to begin a work out regimen. I told Ole Pop that I wanted to buy some weights to work out with and he laughed at me.

"Son you're living on a farm. You don't need any weights you've got all kinds of things to work out with here."

"I know we've got a lot of heavy farm equipment around here but I need a place I can turn into a regular gym where the weights are already there when I need to use them."

"Okay so what you're saying is you need a work out room like they have in the city. I don't see the need in it but let me see what Jesse and I can do."

Ole Pop went down the stairs and told Jesse and I could hear both of them laughing at me and my city ways again but I knew they were just having fun.

Two days later Ole Pop and Jesse took me out to the barn. They had moved a lot of equipment around and made a place for me to work out. It wasn't like the ones in the city because it didn't use regulation weights. In fact it didn't look like it would work at all.

Ole Pop and Jesse had put together a weight room with some of the things we had on the farm. They had a pull down bar with one end attached to the bar and the other attached to a small bale of hay. It didn't look right but it worked just fine. After using it for the first time I could feel it in my back and arms.

Ole Pop told me when I needed more weight all I had to do was go and get another bale of hay and add it to the one already there. It wasn't a regulation weight set but it worked just fine.

The next thing they did was to take the axle from one of their old tractors, cut it with a torch and make it into a weight bar. Then they used spare parts from the tractor to make the weights they added to the end of the bar. Jesse even used a chisel to mark the parts so I would know how much they weighed.

They made several weight stations for me, all of which did the same thing as one of the machines you would find in an expensive gym. Ole Pop laughed when I got through working out with them for the first time.

"Well son how did Jesse and I do?"

"Yeah nephew what do ya think of our gym?"

"Ole Pop I don't know how you and Jesse did it but this works real good."

Jesse starts laughing, "Well nephew me and Buford did something we call Afro Engineering."

"What does Afro Engineering mean?"

"It means we took what we had and made what we wanted. Black folk have been surviving that way for as long as we've been in America. Oh and nephew there's another name for "Afro Engineering" but we're not going to use it."

Ole Pop looked me in the eyes, "What the corporate world calls thinking out of the box, we call surviving. If it doesn't work this way then try it that way. If it doesn't work that way then try it another way until you get what you want."

Jesse smiles and puts his hand on my shoulder.

"Never give up until you have explored every option given to you. If you have a problem try every angle you can before giving up on it."

I remember this conversation every time I work out and I have kept what Ole Pop and Jesse told me that day in my mind as a guide when things get tough.

I continued to work out through the summer and by the fall of the year I had muscled up until my thin body was several inches thicker. Now I was going to be able to try out for the school football team.

I had decided the fastest way to become an insider was to try out for the school's championship football team. When I was younger I played Pop Warner ball and had been pretty good at it. If I were lucky I would make the team and not have to go through the "new guy" thing. I was looking forward to the try out but I really dreaded that first day of school.

The first day of school is already hard enough when you're going to a new school. It's even harder when you're going to a new school not only in a completely different state but also in a completely different part of the country. I was a nervous wreck about going to the new school. However to my surprise as soon as I got on the bus I found out most of the kids in the community knew about me and all of them were friendly.

On that first bus ride I met Nathan Bell and I knew we would become best friends. The seat beside him was the only vacant one on the bus so I sat beside him and he introduced himself as Nathan Bartholomew Bell but told me to call him Nate.

We talked all the way to school and by the time we got there I had become part of his crowd. He was the one who introduced me around school and to the head coach then showed me where every thing was.

That same day I met the woman I was destined to marry. Her name is Vanessa Mae Bell. She was absolutely stunning. There is no way you could have convinced me another girl even existed that was as pretty as this one.

The first time I saw her I just stopped and stared. She was dark skinned, with beautiful oval shaped eyes, long eyelashes and long thick black hair that hung down her back. And to this day I won't let her cut it no shorter than her shoulders.

She had a figure that caused all my hormones to start dancing and singing, long beautiful black hair, but most of all she had a smile that made me want to give her the world if she asks for it.

I met Vanessa when Nathan walked up behind her in the hall and pulled her hair. She immediately turned around and hit him in the gut. I don't mean a little girl punch I mean a good one, the kind of punch that would have knocked the average boy down.

It didn't even faze Nathan. I guess that's because he was six foot four, weighed two hundred and sixty five pounds and he was an all-state defensive end for the schools championship football team. He just smiled and said,

"Whuzzup cuz?"

"Nate if you pull my hair one more time I'm going to knock your teeth out."

He put a big arm around her shoulder and hugged her.

"Yeah but I'll still be pretty and you'll still be ugly even with your teeth."

She giggled and hugged him back, then hit him again and he laughed. We continued down the hall to class and I just had to know who she was.

"Nate, who was that?"

"Oh that's just my cousin Vanessa Mae Bell. We call her Nessa."

"Damn she's fine."

"Yeah you and all the other guys in this school think so, but she ain't having it. She's a hard girl to get to know especially after aunt Fran and uncle Joe got a divorce. Since then most of the time she stays at home, does her work around the house, and reads. I've tried to hook her up with some of my friends but she's just not interested."

"Well you don't mind if I try do you?"

"Naw my boy help yourself and good luck you're going to need it."

The next day I waited until she came out of the lunchroom and walked over to her.

"A beautiful lady like you deserves a good man to take care of her."

She stopped, took her time looking me up and down and then she opened her mouth and let me have it.

"Oh see now what we have here is a man who thinks a woman needs him to take care of her, or a man who thinks a woman will fall

all over him just because he offers to buy her a few nice gifts, or a fake playa with a tired line. Either way you're wasting my time now if you'll excuse me I've got to go to class."

There I stood looking stupid and to make matters worse I didn't know Nate was standing behind me.

"Well hoss, I see you've been introduced to Nessa's bad side. I could have told you the playa role wasn't going to do you any good with her. She hates playas. Uncle Joe thought he was a playa, that's why he got divorced from her mom. Now any man trying to talk to her gets his head taken off. She just ain't havin it."

I figured after that I had lost any chance of ever talking to her again. That was until our English teacher Miss Grant gave us an assignment to write about the worse or best thing that happened in our lives. I chose the divorce of my father and mother.

After grading the papers Miss Grant called me to her desk.

"Andre this is a very good paper and I was wondering if you would read it for the class?"

"I don't know about that Miss Grant."

"I understand if you think it's too personal."

"That's not it. I just don't like reading in front of people."

"But this is such a good paper I think it would do the whole class good to hear it. You'll be surprised how many students will understand what you're saying."

"Well, okay I guess I can do it."

The next day I stood in front of the class and read my paper. The title of the paper was, "A childhood's end."

I was shaky at first but once I got into it I did pretty good. After I finished everyone in class applauded and I happened to look at Vanessa and she was crying.

After class she walked over to me, "That was really, really good writing."

"Thanks. It's hard trying to put what you feel into words on paper. I had so many feelings I had to deal with. I could have written a book about it."

"I know what you mean. When my parents divorced I hated both of them and I wanted to run away from home, but instead I buried myself in my books."

"Well at least you got involved in something positive. I did some really stupid stuff after they divorced. I almost got myself put in jail for fifteen years because I was stupid."

"Really? What did you do?"

"I'm not trying to be rude but I'd rather not say what it was right now but it was so bad that my mom sent me down here and probably saved my life."

"I wish I had someplace to go to get away from my mother and father's problems."

"No you don't, trust me on that. Stay with your mother for as long as you can because believe it or not she's hurting too. She's just trying to be strong so you won't notice it."

Vanessa looked at me for a minute. "You know, I'm going to have to change my mind about you. I thought you were just another playa-wanna-be, but you're a nice guy."

"I can see why you would think that and I want to apologize for the way I approached you the first time. I didn't mean to insult you and as far as the playa thing is concerned, I was that person but that person has been gone for awhile. Now let me introduce myself properly.

I stuck out my hand and said, "Hello, my name is Andre Wright and it's nice to meet you."

She laughed, shook my hand, and said, "Hello Andre, my name is Vanessa."

I walked her to her next class and we started talking from there.

Vanessa and I spent many days studying together and talking about everything you can imagine. Not only was she pretty, she was real intelligent and could talk about things I had never even thought of.

She was a financial genius and had mapped out the way her financial life was going to go. We talked about a lot of things but only argued about one thing. She didn't want anything to do with marriage.

She had formed this shell around herself when it came to the subject of marriage. She told me she would never get married under any circumstance because it was an illusion. She believed there was no way two people could love each other for the rest of their lives. I told her she was just feeling the effects of her mother and father's divorce and she went into a little rage and cursed me out.

I realized then her pain was still too fresh for her to deal with and I decided to let it go for now but over the next few weeks I approached the subject very gently and pretty soon I had gotten her out of her depressed state of mind. That's when we really started to get close.

Now instead of spending all our time studying we did more kissing and hugging and one thing led to another and pretty soon we were engaging in serious foreplay but she would always stop me before it went too far and it was killing me.

Here I was a teenaged boy with all these hormones raging through me and just about the time I was about to release these hormones she would push me away.

Sometimes I would get mad and not call her for a couple of days but I just couldn't live without her so eventually I would call back. I was considering asking her to marry me and I knew she felt the same way and all of this didn't go unnoticed by our friends.

In two months time we had become so close that our friends around school got sick of us always kissing and looking at one another and holding hands, so they started teasing us.

First they called us the "Old married couple," Then they called us "Glue" because we were always together. But Nate came up with the name that stuck. He called us "The shadows."

He said every time he turned around there we were, either I was in front and she was the shadow or she was in front and I was the shadow. I told him he wasn't funny while I was laughing at the same time and Nessa hit him in the ribs like she usually did but it was too late from then on we were known as "The shadows."

One day after football practice I sat down and had a talk with Nate.

"Nate I want you to know I plan on marrying Nessa and I want you to be my best man."

"I kinda figured she had you whipped. What happened to the playa playa I first met?"

"That life is far behind me and I'm glad it is. I probably would have been dead if mom hadn't sent me to Ole Pop."

"Yeah from what you told me you were headed for some bad things. Either jail was going to get you or your boys were. Wonder why they didn't come down here after you?"

"Trey's in jail and he's the only one who would have a reason to come after me. Besides there isn't much I can do to hurt them from way down here."

"Well I'm glad you came here my boy. You're a good friend to have around but you better treat my cousin right or she'll kick your butt."

"Naw she won't, cause I'm scurred of her I ain't gonna mess up."

We both have a good laugh then head out to the football field for practice.

My life was going really good now. I had the love of my life, I was on the honor roll, I was the starting outside linebacker on our undefeated football team, and I was president of the junior class. Not bad for a boy who was almost destined to die or end up in jail. Things were good but you know how the devil is if he doesn't get you one way he always has something else up his sleeve. Trouble was just around the corner and it was headed my way.

Back in Philadelphia Trey's new lawyer has managed to get a new trial for him. New information had come to light that the court needed to hear. The outcome of the trial would bring a major problem back into my life.

The District attorney argued his case as effectively as he could but he really didn't stand a chance. The warrant the police used to search Trey's house and seize his books wasn't valid. It was issued for thirteen sixteen Mortin street not thirteen sixteen Morten street which was Trey's address. Somehow that had slipped by everyone involved in the original case. It wasn't until Trey hired a new lawyer that this mistake was discovered.

Monday morning, November fifteenth Trey walked into the courtroom and listened to the judge bang his gavel.

"After reviewing the case of the city of Philadelphia versus Davon Jackson III and finding that the officers did perform an illegal search and seizure. Mr. Williams I have declared your record cleared and you are free to go."

Trey heads for the door with one thing on his mind, revenge. He was going to find the little bastard and put an end to his life and any one who got in his way. Nobody snitches on him and gets away with it. Now the snitch is going to do some hard time before he dies.

Chapter 11

When Trey walks back into his house all his boys are waiting on him. BnasT was there along with Darrell Stevens who's nickname is "Gator", then there was Gerald Mason, they call him "Wall street" and next was Trey's right hand man Christopher Floyd notoriously known as "Sugah bear."

Sugah bear is Trey's six foot six, three hundred and forty two pound body guard, enforcer, killer. He has a nasty streak that makes him want to break bones. In general he's not the guy you want Trey to send after you.

Trey turns on the stereo real loud so if the cops are listening they can't hear anything and they get close together to talk.

"Trey, Terrell said he'd be here later. His ole lady just got home with the baby."

"Aight."

"So what's up Trey, where we going to start?" You know the Trane street boyz have taken over most of the territory."

"Is that right? Trey looks at Gerald. Wall street how the hell did you let that happen?"

"We can't do nothing. PoPo is all over us. Every where we go there's at least two undercover cops waiting. While you were gone all we could do was keep the territory around here and wait for you."

"Well I'm back and my lawyer has filed a harassment suit against their ass so they'll pull these undercover cops off us but before we do anything else, Gator did you find out where that bitch Andre went to."

"Yeah he went to his uncle's place in Mississippi but we don't know exactly where that is."

"Why the hell not?"

"Because none of the people we talked to have ever heard his mother mention where her uncle lives other than Mississippi."

"Well we're going to find him."

Trey takes his cell phone out and calls Terrell.

"Terrell I want you to park your car down the street from your house then open your garage door. I'll fill you in when I get to your house.

"C'mon Sugah Bear let's go."

Trey closes his cell phone and heads toward the door with Sugah Bear behind him.

"Where we going Trey?"

Trey gives Sugah Bear a crooked smile. "First we're going to play some head games with these dumb ass cops. After that we're going to pay a little visit to Andre's mom and see if I can get her to tell me where Andre is."

Trey and his boys get into the car and pull off. As they pass the liquor store two undercover detectives pull out and follow them. Trey's car has limo tint on the windows which is illegal. The tint is ample reason to stop Trey and his boys but the detectives are looking for more than just a traffic stop.

Sugah Bear drives to Terrell's house and pulls into his garage. He and Trey get out of the car and in full view of the detectives pull the garage door down before walking into the house.

Thirty minutes later the garage door opens and Terrell backs Trey's car out of the driveway. He turns left and heads down the street. After he turns the corner the undercover officers pull out and follow him. Trey cracks the blinds and watches as the officers leave.

"Those dumb asses couldn't catch and cold in the winter. Let's go."

Twenty minutes later Trey knocks on Sarah Wright's door. When she opens the door she is greeted by a large gun.

"Don't talk. If you say anything I will kill you where you stand. Do you understand me?"

Sarah nods her head. "Good now walk with me out to the car and get in."

Trey takes Sarah by the arm and leads her to his car. After they get in he doesn't say a word. He wants her to worry about what is going to happen to her.

Trey and Sugah Bear take her to a warehouse and tie her to a chair. After asking her repeatedly where Andre is Trey loses his patience and slaps her. She starts to cry but still doesn't say anything.

He continues to slap her every time he asks a question and she doesn't answer. He blacks both of her eyes and bloodies her nose. After a while the beating takes its toll and she passes out.

Trey decides to send Sugah bear to her house. He gets to the house and uses her key to open the door. Once inside he turns the place upside down until he finds a box with all the letters Andre has written to her. He takes the box and drives back to the warehouse where Trey has poured water on Andre's mother to wake her up and is just about to slap her again.

"Trey I got the address off these letters he wrote to her."

"Aw ain't that sweet. So your little boy has been writing his momma. Well it's too bad you're never going to see him again."

Trey pulls out a thirty eight and squeezes the trigger one time. Andre's mother slumps over in the chair and Trey and his boys get in the car and leave.

After they are gone a head sticks out of a barrel on the other side of the warehouse. It's a homeless man. He looks around to make sure the men are gone then he runs over to Andre's mom and unties her. He gently lowers her to the floor and places his coat under her head. He grabs her purse and empties the contents on the floor. The last thing to fall out is her cell phone.

At three o'clock in the morning an ambulance arrives at the hospital and Sarah Wright is rushed into emergency surgery. After three hours of surgery she is put into intensive care. Every thirty minutes a nurse comes in to check her vitals.

The doctors are pretty sure that she's out of danger and considering what she went through the Lord must have wrapped his arms of protection around her because the bullet went clean through her without touching her heart and even though she also had a mild concussion and blood loss she survived.

Trey and Sugah bear are on their way to Mississippi and all the way to Mississippi Trey is quiet. He is so set on killing Andre that nothing else matters. They arrive in the town at three o'clock in the morning and get a hotel room.

At ten o'clock they drive downtown to the courthouse and find out where Ole Pop lives. They ask about me and find out that I'm one of the star football players on the championship team. Five minutes after they leave the phone rings at Ole Pops house.

"Hello."

"Buford this is Hershel."

"Hey Hershel how are you doing?"

"Buford a couple of young men came into my store looking for Andre. They looked like they might be trouble."

"Are you sure they were looking for Andre?"

"Yeah but they called him Dre at first until they realized I didn't know him by that name then they gave me his full name."

"Was one of them a short light skinned guy with a big head?"

"Yes he was. Do you know these young fellas?"

"Yeah I know who they are. Thank you for calling and tell your wife I said hello."

Ole Pop goes and gets Jesse, tells him he thinks the boy Andre told them about is in town.

"So how you wanna handle this Buford?"

"Hershel gave them directions to our house so I'm sure they'll show up here pretty soon. If this is going to turn into a fight I don't want it to happen in our house. I think we better wait in the field and see what happens."

Buford and Jesse take their shot guns and head out toward the fields.

Trey and Sugah bear pull off the main highway onto the gravel road and then onto the dirt road.

"Damn these country ass people don't even have roads, just dirt."

Sugah Bear laughs "Good, we can bury Dre's ass six feet deep in it."

They drive as far as they can then they get out and walk through the fields until they come to the house. What they don't know is that Ole Pop and Jesse have been with them since they got out of the car and could have taken them at any time.

Sugah bear walks up to the door and knocks then he hears a low growl and turns to see the biggest dog he's ever seen. He pulls his gun and so does Trey but before they can kill ole blue Jesse makes a sound like a bird and ole blue runs off the porch toward the fields.

Sugah bear picks the lock to get into the house and after looking around and finding no one there Trey decides to head for the high school hoping to find Andre there.

It is about six o'clock and dark outside, and as usual I am sitting on Nate's car waiting for him to come out of the dressing room after practice when this Mercedes with tented windows slowly rolls up the street and into the parking lot. It comes to a stop right beside me and when the window rolls down it's Trey.

"Well, I'll be damned! I finally found yo ass. How you doing Dre?"

I get off Nate's car and begin to back toward the weight room but before I can turn around Trey has his Gun pointed right at me.

"Don't even think about running nigga. I'll wet this whole parking lot up with yo ass. Get in the car Bitch."

"Look Trey I don't want no trouble. I'm sorry about what happened to you but you were the one who told the police the weed was mine."

"Shut up bitch and get in the car before I bust yo ass right here."

I get in the car and we pull off. "I guess yo ass is sorry you snitched on me now huh? Well it's too late, now I'm gonna do what I should have done when I found out you was trying to set yourself up in business. Aw now don't look so surprised, Marcus told me all about your plan to start getting your weed from Li'l C and his boys."

"Marcus is lying man I wasn't going to buy weed from someone else."

"Really then how come Marcus found Nasty Pete's phone number in your jacket?"

"I don't know Trey but I wasn't going to cross you like that. I was making more money working for you than I have ever made in my life. Why would I try to double deal on you."

"I don't know and it don't matter now cause yo ass is through."

We drive for several miles then turn off the main highway onto a gravel road. Fifteen minutes later we pull up in front of a large weathered looking gray barn and get out. Sugah bear leaves the lights on so the front of the barn is lit up and drags me to the wall and ties me up.

Trey pulls up a crate and sits down in front of me.

"Well my boy, it's time to get rid of the snitch. Oh by the way, sorry about your mom. She didn't want to tell me where you were and I had to persuade her to do the right thing. Now she's dead and her baby boy is about to be dead too. It's a damn shame too, cause I understand that yo raggedy ass father ain't doing to good. That means your whole family is about to be wiped out."

Tears run down my cheeks as I hear Trey tell me he killed my mother. Right now at this point if I could get my hands on him he would be as dead as my mother is. I turn my head so I can stare at him and over his shoulder I spot something moving. From behind them I see a dark figure walking out from the shadows and hear Ole Pop's voice.

"Seems like you made two mistakes tonight."

Sugah bear pulls his gun and spins around only to be met with a hard right to the mouth. Ole Pop hits Sugah bear so hard he falls backward into the hay. He rolls over and tries to stand up but Ole Pop walks over, hits him again and knocks him flat on his back. He's not out but he's not quite fully conscious either. However I know how strong Sugah bear is and it won't be long before he's up and ready to continue the fight.

Ole Pop leans over and removes the gun from Sugah bear's hand. Then rolls him over onto his stomach and pats him down to make sure he isn't carrying another one.

As soon as Trey sees Ole Pop hit Sugah bear he pulls his gun and moves toward me but he is met by a shotgun in the face as Jesse steps out of the darkness.

"Young fella, if I was you I wouldn't even breathe hard cause I'm old and shaky. I might just squeeze this trigger and that would make a bigger hole in ya head than ya already got. Now why don't ya drop that gun so no one has to git hurt?"

Trey doesn't move he stands there glaring at Jesse. Jesse pulls both hammers back, looks Trey square in the eyes and says in a very calm voice.

"I said drop the gun."

Trey immediately drops his gun and Jesse eases the hammers down and lowers the shotgun to Trey's chest.

After Ole Pop searches Sugah bear then backs away from him. Sugah bear is still groggy but he staggers to his feet. Trey looks at Jesse and says, "Who the hell are you?"

Jesse points the shotgun back at Trey's head.

"Young fella ain't your momma ever told you it's impolite to cuss your elders especially if they have a double barreled shotgun pointed at your head?"

Ole Pop walks over to me while Jesse covers Trey and Sugah bear and removes the rope that is holding me to the post.

"Andre your mother is alive and in the hospital. The doctors say she's going to make it."

My heart starts beating again. It seems like it hadn't beat since I heard she was dead but now I could feel all my strength come back and I start to walk toward Trey. Ole Pop puts his hand on my shoulder.

"Son let me and Jesse conversate with them for a minute. After we're finished if you still want to whoop his ass you can go right ahead."

He winks at me and I start smiling cause I know what conversating means.

Trey smiles that nasty smile of his and looks me in the eyes.

"Yo punk ass can't whoop shit. Tell this old man to put down the gun so I can beat yo ass like I beat yo momma's ass."

Ole Pop raises his gun and walks toward Trey

"You must be Trey. Damn Andre he's a little fella ain't he? Trey what I need you and your partner to do now is strip to the waste and lie down on your stomach with your hands interlaced on your head for me. I'm sure you've been in that position before."

"Old man I don't know what the hell you think you're going to do but I don't play that shit."

"What shit is that son?"

"That country, cross breeding, screw the city boy shit."

"Oh come on now son don't believe the bullshit you hear about country people. I don't find you the least bit attractive, I just want to make sure you're not carrying another weapon now strip and lie down before I change my mind and shoot you."

They both take off their shirts and lie down. Jesse walks over and hands me the shotgun, I cock both hammers and point the gun right at Trey. Jesse walks over to Trey, bends down and places handcuffs on him then walks over to Sugah bear and does the same.

Trey turns his head sideways so he can see Ole Pop, "I should have known you were PoPo."

Ole Pop looked at me, "What did he just say to me?"

"He thinks you're the police, Ole Pop." Ole Pop chuckled, "Naw son we aren't the police we just know what to do with criminals."

After Jesse handcuffs both of them, He takes Ole Pop's Shotgun. Ole Pop picks Trey up by the waist of his pants like he was a sack of wheat and carries him to the post I was tied to. He puts Trey down turns him to face the post, and ties him to it then grabs Sugah Bear drags him over to the post beside Trey ties him to it. Then he does something Trey didn't expect, he pulls their pants down.

"What the hell you doing old man? You better not be planning on touching me cause I swear I'll kill your ass."

"Well first of all your pants were already down below your ass so I didn't know if you're straight or gay and second of all you're not in a position to tell me what to do. Besides you don't even look like a woman so quite frankly you ain't my type."

Jesse starts to laugh and spit snuff at the same time. "He ain't my type either Buford."

Ole Pops looks at me, winks and laughs then he looks at Jesse.

"Well what do you think Jesse? You think a good conversation will help these young fellas?"

"Naw I don't. I think they're way past that now, but it would sure do my body good to see you do it."

Ole Pop disappears into the night and when he returns he has an armload of switches. Trey turns his head and sees the switches.

"What the hell are you going to do with those bushes old man?"

"I hope I'm going to help you with your common sense but I think it's too late for that so I'm just going to do what your mother should have done to you when you were a boy. I'm going to whoop your ass."

"Old man if you hit me with one of those bushes . . . ."

"No son these are switches not bushes."

"I don't give a damn what they are, don't hit me with em."

"Shhh, now son. I hate to do this but this is something you've been needing for a long time. Besides my brother Jesse here wants to see it happen and I try not to disappoint my family. Now this is going to hurt a lot so don't be afraid to cry."

"Screw you old man."

"Didn't I already tell you I don't find you attractive?"

Jesse laughed and snuff came out the side of his mouth.

"That's the second time he's propositioned you Buford I think he likes the way you look." Ole Pop let out one of his deep rumbling laughs and I start laughing too.

Trey turns red and starts cussing. "When my boys back in Philadelphia get here we'll find out who the bitch is."

"OoooooWeeeeee Buford! This young fella sho got a nasty mouth."

Ole Pop stops laughing, and looks Trey in the eyes.

"Are you sure you want your boys to know that two old men whooped your ass? Besides, you and I both know the only reason you found Andre in the first place is because someone in town told you where to look but after my friends and neighbors around here find out why you wanted him the next set of strangers who come to town won't find out anything. And to tell you the truth I don't think your boys will give a damn about you. If you're gone they'll take your place. The only reason your boys stay around you is because of the money they can make and if they can make more money without you they will. They're not about to come all the way down here. Now I think it's time to pass out this ass whoopin."

Ole Pop picks up the first switch and slides the leaves off it then walks up behind Trey and let him have thirty quick lashes on the butt. I never knew Trey could scream so loud or so high for that matter. If you didn't know better you'd think Ole Pop was whoopin a girl.

Ole Pop walked around to face Trey. Trey's cheeks are wet from tears.

"See son this is called conversating with a child. Grown folk around here conversate with a child so they can talk to them later. Now what I want to talk to you about is my niece and nephew. After I'm through whoopin your ass I'm going to let you go."

As soon as Ole Pop said "after I'm through" you could see the fear in Trey's eyes because he knows Ole Pop is going to whoop him again and he doesn't want to take another ass whoopin. Ole Pop continues talking to him.

"Son, if anything ever happens to my niece or nephew and I even suspect you had a hand in it, I'm going to kill you."

Ole Pop looks Trey dead in the eyes with a killer look I had never seen before then he walks back around behind Trey, picks up another switch, slides the leaves off it and gives Trey thirty more lashes. Every time Ole Pop hit Trey with the switch, a welt pops up on his back. Some of them are bleeding, some are not, but all of them were a deep red color.

After Ole Pop finishes with Trey he walks over to Sugah bear and gives him the same thing. Sugah bear is determined not to cry but after about the tenth lick tears start rolling down his cheeks too.

Here they are, two of Philadelphia's most notorious gangsters, getting their ass whooped by an old man and crying like two big ole babies. I couldn't help but laugh at the fact that I use to look up to these clowns.

After Ole Pop is done he cuts them loose and allows them to put their clothes back on. I hold my shotgun tight just in case they decide to do something stupid but by this time they are in no mood to fight.

Ole Pop goes and gets the truck and makes Trey and Sugah Bear lie down in the back. Jesse takes his shotgun and gets in the back with them. We ride for several miles but we never get back on the main road, in fact it looks as if we're going deeper into the woods. After about twenty miles Ole Pop stops in the middle of a field, gets his shotgun and gets out.

"Okay fellas you can get out now."

Trey gets out first, "I thought you said you were going to let us go."

"I am young fella."

Ole Pop tosses a canteen at Trey. "There's water in that canteen, if you use it wisely you'll have enough to get you to a main road. Don't forget, if anything happens to my niece or nephew I'm coming to get you, now start walking."

"Which way is it? It's dark out here, how are we supposed to find the road?"

"You found your way down here didn't you. You should be able to find your way back now like I said, start walking."

Trey and Sugah bear turn around and start to walk away. Suddenly Sugah bear whirls around and tries to grab Jesse's shotgun but the old man is too fast for him. Jesse sidesteps Sugah bear and hits him on the back with the butt of the gun. Sugah bear goes down on one knee and Jesse cocks his shotgun.

"Buford I don't think you conversated with these young fellas enough. Either that or they ain't got enough sense to pour piss outta a boot. Which ever it is this big'n here is gonna git himself killed if he tries that agin. Now git up and git movin."

Trey helps Sugah bear up and they start walking. We stand there until they're out of sight then we get in the truck and leave. For the first few minutes I sat in silence thinking about what just happened until Ole Pop interrupts my thoughts.

"What are you thinking about son?"

"How did you know I was in trouble?"

"The hospital called about your mom and I was just getting ready to come and get you when Hershel Hall called and told me there were some young fellas looking for you and they were headed to my house. Me and Jesse went into the field and watched them as they went into the house looking for you. I thought about catching them and taking them to the sheriff but I didn't have a real reason except for trespassing or breaking and entering and that would only keep them in jail a couple of months. I decided to wait until they came back and tried to kidnap you before I jumped them.

After they left, me and Jesse got into the truck and followed them because I wanted to know where they were staying. Unfortunately I didn't realize they would go to your school and when they did all I could do was follow them, and hope they tried to find a secluded place before they did anything to you, and they did exactly what I wanted them to do."

I had forgotten about mom in all the confusion.

"Is mom alright?"

"She's in stable condition. They said she was lucky but I say she was blessed that the bullet went right through her without touching any vital organs. The doctor said all she needs now is some rest."

"Ole Pop I don't think you should have let Trey and Sugah bear go. When they get back to town Trey's going to call some more of his boys and they're going to come down here looking for me, you, and Jesse."

"I don't think you need to worry about that or don't you remember what happened to you when you went out into the woods without knowing where you were going. The land I left them on has more wolves, deer, bear, coyote and snakes than the woods you were in. Both of them are bleeding from the conversating we did so the animals in that field will certainly pick up their scents. Quite frankly son, I don't think they'll survive the night."

The next day Ole Pop went to Philadelphia to be with mom. He wouldn't let me go because he knew Trey's boys would find me there. So I had to wait until Ole Pop called home to find out how mom was doing. And he made sure to call every day. Each day I prayed for mom and then I prayed that Trey's boys would leave us alone.

A week later a pair of hunters find two bodies in the field where we left Trey and Sugah bear. Their bodies had been torn to pieces by wolves and picked at by coyotes and buzzards. The coroner had to use their dental records to identify the bodies as Trey and Sugah Bear.

Three days after they were found a couple of Trey's boys came down to pick up the bodies. While they were here they asked a few questions but our neighbors and friends wouldn't tell them anything.

Trey's boys finally gave up and left town with the bodies and that was the last I heard of any of Trey's people until a year later. One night mom called me and told me that B NasT had been shot and killed in a bad drug deal, and the other four got caught in a drug sting operation. Each of them was sentenced to fifteen years in a federal penitentiary.

I often wish B NasT had been sent to Ole Pop with me then maybe he wouldn't have been killed for nothing. It's a shame for young black men to die like that.

Chapter 12

When Ole Pop finally came home he brought mom with him and she stayed for a month. During that month she got to meet my Nessa. They hit it off real good. They got so close that both of them started double teaming me, Ole Pop and Jesse about how and where we ate dinner.

I mean we were men so we ate with our elbows on the table or in the living room watching television especially if a football game was on but mom and Nessa wasn't having it. They insisted that we all eat properly at the table together like a family.

I told Ole Pop that he needed to take control of his house but he said.

"Son there ain't nothing more determined than a woman trying to correct a man's thinking." So we had to sit and take the abuse.

Ole Pop didn't say anything until they started changing the scenery around our house. He told them we didn't need a whole lot of fancy things to eat with, but that didn't stop them. First, doilies, and coasters appeared out of nowhere. Then new curtains on the windows and all the while we were arguing about them changing stuff. But it just went in one ear and out the other. Every time mom and Nessa went shopping something new would show up in the house.

Ole Pop and I finally just gave up arguing with them and let them run the house. Jesse didn't give up though. Every time they brought something new he would say, "Here they come again with something else they done wasted their money on."

Mom would kiss him on the forehead and say,

"Oh now Jesse, you know you like having me around. It reminds you of the good old days."

Then Vanessa would put her arms around Jesse and kiss him on the jaw.

"C'mon Mr. Jesse you know it looks good in here now."

He would half-heartedly try to elbow them away.

"Gone now, I don't want all that slobba on me."

But his smile would give him away every time. He actually loved having them around as much as we did, he just liked to argue.

After a month of having mom around it was time for her to go. Just before she left she kissed me on the cheek, and with tears in her eyes she told me she was proud of the way I had grown up in such a short time. I told her that thanks to her and Ole Pop my life was saved because I could have been where

B NasT is today.

She smiled and said, "I know."

Then she got in her car, waved at me and drove off. I know it had to be hard for her to leave me because it was hard for me to see her go but I belonged here with Ole Pop because I still had a lot to learn.

Things around the farm calmed down and I settle back into my regular routine. The school year is almost over and since I'm doing good in school and I do my chores around the farm Ole Pop has agreed to let me have a part-time job so I can get some spending money. He and Jesse have even fixed up one of the old cars they had around the place and let me drive it. Now I really was something.

Every Saturday night me and Nessa and Nathan and his date go to the movies and then go hang out at the mall. Life is good for me. I have a girl who loves me, I'm on the honor roll at school, and Nathan and I have been voted the co-captains of the football team. It just can't get any better and to top it off Nessa and I make love for the first time after the prom and she told me she would never love anyone like she loved me.

She is the love of my life, the only woman I want to be with and I want to make love to her as often and for as long as possible. Like I said my life was great. So when Ole Pop told me in his most stern voice that he wanted to talk to me I didn't have a clue what I had done.

"Sit down here son we need to talk."

I walked over to the couch and sit down beside him.

"What did I do wrong?"

"What makes you think you've done something wrong?"

"Well you never look that serious unless I've done something wrong."

"This time I hope I can keep you from doing something wrong. I want to talk to you about time.

When you first got here you couldn't wait to leave. You hated it when your mother dropped you off with me and Jesse and the longer you stayed the more you were convinced you were going to run away. You had only been here two or three days but you were sure this was not the place you were planning on staying for very long. But as time went on you actually came to like it here. And all it took was a little time. And that's what I want to talk to you about."

Ole Pop let that sink in before moving on.

"It takes a lifetime to correct the mistakes we make in life but it only takes a few seconds to make life changing decisions. If a young man takes a gun and shoots another person it only takes a few seconds to squeeze the trigger but it will take a life time to make up for the mistake of killing another human being. The same thing can be said about love. Son I know the young lady you're with is the best thing that ever happened to you but if you really believe that then you are going to have to be careful with her. She's a precious jewel and she doesn't need any man laying with her and creating a baby without making a real commitment to her."

I look at Ole Pop in amazement. How does he know everything about me all the time? He must have my clothes bugged or something. I drop my eyes to the floor and sit there thinking for another few seconds before his voice brings me back to the conversation.

"If she's worth your love she's worth waiting to make love to. I know you've probably already done that and I know you already know the consequences of it but I want to leave you with this thought. It takes a few seconds to deliver sperm to an egg but it takes a lifetime to raise the product of that delivery. I want you to remember that before you lay her down again."

I shift around in my seat. This is not a subject I ever expected Ole Pop to talk about but he was right. I'm not ready to take care of a baby and I know it but it's kinda unnerving how he always seems to know what I'm doing or about to do. I wish he couldn't do that so well, it scares me sometimes.

Now don't get me wrong Ole Pop has had my best interest at heart as long as I've been here but there is something spiritual about the way he can always step in and give me a talking to just about the time I'm about to make a mistake. So if he's giving me a talk about sex then I must be getting ready to make a mistake. But I had to ask the question.

"Ole Pop why are you talking to me about this?"

"Because I see the way my nephew looks at his young lady and I know his young lady feels the same as he does it's all over her face when she looks at you, and son, believe it or not I was young once. I remember the first time I fell in love and how it felt to make love to someone who loves you back. Unfortunately at your age the only way you know how to share your love is to lie down and have sex. You don't understand that to love a woman is to treat her like a beautiful flower.

Ole Pop smiles at me before going on. "To love a woman is to be able to hold her in your arms but respect her enough to wait until you're old enough to make a real commitment. I know it's hard. She's beautiful, soft, warm and willing but the both of you have to show some restraint because the child you bring into the world deserves all the love, protection, and nurturing two parents can give it. Not one parent but two parents. Don't you remember how sad you were when your mother and father divorced? Now just imagine how a child feels who has never had both parents in the home."

"Okay Ole Pop I understand what you're saying but what makes you think Nessa and I are having sex?"

Ole Pop looks me dead in the eyes, "Well are you?"

I swallow hard as I look at him. There he goes looking like Moses again. How do you look Moses in the eyes and lie to him. The only thing that would be harder is looking Jesus in the eyes and trying to lie to him.

I drop my head, "Well maybe once."

Ole Pop put his arm around me. "Son I'm not trying to embarrass you, I'm just trying to make sure you make the right decisions for your life as well as hers. She's vulnerable because of her parents divorce and she needs the love and warmth only the man she loves can give. She loves you so much she'll give you anything you ask of her including a child but you know you're not ready to take care of a child. And first Timothy says "But if any provide not for his own, and specially for those of his own house, he hath denied the faith, and is worse than an infidel." And according to what I know about the Bible, an infidel is one of the lowest creatures on earth.

I lock that thought away. It will stay with me for the rest of my life. Ole Pop goes on with his teaching.

"Now I'm not trying to keep you from having fun but there are more things you can do together than just have sex. Don't put her at risk of having to take care of a child and missing her chance at education and don't burden your life with a child you're not ready for. I hope I've said something to help you but remember the decision is up to you. Today's decision creates tomorrow's future."

Ole Pops gets up and walks away leaving me on the couch to think about what he said.

That next Friday is the school picnic. The high school lets out early and the students and the teachers all gather at the park. We have a faculty student softball game and after the game we eat hotdogs, hamburgers, Ice cream and cake.

Nessa and I are on the clean up committee so long after all the other students are gone we are still at the park. By the time we get through cleaning up it's about dark. We get in my car and head home but before we leave the park Nessa ask me to drive around because she's never seen the whole park so we drive and talk.

After a while she tells me to pull over in a nice secluded area. We sit and talk some more then we kiss and as we kiss we get closer and my hands automatically go to her top. I start to kiss her on the neck and fumble with the buttons. She leans back against the seat and allows me to open her top. I lean down to kiss the valley between her breast and all of a sudden the conversation Ole Pop had with me starts replaying in my head. Of all the times for me to hear Ole Pops voice it would be now.

I stop what I'm doing and sit back in the seat. Nessa looks at me with a concerned look, "What's wrong baby?"

"Nothing I just have a lot on my mind."

"Like what?"

I turn and look at her and smile. "You are the most beautiful woman I've ever known."

"She smiles and leans over and kisses me softly on the lips but I pull away.

"But I can't do this right now."

"Do what right now."

"Make love to you like this. You're special to me and in this car is not the way I want to make love to you."

Nessa starts buttoning up her blouse. "Ooooo, that's so sweet. So where is the right place?"

"Well it's not so much of a place it's a, well it's a . . ."

I drop my head then look up at Nessa. "I think we need to talk."

I tell her about the conversation Ole Pop had with me and then I tell her she's going to have to be strong for the both of us because she's so beautiful and I love her so much that if we get into this situation again I will make love to her no matter what the consequences are. She agrees and from that day until we get engaged she puts everything on lock down. Well that's not actually the whole truth.

Every once in a while our hormones run wild and we just can't help ourselves but we make sure to take every precaution and we try our best to limit the times it happens.

Not making love often was the hardest part of being with Nessa, but Ole Pop was right it was worth the wait. Now I have a woman who respects me and I respect her and she lets me make love to her often. She says she's letting me catch up for the years she had everything on lock down.

I laugh and tell her that's five years plus interest so I get at least three extra years. She says she doesn't remember seeing that part in the contract. I tell her it was in the fine print and she hits me in the ribs. I'm glad I took Ole Pops advice and treated her like the special flower she is.

I said those years were the hardest of my life but one of those years was harder than any of the rest. That year my father died and even to this day I miss him. I know he did some things wrong but he was still my old man so it hit me kinda hard when he died. That was a very hard year for me. It's a shame he had to die alone.

Chapter 13

My pops passed away alone at his house. His sister, my aunt Mary found him sitting in his chair in the living room of his house with a pile of beer bottles around him. No one deserves to die alone without any family around but it was the choice he made for himself.

After he and mom separated I never really got the chance to see him much. The last time I stayed with him all he did was come home, drink a six pack of beer and pass out in his easy chair. I didn't know the pain he was enduring. If I had known I would have tried to help but he wouldn't talk to me and after the break up he and mom stopped communicating.

His sister, my aunt Mary would sometimes call my mother and tell her about what he was doing to himself and mom would try to call and talk to him but all he would tell her is that he was fine so there wasn't much she could do to help.

After he died and I got to Philadelphia, mom, Aunt Mary and I began to clean out the place and Aunt Mary sat down and told me all about some of the things he had done before he died.

The first story she told me was about the five cars he wrecked. In four years time my father had gotten drunk and totaled out five cars. Aunt Mary said it was a wonder that he got out of three of those cars alive.

The first one he drove into a telephone pole. When the police got to the scene he was standing out in front of the car trying to get the hood up even though the motor had been pushed into the back seat and the front end of the car was wrapped around the pole. The police said they had the hardest time getting him to understand there was nothing he could do to get his car started again.

When they brought him home all he had was a scratch on his head. The officers told my aunt that it was a miracle he survived. If it had been anyone else they would have been dead. That didn't stop him from driving though. He just bought another car and kept going.

Two months later he ran the new car into a concrete ditch on the side of the interstate. Once again he was blessed with a minor cut on his leg while the car was totaled. It took two tow trucks an hour to get the car back up on the road so they could tow it away. According to my aunt my dad was blessed that he didn't kill himself or someone else.

After telling me about the cars she started laughing and talking about the other things he did. She told me about the time his neighbors called her and told her he was lying out in the front yard. When she got there he was lying in the front yard dressed only his underwear and it was ten degrees outside.

She just knew he was either dead or unconscious but when she got to him she could hear him snoring. She woke him up and got him into his house and his bed and the next morning he got up and went to work like nothing had happened. My aunt said if it had of been her she would have been in the hospital with double pneumonia.

From what she told me about him he never missed a day of work. How a man could get drunk every day for the last four years and never miss a day of work was almost unthinkable but he did it. We found all four of the certificates his company gave him for not missing a day each year.

She told me about the many times she found him in his truck asleep after work. He was so drunk he never made it out of the truck. And even through all this she said he always found the time to come to see her and take care of things that needed to be fixed around her house.

She told me he was a gentle soul who she is sure regrets having the affair that led to his break up with mom. She said that mom and I were all he talked about. She wished I could have grown up with him.

After that we started to clean up the house and while going through his closet I found what looked like a diary. I opened it and a picture of me when I was a little boy fell out. I looked at the picture then sat down to read the diary.

On the first page he talked about how he had ruined the only good thing in his life and how he missed me and mom. The next few pages are taken from his journal and it chronicles his decline.

Journal of Joseph Wright

1st week of May 2004

Damn how could I have been so stupid as to cheat on my wife? Now all I have is this broke down old car and raggedy apartment. I've lost my wife, my son, and my self esteem. If I had the chance I would turn back the hands on the clock and never make the mistake but now all I can do is deal with the fact that I messed up. I'm writing this in hopes that one day Andre will read it after I'm gone. Son I want you to know that I never stopped loving you but I made a mistake and I just couldn't correct it. Now I'm on the verge of making another mistake and I can't help that one either. I hope one day you can forgive me. I love you son.

2nd week of May 2004

I started drinking again. Now I'm really screwing up my life. I thought I had whipped the alcohol demon after I left the army but its back and getting stronger by the day. I have to stop this before I kill myself. The army doctors told me if I didn't stop drinking I would lose my kidneys so why can't I stop this.

3rd week of May 2004

Andre came over for the weekend but I don't think I talked to him twice. All I did was come home and drank until I passed out.

What kind of roll model is that for my son? The next time he comes I'm going to do better.

1st week of June 2004

Screw it. Sarah came to pick Andre up and smelled the alcohol on my breath and asked me if I was drinking again. I told her to mind her own damn business and she said if I hurt Andre because I was driving and drinking or anything like that she would ask the court to stop my visitation rights. I told her I didn't give a damn about visitation rights. I didn't know Andre was listening until I turned and saw him looking at me. I tried to explain to him that I didn't mean it but he just walked out the door and I haven't seen him since.

3rd week in June 2004

I'm sitting here now with my second six pack and I'm feeling good so I decided I'd write this in my journal. Ain't nothing wrong with having a drink now and then. Shit I ain't doing too bad. I just finished two six packs of beer and I can still sit here and write. Hell I don't need nobody in my life I can take care of myself.

July 2004

What the hell am I thinking? I wrecked the car three days ago. I totaled it. It's a miracle I walked away from it. Now all my neighbors know I have a drinking problem and my sister Mary had to come over here and help me. That's it I'm never going to drink again. Andre I'm going to be the dad you remember son.

August 2004

I lasted one week without a drink. So I know I can control it. I've had a lot to drink tonight but I can handle it. I'm a grown ass man and I can drink if I want to. Oh yeah I'm supposed to be writing this to my son. Hey Andre I hope when you read this you understand that your old man didn't mean you any harm but it ain't nothing wrong with a few drinks.

September 2004

I found the journal when I woke up on the floor beside the bed. Now I'm sitting here with the worst hangover I've ever had trying to figure out why in the hell I'm trying to kill myself. I don't want my son to see me in this condition but I do want him to know who I am.

Andre your father is human and I make mistakes. It gets lonely around here at night with no one to talk to. I always hoped I would get the chance to see my son grow up and play sports but now his mother has called me and told me he got busted for possession.

I can't help but think it's my fault. If I hadn't had that affair maybe we would all be together and he wouldn't have to pay the price for my mistakes. It hurts too much to think about so tonight I'll do what I've done for the past month. Get three six packs, climb into my chair and pass out.

December 2004

It's been a long time since I've written anything in this book. I had forgotten all about it until I found it in the bathroom drawer. What have I done with my life? How do I explain any of this to Andre? At least Sarah had enough sense to send him to Ole Pop and Jesse. If any body can straighten him out those old men can. I hope he turns out to be the intelligent strong young man he started out to be before I screwed things up for him.

March 2005

I can't remember ever being this alone. There's no laughter here. I miss my wife, I miss Andre, most of all I miss the man I used to be. I don't know how much longer I can stand being alone like this. I just wish I had my family back.

If I could just put this bottle down I could do better. Sarah called to ask me how I was doing and I was so drunk I couldn't even carry on a decent conversation with her. I'm so out of control I can't even slow down. I'm heading down hill and it's going to be too late to stop after while.

July 2005

Its been a while since I've written anything down. Damn, I've drank so much and so often that I've had to switch from six packs to forty ounces. I know I shouldn't be writing things like this down for Andre to read but he needs to understand that his father is an alcoholic and that if he doesn't be careful he could end up like this. Son I don't want you to end up like me. Please keep yourself straight and don't follow in my foot steps. Alcohol is not the answer for you so don't be like your father stay far away from it.

January 2006

Well I just wrecked my car again. The police charged me with reckless driving and I'm going to have to go to driving school and alcohol therapy so I can keep my license. Maybe this is the wake up call I need. If I can make it through all the classes and get my self clean maybe I can get my family back.

June 2006

Been clean for two months now and my head is starting to clear. I went to the doctor today because my back has been bothering me. They ran some test on me and told me to come back Friday. They should have the results then.

Talked to Sarah several days ago and Friday we went out to dinner. It was good to see her laugh. She even gave me a hug before she walked into the house. I just know I can beat this addiction and get my family back. Things are looking up.

October 2006

My doctor told me that my kidneys are gone and I am going to have to go on dialyses. Just when I thought I was about to get myself together things go bad. I don't know what I'm going to do now.

Dialysis is a big deal. If I hadn't drank so much then I wouldn't be going through all of this. I hope I'm around to see Andre graduate.

November 2006

I tried dialyses and its hard to do. I've never been fond of needles and I like them even less now but I guess I'm going to have to do this until they find a suitable donor for me. Maybe this will keep me sober. I can only hope that it does.

February 2006

Last night I drank a beer. The doctors told me that I have to stay away from alcohol completely but they don't know how hard that is to do. Sometimes a man needs a drink especially after one of those long dialysis sessions. They are so draining all I can do is come home and lay down. I feel like I'm so old I could just lay down and die and since it's obvious that I'm heading to the grave I may as well enjoy myself on the way down.

May 2007

I missed Andre's eighteenth birthday today. I had my bags packed by the door. But I had some time before I needed to be at the airport so I decided to drink a couple of beers. A couple turned into four six packs. Before I knew it I was out. Two days passed and not only did I miss my flight but I was out so long I missed my son's most important birthday.

Andre deserves a better father than me. I hope if he reads this he realizes I didn't miss his birthday on purpose it's just that I'm weak with no self control and this bottle is going to be my death.

June 2007

Why does every body have to be in my business? My sister came over today and cursed me out for no reason. So I missed Andre's graduation. I sent him two hundred dollars. He can do more with the money than with me so he'll be alright.

And yeah I missed dialysis once or twice, who cares, I still feel good and there ain't nothing wrong with taking a drink every once in a while. She keeps telling me I'm killing myself. Well what if I am? Who am I trying to stay alive for anyway?

July 2007

Woke up this morning with my back on fire. It felt like someone had placed a hot branding iron in the middle of my back. I got up and almost crawled to the bathroom to use the toilet.

When I got up from the stool there was blood all over the place. I went to emergency and the doctors put me in the hospital. They wanted to keep me there but I decided to go home.

My sister came by to give me some grief about my decision but I told her I didn't want to hear it and put her out of my house. If I'm going to die it's going to be on my terms.

August 2007

This is my last entry. There's no need in writing anymore. With my kidneys gone it's only a matter of time before I'm gone, especially since I can't stop drinking.

Last week I drank until I passed out and I missed two of my dialysis sessions. It's no use trying to save my life. It's not worth saving. Andre I tried to be strong but it wasn't enough please forgive me son. I love you.

Joseph Wright

My father died two days after his last entry in the journal. He loved me and I didn't get a chance to be with him. I didn't even get the chance to say goodbye.

I sat on the bed with tears running down my cheeks when mom and aunt Mary came in I gave mom the book. They both read it at the same time and they started crying too. I wish I had known he was hurting that much maybe I could have helped him.

When we got back to Mississippi I showed the book to Ole Pop and told him I wish I had been there. He told me there are some journeys a person has to make by themselves and it doesn't matter who is around them when they make the journey it still has to be made by them alone.

Then he told me to make sure my journey to become a man is a good and true one so I can honor my father's life as well as his death. I have tried to do just that.

I put the book in my dresser and every once in a while I take it out and read it. I have even read some of it to my son and I took what Ole Pop told me to heart and I never try to do anything that would dishonor my father's name.

Chapter 14

Six months after my father died two other tragedies struck my life. It was as if my life suddenly headed down hill really fast and I couldn't do anything but watch.

During football season of our senior year Nate and I and several others on our football team received lots of attention from several major college teams. Nate was the number one defensive tackle in the nation and I was ranked as one of the top five linebackers. Nate and I had decided that we were going to go to school together but things didn't work out that way.

Nate didn't have a father figure at home all he had was Uncle Henry. Henry was his uncle on his mother's side. Uncle Henry was one of those get rich quick people. All he thought about was the money. Nate really wasn't that type of person but since his uncle meant a great deal to him he listened to what he had to say.

Uncle Henry lived in another state and he would sometimes show up when he got himself in trouble and needed somewhere to hide. He was all flash and no substance but Nate looked up to him because he was cool and looked like he had himself together.

To tell the truth, I looked up to him too. He wore the latest styles and always had several business opportunities he was working on. Every time I saw Uncle Henry he was on his cell phones talking to several business associates at the same time and every time he came to town he was driving a new car.

I didn't want to be like him but there were certain things about him I wanted to emulate. I expressed this to Ole Pop. We were

washing dishes together and Ole Pop stopped drying the plate he
had in his hand and looked at me for a minute.

"Have you noticed that every time Henry comes to town Nate
changes?"

"What do you mean?"

"Well he changes from that good natured young man we
all know to a person who believes all his troubles are caused by
someone else."

"Yeah I know Uncle Henry talks a lot about how the white man is
always trying to keep the black man down but some people are just
like that and beside it's true."

"Yes, sometimes certain white men will do evil things to hurt a
black man but you can't blame a whole race of people for the things
one person in that race does and you can't blame your own short
comings on anyone but yourself. Henry has all the flash that some
young men want to emulate but if you look a little closer you will
see that the flash is hiding weaknesses in his character. I just hope
Henry doesn't convince Nate to do something that will mess up his
future."

I thought about what Ole Pop said for the rest of the night.
I knew Uncle Henry was all about being for himself but I didn't
think he would do anything to hurt Nate. I found out later that
just because someone is your kin doesn't mean they have your best
interest at heart.

Nate and I had kinda set our minds on going to the University
of Mississippi. We were going to room together then we were going
to get drafted and go to the pros. But somewhere between football
season our senior year and graduation Nate changed.

I begin to notice the change when Nate started going to these
private dinners with the coaches of several major college programs
and one college program in particular. This program had run into
trouble with the NCAA before.

All of us had been warned by our head coach that taking
anything of value from any college coach or any of their
representatives would result in our being in violation of NCAA
policy. But Nate's uncle convinced him there was nothing wrong
with talking to this coach.

At first Nate and I talked every day about the things some college coaches did to try to get us to sign with them. We both had a lot of stories because we received a lot of letters from several colleges.

One college in particular almost changed both of our minds about going to The University of Mississippi. They began sending us letters our junior year. Both of us received at least twenty letters that year. By the time our senior year rolled around we had received at least fifty letters from them and several visits.

Nate and I both were impressed with the fact that this college wanted us so bad. They were in the running for the national championship every year and if we started for them we would be guaranteed a spot in the NFL.

I was about ready to sign with them until Ole Pop talked to our head coach and then did some research himself. He found out there were rumors floating around about their program engaging in illegal recruiting practices to get high school players to sign with their program.

I talked to Nate about what Ole Pop had found out but he said it was just a rumor. He also told me that his Uncle was working out a deal with the coach and he was going to get paid. I asked him what he meant by getting paid but he wouldn't tell me. I went home and told Ole Pop about it and he said, "Henry is going to cause that boy a lot of grief."

Even after hearing about the deal I was still leaning toward signing with them until one of their boosters paid me a visit. After that visit I knew what the program was all about and I didn't want any parts of it.

The booster came to Ole Pops farm with a brand new Mustang convertible with two nice looking cheerleaders. He walked into Ole Pop's house with the cheerleaders and as soon as he sat down Ole Pop and Jesse went to work on him.

He only got a chance to say, "Hello gentlemen my name is Clarence Hill" Before Jesse and Ole Pop begin to make a fool of him.

It was obvious the recruiter believed the country stereotype. It was also obvious the stereotype tripled when he saw the farmers were black. So Jesse did what he did best. He fed into the Stereotype.

"Dang Buford dats a nice car out there. You reckon he'll let Andre drive dat thang?"

The recruiter smiles. This is going to be easier than he thought.

"Oh yes sir we'll let Andre drive it if he wants to."

"Dang young fella you think I could git a car like dat?"

"Yes sir that might be possible."

Ole Pop looked at Jesse then at the recruiter.

"And what can the university do for me?"

"I don't know sir that would depend on what you need."

"Well lets say I needed some help around the farm could your university do that for me?"

"What type of help are we talking about?"

"Well let's see. There are some mechanical problems I might need help with. Could you help me with that?"

"Yes sir we may have someone who could help you with those problems."

"And how much would it cost me?"

"Oh you don't have to worry about that we would make some arrangements for you."

I look on with my mouth open. Jesse looks at me and laughs.

"Close your mouth nephew we're tryin ta come ta an agreement heah."

It looked like Ole Pop and Jesse were negotiating to sale me like a piece of meat. I couldn't believe that someone would walk into our house and offer my uncles a bribe for me to go to their college.

Ole Pop looked at me and winked and I knew he was about to tell Mr. Hill what he could do with his offer.

"Well son it's nice of you to offer your assistance but I don't need the help"

Jesse smiled at him and in perfect English said.

"And I don't need the car. It's pretty though. However I don't think the car is what Buford and I want for our nephew is it Buford?"

"No it's not. He's not in the market for the car. What he needs is an education and I don't think these two young ladies or the car is the type of education he needs."

Mr. Hill blinked like he had just been hit with a right cross then began to try and explain himself.

"Mr. Anderson I think you have the wrong idea about my visit."

Jesse laughed and looked at me. "See nephew this is what we call back tracking. Mr. Hill came here hoping to find two greedy country folk who would go along with his plans for you. What he found was two old men who are serious about your education now he has to back up and try to make this bad situation look good. However he's about to find out Buford isn't going to let that happen."

Mr. Hill had been looking at Jesse and I as Jesse talked to me but Ole Pop got his attention by putting his hand on his shoulder.

"Mr. Hill I'm over here."

Mr. Hill turned and looked at Ole Pop then got himself seriously embarrassed.

"Mr. Hill I don't think I have the wrong idea about you but I do think you have the wrong idea about us. It looks to me like you think we don't know you're hoping to attract my nephew with the lure of fast cars and pretty women."

Ole Pop looked at the cheerleaders and said.

"No offense young ladies."

Then he looked back at Mr. Hill. "My nephew doesn't need a lot of flash or cash or what ever else you're here to bring him."

Mr. Hill tries to interrupt Ole Pop but Jesse takes over the conversation.

"And please don't try to tell us you're not here for that. If you were here for legitimate reasons you would have brought a briefcase with information about your academics instead of the bright red mustang parked in our front yard. So don't insult me, Buford or my nephew further with a denial of your purpose."

As if on cue Ole Pop takes over. "Now while we have appreciated your visit I think it is over. Please be so kind as to shut the door on your way out."

Ole Pop looks at the two cheerleaders. "It was nice meeting you young ladies. Oh and a word of advice. You are very pretty young ladies. Don't allow someone to parade you around like pieces of meat on display. Your parents wouldn't approve."

The cheerleaders smile as they and Mr. Hill get up and walk out of the front door and I didn't get another letter from that university.

As soon as the visit was over I called Nate to tell him what happened but he wasn't at home. His mother told me that he had gone to lunch with the coach of the same college I had just had a visit from. I later found out that his Uncle Henry had called the coach and asked for the meeting.

When I finally caught up with Nate he was quiet and defensive about the meeting. When I told him about the meeting I had he said that Ole Pop didn't know what he was talking about and that I needed to mind my own business. We almost got into a fight about it but I decided it wasn't worth it and just walked away. From that point on our friendship was strained.

Several weeks after our last talk Nate came to school driving a brand new Mustang. It was the same mustang the recruiter drove to our house. A couple of weeks later the college recruiter flew Nate to their university and called a press conference and Nate announced that he was going to their university. His uncle Henry was standing right beside him grinning.

Graduation came and Nate and I went our separate ways. My freshman year was filled with studying, practice, and weight training. I didn't get much playing time because there were two senior linebackers in front of me and they were pro prospects. So I spent most of my time on the bench.

Nate on the other hand was tearing it up. As a freshman he was starting at Defensive end and by the middle of the season he had ten sacks and even more tackles. He was on ESPN more than the announcers were. He was considered one of the best young defensive linemen in the country.

When he came back to town everyone was congratulating him. We ran into each other at the store next to the school. I couldn't believe it when I saw him because he was huge. I mean he was always a big man but he was huge now. There was something unnatural about his size. I asked him what he was doing and he said he worked out a lot but I knew it was something different.

The next year I made the first team. It took me a while to get used to the speed of the game but when I finally did I was able to make some big plays. I caught a few interceptions, and had several sacks. By the middle of the season I was considered one of the top linebackers in college and my name began to show up on ESPN a lot.

One night I was looking at ESPN when the story broke about Nate. He'd been caught when the NCAA gave him a random drug test and he tested positive for steroids. That led to an investigation of Nate and his university's football program.

The investigation uncovered several recruiting violations including the car and money Nate received for signing with the program. A year later Nate was back home for good.

We found out later that after several months of NCAA investigations and a lot of bad press the University needed someone to take the fall and that someone was Nate. They hung him the sacrificial lamb even though everyone involved in the violations knew he wasn't the bad guy.

The university did some fast foot work and certain witnesses and the drug test for several other players mysteriously disappeared. The university did everything they could to hide as much as they could from the NCAA investigators. Of course the alumni association rallied behind the coach and his program and in the end Nate and three other players lost their scholarships.

That same coach who promised Nate all the good things in life was the same one who abandoned him when it looked like his program was in trouble. In the end Nate and the other players were suspended for one year and the coach and his program got two year's suspension.

Of course two year's suspension for a football program is no where near as bad as one year of a football player's life especially if the football player can't play ball anywhere. The sports media forgets about him and the pro scouts do to.

To top it off, since Nate didn't go to class much his freshman year he was put on academic probation by the University. They really didn't want him there anymore because of the scandal and this was their way or getting rid of him.

He tried to get his studies back up but the university didn't offer to help him in any way. Since he was put on probation he couldn't have any contact with the team and he couldn't receive any of the special help college ball players receive. He had to catch up on his own and that was the worse part of it.

Nate never was the best student. Most of the time Nessa and I helped him with his work. That's not to say he was stupid or anything like that. It's just that his mind was geared a little different from everyone else.

Nessa convinced him to see the learning specialist at our school and after several test she discovered that Nate had a learning disability. She suggested that Nate come to the learning center every day after school so she could work with him but to Nate it sounded like she was saying he was slow. He wasn't about to let anyone call him slow so he never went.

Now he was on his own trying to get off probation. Unfortunately he wasn't up to the challenge. His grades never improved and at the end of the year his scholarship was pulled and he was kicked out of the university.

The coach didn't even bother to tell him. An assistant coach called him at the dorm and told him to pack his things and leave. They even had security escort him out just in case he didn't want to leave. They were nice enough to provide him with a bus ticket home.

He came back home with no football career and no education. He went to a small division one college in our state and started there but he hurt his back the third game into the season and because of the damage steroids had done to his body he didn't heal properly and pretty soon he was out of football altogether.

The money was gone along with the car and his prospects of becoming a millionaire pro ball player. Of course as soon as his career was over his Uncle Henry was gone and after that Nate's life went down hill rapidly.

I tried to see him several times but he wouldn't see anyone. Finally he left the state and found a job in Alabama as a security officer. A year to the day after his career ended he was found dead in his apartment of an overdose of Cocaine.

I went to his funeral with Nessa and couldn't believe how weak and feeble he looked. For the next month all I could do was think about him and wonder why all of this had to happen to him.

The next football season came around and I was selected as the number one linebacker in the country. I decided to dedicate that season to Nate. I wore his number on my socks in every game I played.

I was having a great year until I was blind sided by an offensive tackle and I heard something snap in my leg. After the play was over I tried to get up but I couldn't. I couldn't even feel my leg. It was as if it wasn't there. The team doctor and trainer put me on a stretcher and carried me back to the field house for x-rays. I found out later that I had torn several ligaments in my knee and my leg had been broken in several places.

After they fixed the tears and breaks in my leg I started my rehabilitation so I could get ready for the next year. After six months I was running and practicing and I was feeling pretty good until spring practice and the first contact of the season.

On the first hit I felt my leg give way and I couldn't move it again. I had torn the same ligaments again and this time the doctor told me I wouldn't be able to play football again.

I was angry as hell. How could this happen to me? Wasn't it enough that I had lost my best friend? Why in the hell was life trying to beat me down? I didn't want to eat or talk to anyone including Nessa.

I shut her out of my life for a month. She waited patiently for me to deal with my pain but eventually her patience ran short. One day she came to the house and she was in no mood to hear all my complaints and deal with my attitude.

She walked into my room, sat down and quietly said, "Baby I need to talk to you."

"I don't feel like talking."

"Okay then just listen. I know you're hurt about your football career but you have more going for you than just foot ball."

"Look I told you I don't feel like talking. You don't know how I feel so just drop it."

"I know I love you and you've shut me out of your life and that's not fair."

"Fair!! What the hell do you know about fair? I put in a lot of work to become one of the best football players in the country and now I can't do it because of my leg. You don't know what it's like to lose something you've worked your whole life for."

"First of all Andre, don't yell at me I am not your child. And why don't you stop feeling sorry for yourself? You have not been working on this all of your life. You just started when you came to school down here and you have over come bigger things in your life than this so why the big deal about this?"

I got up off the bed, walked to the door and opened it.

"See there you go talking about shit you don't know nothing about. Why don't you just leave?"

Nessa got off the bed, walked over to my dresser to get her purse.

"Okay I'm going to leave but I want you to know you're acting like a big baby. You still have your scholarship and you can still go to school and get your education so why don't you stop all this whining and moping and act like a man?"

"How you gonna come in here and tell me what to do? You ain't my mother and we don't have no papers on each other."

"I don't need papers on you to know when you're acting like a baby and if I were your mother I would whoop your butt and tell you to get over it."

I started walking toward her and raised my hand.

"Who the hell do you think you're talking to? Get the hell out of my house before I knock your ass out."

I didn't know Ole Pop was across the hall in his room and had heard the whole conversation. As he walked into my room I heard his booming voice ring all over the house and it didn't sound as if he was happy.

"Boy what do you think you're going to do with that hand? And this is not your house its mine and Jesses. She can stay as long as she wants."

I turn and look at Ole Pop then grab my coat and try to walk out of the room but Ole Pop stops me.

"You owe the young lady an apology and you're going to give it to her or I'm going to go get my shotgun and blow your damn brains out."

I knew Ole Pop was mad but I didn't know how mad until he cursed. He very rarely cursed and he certainly didn't curse at the people he loved but I had crossed the line and I was going to listen to everything he had to say.

His eyes never left me as he continued to explain to me the mistake I had just made.

"The only thing she's guilty of is trying to love your dumb ass and this is the way you repay her. If I was her I'd leave your butt and never look back. Oh, and the next time I hear about you cursing or raising your hand to any woman give your heart to God, cause your ass will belong to me."

From behind Ole Pop I hear another voice say

"Me too."

Jesse is standing just outside the door and he sounded madder than Ole Pop. Now I had both of them mad at me. I turned and mumbled an apology and then walked past Ole Pop and Jesse who looked like they wanted to get some switches and conversate with me.

I knew the whole house was mad at me but at that present time I didn't care. I hit the front door and turned the corner and started walking toward the fields and Old Blue joined me. He looked up at me like he wanted to say, "What has your dumb ass done this time?"

I rubbed his head and kept walking. I walked for several miles until I got things sorted out in my head.

When I got back Nessa had cooked dinner and Ole Pop, Jesse and Nessa were sitting down to the table eating. I washed my hands, got me a plate and sat down with them. Jesse looked at Ole Pop.

"Well I guess he ain't so mad he can't come in and eat but you'd think he would at least say something before he did."

I looked at Jesse then at Ole Pop and then at Nessa.

"Look Nessa I'm sorry about what happened. I had no right to talk to you like I did and you're right I need to get on with my life. I hope you'll forgive me."

She looked me in the eyes, "Andre you know I love you so you know I forgive you but if you ever raise your hand at me again I'll be gone before you can take another breath and I won't be back."

Jesse started laughing, "Well Buford I think the boy might be in good hands."

"Oh I wasn't worried about that. I knew she could handle him. Around his friends he may be the big man but we all know who is the CEO of the Wright company. Besides he's always been a little soft when it comes to her anyway."

Jesse laughed so hard he swallowed some of his snuff and got choked but not choked enough that he couldn't say, "That's good cause if he keeps writing those checks his butt can't cash she's going to take one of them and knock him upside his head with it."

Now it was Ole Pops turn to laugh. I looked at both of them and shook my head.

"I see you old men gots jokes tonight. I want you to know I'm running things around here."

Nessa punches me in the ribs with a loud thump and Jesse looks at me still laughing.

"Dang nephew your ribs ought to be broke. I heard that punch all the way over here. Now who did you say was running things in here?"

Both Ole Pop and Jesse keep the joke going while we finish dinner. After dinner Ole Pop and I had a talk and I finished getting over myself and preparing to move on with my life.

Chapter 15

Mom became severely ill six months after dad died and I had no choice but to go back home and take care of her. Since I was living in the football dorm while I rehabbed my leg again Ole Pop didn't know. Mom and I decided not to tell Ole Pop about it because he was having health problems too and Jesse was too old to look after her and Ole Pop.

Ole Pop found out about it anyway. I wasn't home a week before he knew I was there. I don't know how he does that. Sometimes I think he has a direct pipeline to God.

As soon as he found out he came up to Philadelphia to take mom back to Mississippi. She tried to argue but Ole Pops started putting her clothes in bags and chewing her out at the same time.

"Sarah there's no reason you can't come home and rest."

"Ole Pop I don't want to be a burden on you and Jesse."

Jesse stops helping Ole Pop pack boxes.

"Look heah missy, I'll tell you when you're a burden on Jesse now come over here and tell me which clothes to put in this here box."

"You really don't have to do this. In another few months I'll be back on my feet and Andre can go back to school."

Ole Pop stops and looks Mom in the eyes.

"Sarah, Andre has already missed a week out of school he doesn't need to miss two. You and I both know that an education is one of the survival kits a young black man needs to make it in this country. Now come on home and let Andre go back to school."

"Ole Pop I'll be alright. I can go back next semester."

"I know you can son but I want you to go on and finish and then I want you to go on to graduate school. And there's no need to delay your return when Jesse and I can watch after your mother and you can come home on the weekends and take care of her. Now help me move these boxes into the truck."

Mom and I look at each other and nod. We both know that once Ole Pop and Jesse get something in their heads nothing short of the Lord coming down and talking to them is going to change their minds. So we go to work and in a short time we have mom's things loaded up and we're headed back to Mississippi.

As soon as mom got home Nessa came over to help her get everything organized around the house. The first thing they did was put the curtains back up to the windows. And as soon as they did the argument started again. This was the second time Ole Pop and Jesse argued with Mom about those curtains

Ole Pop took the curtains down after Mom went back to Philadelphia. He said he didn't have time to wash curtains and take care of a farm too. Mom didn't listen, she found the curtains and put them back up.

Of course Jesse started right in complaining again. However as soon as he did mom and Nessa would sneak up on him and hug him and kiss him. That would make him stop complaining about the curtains and start complaining about them trying to butter him up.

"Yall can go on somewhere with all dat butterin yall is trying to put on me. I ain't goin for it."

I don't know which one he loved more, mom and Nessa or complaining about mom and Nessa.

One night Ole Pop sat down with me, mom and Jesse and expressed his concerns about Nessa. It appeared to him that she never wanted to go home. He said He didn't mind her being here in fact he enjoyed having young people in his house again but it wasn't right for a young girl not to be around her mother more.

He asked me if I had seen any changes in her lately and I told him yes. She was much more moody than she had ever been and sometimes she would snap at me for no reason at all and sometimes when I picked her up from her house there would be tear stains on her face like she had just gotten through crying and then it hit me. It had been months since I had been in her house. Every time I came to her house she was always outside on the porch.

I told Ole Pops and he said that He thought he saw Nessa's mother in the liquor store the other day and he hadn't seen her at church in a while. He had the feeling whatever was wrong had something to do with Nessa's mother.

The next night when I pulled up in front of Nessa's house I got out of the truck and walked toward the house. Nessa stopped me and asked me where I was going.

"I'm going to see your mother I haven't said hello in a while."

"Mom is sick with the flu and doesn't really need to be disturbed right now. Besides I don't want you to catch what she has.

After our date I went home and told Mom about it and she said she and Nessa's mom were close in high school. She decided it was time for her and Nessa's mother to talk so the next day mom paid her a visit.

After the visit mom came home and told Ole Pop Nessa's mom was drinking heavily. Ole Pop asked her if she could get her to agree to go for counseling and she said yes.

Mom convinced Nessa's mother that Nessa needed her. Mom also told her she would go to the meetings with her for support. Ole Pop told mom that he would do everything he could to help her.

That night mom told me to go get Nessa and bring her back home. When I got there she took Nessa up to her room and they stayed up there for a couple of hours. I asked Ole Pop what was going on and he sit me down and told me about Nessa's mother's drinking problem.

Being the child of an alcoholic I felt her pain. I also felt a little stupid for not recognizing that her mother was an alcoholic. She showed all the classic signs. I just didn't notice.

When mom got through talking to Nessa, Nessa came down the stairs with tears on her cheeks and I walked out on the porch with her so we could talk.

I told her that I loved her and would always be there for her and then I held her in my arms and let her cry as long as she wanted to.

For the next two months mom and Nessa's mother went to the rehab center for counseling and gradually Nessa's mom got better and Nessa became her old self again and everything was fine until

the eighteenth of October. That's the day things went terribly wrong.
So wrong in fact that I thought I was going to lose my Nessa. Thank
God Nessa didn't see it happen. It was bad enough that she had to be
the one to find them.

That October night Nessa's father came back to the house for
the first time in several years. He was broke, drunk, and mad. The
neighbors say he stormed into the house screaming about how it was
still his house and how he would come there any time he pleased.
Nessa's mother tried to calm him down but the more she tried to
talk to him the crazier he got.

According to the neighbors he started yelling that it was her
fault his marriage to his young secretary didn't work out. He kept
screaming that if she had stayed out of his business he would still be
happily married. She told him she was sorry but he had to pay child
support for Nessa. He said he didn't have enough money to run two
families and that's why his wife left him and now his life was ruined
all because she wouldn't leave him and his family alone then he
pulled out a gun.

The neighbors said they could hear Nessa's mom pleading with
him not to shoot her and that's when they called the police. Seconds
later they heard two shots and then silence. Unfortunately right after
the shots had been fired Nessa pulled up in her mother's car.

The neighbors ran out of the house and hollered for her not to go
in but they were too late she had already opened the door and found
her father lying in his own blood in the living room and then she ran
in the kitchen and saw her mother lying face down on the floor. She
screamed and fainted and that's the way the neighbors found her.

There was an official investigation that concluded that Nessa's
mom was killed by her father and then he shot himself. When Nessa
got out of the hospital I brought her back to Ole Pops place. She
was totally devastated and all she kept saying is, "Why is all of this
happening to me?"

After the funeral Mom and Ole Pop petitioned the court for
custody of Nessa and since she didn't have any grandparents the
court agreed and she came to stay with us.

For the next month she wouldn't go anywhere but to school and
back and she didn't say much. Mostly she just sat out on the porch
and looked out over the fields. I tried my best to keep her company

but something inside of her had withdrawn and I didn't know if I could get it back. Ole Pop sat and watched her as she grieved and when he thought the time was right he took her to his study, shut the door and talked to her.

She later told me what he said to her. She said when he called her into the study to talk she thought she was going to get the standard speech about how her mother and father would have wanted her to go on with her life and that no matter how sad she feels she needed to get on with her life but instead he asked her how long she was going to let the world walk all over her?

When she asked him what he meant by that he looked her in the eyes and said.

"Vanessa I know you're hurt but do you realize there is a whole world out there just waiting to see what you're going to do with your life. There are people out there hoping you'll come through this. I happen to be one of those along with Sarah, Andre, and Jesse. Then there are the ones out there who don't like you. They're the ones who hope you drown in sorrow and die. You know the ones I'm talking about. The young ladies who don't like you just because you're you, the boys who don't like you cause you won't lay down with them, the old people who don't like you because of something that happened between your parents and them and the ones who don't like you because they don't like any body.

Don't let these negative people win and don't let this negative situation ruin your life. You've got a choice to make. Either stand up and take control of your life right now or lie down and let life take control of you and one other thing. I'm going to tell you the same thing I told Andre when he first got here. If you lie down the world is just going to continue to stomp you but if you stand up while life is kicking your butt it will have to kick up at you and the harder it kicks you, the higher you're going to climb."

After saying that Nessa looked at me and said, "And what he said makes sense so I'm going to stand up from now on."

When I heard her say that I smiled because I knew he had reached her. I am constantly amazed at how this old man can motivate people into becoming more than they thought they could be.

After that my old Nessa returned she was intelligent, beautiful, funny and sexy but she still wouldn't let me have what I wanted no matter how much I schemed, begged or pleaded. She reminded me of what I told her and held me to it. Besides Jesse, mom and Ole Pop kept a careful eye open for two young adults with raging hormones and Ole Pop would have killed me if he had caught us doing anything other than kissing, which he did catch us doing several times.

Sometimes Nessa and I would be out on the porch in the swing kissing and Ole Pop and Jesse would walk around from the side of the house where they grew tomatoes and catch us. He would chuckle and say, "Boy quit sucking up all the girl's air."

Then Jesse would laugh and say, "Yeah boy turn her loose and let her breathe."

Nessa would get all embarrassed and try to apologize and that would only make Ole Pop and Jesse laugh that much more.

I would laugh too unless mom was around, she wasn't having it. She was bound and determined there would be no babies born to any unmarried young adults in this house and you would think she was trying to protect her son but that wasn't the case.

I was the one who always got chewed out because she didn't want Nessa to go through the misery of being an unwed teenaged mother. Mom was always kinda hard on me ever time she caught us and I didn't understand it but Ole Pop would tell me not to worry about it.

Most times though Ole Pop would kind of calm her down and tell her that sometimes you have to trust them to do the right thing and for the most part Nessa and I did the right thing.

Sometimes I would sit out on the front steps and rub Ole Blue's head and think about where I was a couple of years ago and where I am now and realize how blessed I am that life is real good for me now. There's no telling where I would be if mom hadn't brought me to Ole Pop. Through his and mom's prayers for me I just might make it through.

But for some reason it still bothered me that mom was so hard on me when she thought Nessa and I were going to make a mistake. Why didn't she ever say anything to Nessa? Why was she always on me? Something about the way mom acted just didn't sit right with me.

I tried to sit down and talk to her about it but every time I did she would end up getting mad and walking away from me and that just made the whole thing bother me more.

Finally I sat down and had a talk with Ole Pop. After listening to me he told me he didn't realize our conversations concerned me so much. I asked him why mom got mad every time I tried to talk to her about it and Ole Pop dropped his head for a minute then slowly raised his head and looked at me.

"Sometimes when a person loves you they try to shield you from certain things and in doing so they cause bigger problems than they are trying to hide. Let me talk to your momma and see what I can do."

I wondered what he meant by shielding some one. Shielding them from what? There was something going on. I didn't know what it was but I would soon find out.

A couple of days later I came home from class early. I walked up on the porch and I could hear mom talking real loud. She was telling somebody that it was her business and they needed to stay out of it. I opened the front door and saw her walking away from Ole Pop.

I stood there kind of in shock. There was no one else in the room but her and Ole Pop but I just know she couldn't have been talking to Ole Pop like that. She loved that old man more than I did. My mom would never disrespect Ole Pop like that.

I walked into the house and looked at Ole Pop. He just shook his head, turned and walked into the kitchen. What was going on here? Something just wasn't right and I needed to find out what it was.

I followed mom up the stairs and walked into her room.

"Mom why were you hollering at Ole Pop?"

"I wasn't hollering at Ole Pop and our conversation is none of your business."

"Mom something is bothering you and it has been bothering you for a long time don't you think we should talk about it?"

"There is nothing wrong with me and there is nothing to talk about so just drop the subject."

"Drop what subject? Mom what is this all about? You've been real moody lately and you are always hollering at me when you catch me and Nessa kissing. We are in love mom. We like to kiss and hug but you make me feel like I'm doing something dirty."

"Andre I don't want to talk about this now."

"But mom I need to know why you're so hard on me about this. Are you hiding something I need to know?"

"Andre I said I don't want to talk about this. Now get out of my room."

"Mom I'm your son and I love you and I deserve an explanation about this."

"Andre, don't forget who is the mother and who is the child. Now I said get out of my room."

From behind me I hear Ole Pop's deep voice.

"Sarah it's time you got this burden off you. It's time for Andre to know the truth. If you keep this inside of you it will eventually drive a wedge between you and Andre."

Mom gets up off her bed, grabs her coat and heads for the door.

"I wish all of you would just stay out of my business."

She stands in front of Ole Pop who is taking up the whole door and looks at him with a look I've never seen in my mom eyes before. Ole Pop slowly shakes his head then moves out of the way allowing mom to leave the room.

As she heads down the stairs I walk toward the door. I'm going after her to find out what this is all about but Ole Pop steps in front of me.

"Let her go son."

"Ole Pop what is going on?"

"I can't tell you. Only she can tell you about this. I know it's hard but you're going to have to be patient with her until she sees fit to sit down and talk to you about it."

Ole Pop turned around and headed down the steps leaving me alone in mom's room. What could be so bad that it has mom hollering at both me and Ole Pop? This was going to be on my mind for a long time.

Mom left at seven and now it was eleven and she still wasn't back. She never stayed out this late without telling us where she was. I was beginning to worry that something had happened to her but around eleven forty five I heard the front door open then the sound of her feet on the stairs.

I wanted to walk to my door, open it up and tell her we needed to talk but I knew that probably wouldn't do any good so I continued to lie on my bed worrying about her.

Twenty minutes later my door opens and mom walks into the room followed by Ole Pop and Jesse. Ole Pop and Jesse sit in the chairs across from my bed and mom sit down beside me on my bed.

There were tears in her eyes and her hands were trembling as she rubbed my head.

"Andre I have something to tell you and its going to be hard for me so promise me you'll be quiet until I finish."

"Mom what's wrong?"

"I'm wrong Andre but I'm going to correct it right now. Andre this is hard for me to say to you but the man you think is your father isn't your father by blood."

Those few words hit me in the gut like a straight shot from a professional fighter. Is she telling me that my father isn't my father?

"Are you saying dad wasn't my father?"

"Yes Andre."

"How did this happen mom?"

"When I was eighteen I met an older man and fell in love with him. I couldn't see that he really didn't love me but Ole Pop could. He tried to tell me about this man but I wouldn't listen. Just like you I was hard headed and disobedient and one night I slipped out of the house and went to a party with him. I drank too much alcohol and one thing led to another and I woke up in his bed the next morning.

He told me nothing happened between us but he lied. By the time I found out I was pregnant with you he was long gone. It wasn't long after you were born that I met your father. You were two years old when we got married."

"Why are you just now telling me this?"

"Because your father didn't want you to know. From the time you were three months old until now he has been the only father you have ever known. He didn't want you to have to deal with the rejection of someone who was supposed to love you so he wouldn't let me tell you."

"What is my blood father's name?"

"Carl Perry."

"What does he look like?"

"He's shorter than you and light skinned and he wears glasses."

Jesse spoke up then, "Actually nephew you don't look nothin like him. In fact you look more like Joseph than you do that other fella. Just like I told Sarah if a man buys enough milk for a child eventually that child will start to look like him."

I look at Jesse then back at mom. "Mom is that why you've been so hard on me lately?"

"Yes Andre I just don't want Vanessa to end up like I did."

"I wouldn't get Nessa drunk and take advantage of her like that."

"I know you wouldn't Andre but if the two of you had sex and she got pregnant the results would be the same. She would feel stained somehow and she would wonder if you still wanted her."

"Do you mind if I ask you another question?"

"You can ask me anything Andre."

"Is that why you couldn't forgive pop for his mistake?"

Mom turned her head from me but I could see the tears falling from her chin into her lap. I almost wished I hadn't asked the question. It was almost a full minute before she could speak.

"Yes Andre that had a lot to do with it. I had been betrayed once by a man I thought loved me and to have it happen again was totally devastating."

I leaned over and hugged mom while Ole Pop and Jesse got up and quietly walked out of my room. Mom and I talked for the better part of two hours and in the end we grew a stronger bond than we had before and as far as I am concerned Joseph Wright is the only father I have had or will ever have.

After our conversation mom returned to her cheerful self and she made a decision that made all of us extremely happy. She applied for a professorship at Ole Miss where I was attending and she got the job. Several months later she sold the house in Philadelphia and Ole Pop and Jesse had her house built on their property.

Ole Pop and Jesse teased mom because she had all the modern conveniences including cable television. Jesse kept saying to her.

"See that's what's wrong with you city folk, you're too spoiled."

But he was the first one over there on Thursdays to see his favorite show.

After Mom told me the truth about my birth I was glad she didn't have to carry that burden around any longer. I vowed to make sure she didn't have to worry about me and Nessa again. Still I wondered what Carl Perry looked like and if I looked anything like him.

It's funny how the Lord works. I didn't know it then but this man would show up later in my life at a crucial time to deliver a message I would need to hear.

Chapter 16

Now I'm a senior in college and I have applied and been accepted into law school at Ole Miss. Ole Pop and Jesse are both older but that doesn't stop them from working on the farm. They still go out every day and work, but now Ole Pop has put me in charge of heavy shit.

I know that sounds wrong but you would have to understand Ole Pop's sense of humor. Ole Pop has been a big man all of his life and he claims he suffers from a disease that only big men can get. It's called "BM syndrome."

BM stands for "Big Man" and BM syndrome means if anyone has something heavy to lift or move they will automatically come to him and say, "Hey "Big Man" could you take this grand piano to the top of the building for me please."

While he was telling me this he was laughing because he said most of them would get insulted if he said no. It was like he was obligated to lift all their heavy stuff just because he was big.

He said that lifting heavy stuff is what big men are expected to do. That's why Ole Pop decided to make me the "BOHS" which meant "Boss of Heavy Shit." He pronounced it "Boss" and now anytime he needs something really heavy lifted Ole Pop will say, "Go get the BOHS."

Mom didn't like the name but it stuck because it fit me. By this time I am six foot six and I weigh about two hundred and fifty five pounds. So anytime something heavy needs to be lifted I have to do it.

Actually it is an honor to be the one to replace Ole Pop as the big man on the farm. Back in the day everyone knew that Buford

Jefferson Anderson was the one you called when you needed some heavy lifting done.

Now however Ole Pop can't physically do all the things he could do when he was a young man but his mind is still strong and sharp. I found out just how sharp that summer. That's when several strangers came to challenge Old Pop and Jesse's minds.

It was late Saturday evening, right after we got back from the fields when a brand new shiny black Mercedes pulled into Ole Pops yard. A tall, older white man got out of the car, walked up to the steps and looked at Jesse and Ole Pop.

"Hello, is either of you Buford or Jess Anderson?"

Jesse looked him in the eyes. "Who's asking?"

"My name is Claude Brekley and I represent a corporation that is prepared to offer you seven hundred thousand dollars for your farm."

Jesse spit in his cup as Ole Pop stood up and shook Mr. Brekley's hand.

"I'm Buford Anderson and this is my brother Jesse. But the farm is not for sale."

"Wait a minute now that wasn't our final offer I can go up to seven hundred and fifty thousand dollars."

Jesse laughs, "Buford I think he might need to go to the doctor and have his hearing checked. Didn't you just say the farm isn't for sale?"

Mr. Brekley turned to Jesse to say something to him but thought better of it and turned back to Ole Pop.

"Mr. Anderson are you sure you want to turn this money down? I mean after all you're not getting any younger. How long do you think you can keep this farm running?"

"Mr. Brekley I think it's nice that you're thinking about my health but I think my brother and I can manage."

Jesse leaned over and spit into his cup again. Then smiled his best country smile at him.

"We've made it this far we sure as hell can make it further. And why are you all of a sudden comin round here tryin to buy somethin?"

"We're just trying to help you gentlemen out. Farming is becoming a big business run by the government. I know it must be hard for you gentlemen to compete with the big companies. Besides this is a very generous offer. Probably the best offer you'll ever get for your land."

Ole Pop let out one of his low rumbling laughs.

"If you really want to help us why don't you go down there to my corn field and spread some of that horse manure on my corn. I'm sure the corn would appreciate it more than I do. I know you don't believe this but we are intelligent men and my brother and I would appreciate it if you told us the truth. Wouldn't you appreciate that Jesse?"

"I sho would. Da truth would do my whole body good right bout now. And if dey spread dat manure on da corn I won't have tuh do it"

"What do you mean Mr. Anderson? I am telling you the truth."

Ole Pop looks at Jesse and shakes his head as if to say, "Now this is a damned shame" then explodes Mr. Brekley's offer.

"Uh huh so I guess the fact that interstate fifty five is coming through here wouldn't have anything to do with this buy out huh?"

Mr. Brekley's mouth drops open. He looks like he's just been caught in the cookie jar and Ole Pop has a switch about to conversate with them.

Jesse starts laughing. "Look at him with his mouth open Buford. Son you'd better close your mouth before one of dem big mosquitoes takes a bite outta ya tongue. Now why don't you get back in da car, go on back to ya bosses and tell em da bad news."

Mr. Brekley doesn't say another word as he turns and walks off the porch. We watch as he drives away then I looked at Ole Pop.

"His bosses are going to be unhappy with the man when he gets back. They might even fire him for losing the land for them."

"They're not through yet. We're talking about a lot of money or they wouldn't have come. Men in suits who work for corporations only understand the bottom line. They really don't care how they get this land and they don't care who gets hurt in the process. They'll be back and the next time they'll have a much better offer and when Jesse and I turn that down they'll start working on a way to force us out. I'm afraid this isn't going to do nothing but get uglier."

I didn't understand then but it didn't take long for me to find out what Ole Pop meant. The next day Ole Pop made a few phone calls then told me to get in the truck and take him and Jesse across town.

We arrived at a huge house on the river. I didn't even know that Ole Pop knew anyone who lived in this area.

The house sat on a piece of land that jutted out into the river. It was an old plantation looking house but inside it had all the modern facilities.

When we walked up to the house we were greeted by and older white gentleman and Ole Pop introduced him to me as retired Major Aaron Kendall. He told me they had served in Viet Nam together.

We were led into a room that had several computers in it and we sat down.

"Buford it's been a long time since we spoke what makes you come to see me now."

"Aaron I had a visit from some men claiming to represent a corporation that wants to buy up my land and all the land in the area. I know the interstate is coming through my area but they offered me a lot more money than the land is worth. There has to be more to it than just the interstate."

"Let me check it out."

Aaron turned around and got on one of the computers behind him. It took him all of fifteen minutes to come up with a complete answer to Ole Pops question.

"Buford I'm afraid you and Jesse got trouble coming yalls way. Did you know the land you live on once belonged to the Choctaw Indians?"

"No I didn't. Jesse and I bought it from several farmers in the area who were tired of farming and wanted to either retire or move to another state."

"Well a thousand acres of it was originally owned by the Choctaw Indians. About a hundred and fifty years ago the American government moved in and took the land. To keep the chief of the tribe happy and to avoid any conflict they promised him in writing that even though the land would belong to America it would still be under Choctaw law.

"Okay but why is that so important?"

"If the Choctaw nation can get it back they can build a casino on it."

"So if someone of Choctaw descent can get the land they can make a lot of money?"

"That's right and one other thing. The State government has just agreed to a tax break for a corporation that owns two casino chains. Now with the interstate going through there and a casino in the area there could be billions of dollars just waiting to be made so you better be careful. With that kind of money at stake it could get dangerous."

"I knew there was more to this than just the interstate. So they want my land huh? Well I know I can't fight them but before I go I'm going to make them pay for it."

Two days later the Mr. Brekley comes back to talk to Ole Pop.

"Mr. Anderson I'm here to double our offer to one point five million dollars. I don't think you'll get another offer anywhere that is this fair."

"So this is the best offer I'm going to get from your corporation?"

"Yes sir you're not going to get a better offer than this."

Ole Pop turns to Jesse. "What do you think Jesse, should we sell the place?"

"Well I don't know Buford, it seems like a good offer. I mean it looks like a fair price for a farm but I'm not so sure it's a fair price for land the interstate highway is going to run through."

"Yeah you're probably right and it's definitely not a good offer for land a casino is going to be built on."

We all look at Mr. Brekley turn red as a beet. His mouth opens to say something but then he closes it. Jesse starts laughing and almost spits snuff on his shirt.

"Look at em Buford. He didn't think old country black folk like us would have enough sense to find out why his corporation wanted to buy this land."

"And you know that's a shame. If I didn't know any better I would think he thought we were stupid but I know he doesn't think that."

Mr. Brekley has just realized Ole Pop and Jesse have been making a fool of him from the beginning. That realization brings sweat to his forehead. Without another word Mr. Brekley turns and walks off the porch.

Ole Pop looks at Jesse, "Well it won't be long now before they come with all the lawyers in the world. I guess I need to call Henry."

"Yeah ole Henry will know exactly how to handle this."

I look at Jesse, "Who is ole Henry?"

"His name is Henry Bernard McNeal and he's one of our oldest friends. He's a corporate lawyer specializing in contracts and negotiations. He'll know what to do." Ole Pop gets on the phone and calls Henry and sets up an appointment for the next day.

That night Ole Pop and Jesse sit down and tell me they want me to go with them every time they have to do any business because if anything happens to them I will have to be the one who takes over.

Then they drop a bomb shell on me. Ole Pop tells me when he and Jesse pass on they are leaving all their assets to me. I look at Ole Pop and then at Jesse. Jesse smiles and says.

"I didn't think you would be the one when you first got here cause you was as mad as a wet hornet. You remember don't you Buford? Kept talking bout how country it was down here and how he couldn't wait to get back to the city."

"Yeah he was kinda hard headed wasn't he Jesse? I thought a few times I was going to have to knock him out just to get his attention. But he turned out pretty good."

"Yeah he ain't bad for a city boy. He's still a little slow about shucking corn."

"That's cause he's always looking around for them yellow jackets."

"Dats right he did lose a fight with one of dem when he first got here. He sounded like a freight train running through the corn."

Ole Pop starts laughing then I start laughing.

"You two old men ought to get your own comedy show."

Then Ole Pops gets serious, "Son, I want you to know that Jesse and I can't think of anyone else we want to take care of our legacy. You will be the one who will keep our names alive. We've tried to live a life that is pleasing in God's eyes and when we're gone I expect you to keep that legacy true. I know this seems like a lot and no one wants to talk about losing someone they love but this is necessary."

Ole Pop goes to the desk, gets out some legal papers, sits down and shows them to me. They are the legal wills of Buford Jefferson Anderson and Jesse Ustes Anderson. Ole Pop gives them to me.

"Bring these with you tomorrow so we can sign them and get them notarized."

The next day Jesse, Ole Pop and I arrive at Henry's office and Ole Pop tells him what's been happening.

"Henry now that we know why they want the land I'm pretty sure they will resort to some legal tricks to get it if I don't sell it to them at the price they want."

"You're right. In fact they probably have enough money to influence the city council into either making you sell the land or just taking it."

"So what can we do? I already know I'm going to have to sell the land but I want to do it on my terms."

"Hold on now Buford you might not have to sell all the land. Didn't you say that all together you and Jesse own about fifty five hundred acres of land?"

"Yes we do but most of it is undeveloped land."

"How in the world did you and Jesse manage to get that much land?"

"After Jesse and I got out of the army we came back home and found little farms that were for sale. During that time there were a lot of farm owner's in the area. When farming became a corporate game regular farmers couldn't make a living and one by one they started moving on. Most of them knew Jesse and me so when they decided to sale their land and move on they would let us know.

Jesse and I had made some wise investments after we got out of the Army and managed to come up with a pretty good amount of money so we were in position to buy our neighbors out at a fair price. After we bought out so many of them, we combined our land and turned our farm into a successful and profitable venture. When the last remaining folks sold their farms, we bought them too. Eventually we found ourselves the owners of a pretty large piece of real estate."

"And that is going to work to your advantage. You have enough land to split it up so they can get what they want and you can keep part of the land. Now this means that if they ever want to expand on the casino they're going to have to come back to you again. They're not going to want to do that and they'll do everything in their power to get you to sell them all of the land or barring that they'll try to take it but I think I've got an answer for all of that."

Henry outlines the plan he has in mind and when he finishes Ole Pop and Jesse are very happy with it. After that piece of business is finished Ole Pop and Jesse sign the wills and Henry's secretary notarizes them and we leave for home.

Two days later a long white limousine pulls into Ole Pops yard. The front doors open and two men step out of the car. Both of them are carrying brief cases. One of them opens the back door for another man to get out. It is clear as soon as he steps out he is the boss.

He walks up the steps followed closely by the other two and introduces himself.

"Hello my name is Brian Adams and I'm looking for Buford and Jesse Anderson."

"You're looking at them."

"Gentlemen I'm the CEO of the Wentell Gaming and Entertainment Corporation. I'm here to negotiate with you for your land."

"Well you've come to the wrong place. Since you decided to offer what you call a fair deal to us, we did some checking and found out that your fair deal wasn't as fair as you made it out to be."

"I'm sorry about that my associates made an error in calculations that's why I came here myself so I could correct the mistake."

Jesse turned to me and says, "See nephew this is what's known as passing the corporate buck. He's the one who gave the orders. But now he's claiming it wasn't his fault. "The buck stops here" is not on his work desk."

The Brian turned to Jesse, "No, actually they made a mistake in calculations."

Jesse smiles and as country as he possibly can he says, "Is dat right? How bout ya goin down to da cornfield and spreadin dat manure in da same place ya workers did?"

Brian smiles at Jesse as if to say, "I've been warned about you" then turns back to Ole Pop.

"Mr. Anderson my corporation would like to offer you and your brother two million dollars for your land."

"Like I told you the first time you're at the wrong place."

"You do own the land don't you?"

"Yes we do. However after finding out why you want our land we have decided hire a lawyer. So if you want to buy this land you'll have to contact Henry McNeal and associates. They'll be handling our business from now on."

"Mr. Anderson surely we can handle this without getting a lot of lawyers involved."

"Is that right? Why don't you and your friends have a seat Mr. Adams?"

They all sit down and Ole Pops looks Brian in the eyes.

"Mr. Adams I assume that you have a college degree."

"Yes I do."

"Uh huh, and what did you get your degree in?"

Brian looks at Ole Pop and realizes that he's in over his head but he tries valiantly to come out on top.

"What do you mean?"

Jesse winks at me then looks Brian in the eyes.

"Come on now Brian, Buford asked you a straight forward question. And my nephew and I would also like to know what you got your degree in?"

Brian pauses as he contemplates his next move. He knows these old men are very savvy so they probably already know the answer to the question lying to them won't work. His next answer has to be the truth.

"Political science."

Ole Pop sits back in his chair. He has Brian on the ropes. Now all he has to do is deliver the knock out.

"Uh huh and where did you go to law school?"

"What makes you think I went to law school?"

"Mr. Adams I know your employees already told you we know how to use the internet. So lets cut the bullshit and get right down to the truth. Where did you attend law school?"

"Why are you asking me about my education?"

"If I remember correctly you asked me if we could handle this land deal with out lawyers. I'm trying to understand why you want me to do that especially since you're probably a corporate lawyer yourself. You wouldn't try and take advantage of two old country farmers would you?"

Brian stands up and the two men behind him stand up also.

"Mr. Anderson you will be hearing from me again."

"Then you'll be wasting your time. I already told you that you need to contact my lawyer. Ya'll have a good day now."

Brian's face gets flush as he heads back down the steps. He has had his pants pulled down and his butt spanked in front of his own people. That wasn't supposed to happen especially by two old country black men. The man was not happy when he left.

The next day around dusk dark Councilman Orton comes to the farm to talk to Ole Pop. Ole Pop, Jesse, mom, Nessa and me were all out on the porch watching the sun go down when he pulled into the yard.

He got out of his brand new E class Mercedes and walked up on the porch and without even saying hello he got straight to the point.

"Mr. Anderson I understand that you're kind of reluctant to part with your land."

"And where would you get a notion like that?"

"I have certain sources that have asked me to help in the negotiations."

Once again Jesse turns to me, "See nephew that means that he's going to make a lot of money if he can get Buford to sell his land cheap."

It is a thing of beauty when Jesse and Ole Pop get together and match wits with people who are supposed to be smarter than they are. Councilman Orton, just like Mr. Brekley and Mr. Adams is in over his head. The only difference is Mr. Brekley and Mr. Adams knew it. Councilman Orton doesn't have a clue so he presses on.

"Now Mr. Anderson I'm not here to talk about profit I'm here to explain to you and your brother how a casino could help our county grow. As you know we're one of the poorest counties in Mississippi. A casino would help pay for schools and better roads and health care for the county."

As soon as Jesse hears this the smile that is usually on his face disappears and in a most serious tone he addresses what he has just heard.

"You don't really expect us to believe that do you. We all know that a casino will only bring money to the politicians and owners of the casino while every one else will end up working for the casino or losing their money to it. Tell you what, that manure stinks so bad I don't even want it in our cornfield."

Councilman Orton completely ignores Jesse which is a major mistake.

"Now Buford, I hope you don't mind me calling you Buford, if I can have just a few more minutes of your time?"

"It won't do you any good. I already told those other fellas they need to see my lawyer if they want to buy this land."

"They did and they feel that fifty Million dollars is too much to pay for only half of your land."

Now Jesse's smile is back as if to say, "So you want to ignore ole Jesse."

Once again that country drawl is back as Jesse says, "Ooooooowee Buford! Did he say fifty million dollars? Dang dats a lot of money?"

"Yes it is Mr. Anderson. Actually it's too much money." Councilman Orton has just taken the bait.

Jesse pulls a computer print out from behind the chair he's sitting in and with the clearest English and diction begins to quote statistics.

"Not according to these projections we pulled off the government web site. According to this, the casino stands to make five hundred million dollars in its first year. This report further states that the consultant firm Wentell Gaming is using to procure the land for the casino belongs to you. That firm stands to make fifty million dollars if the deal is successful."

Jesse looks at Councilman Orton and smiles real big then drops back into his southern drawl.

"Now wut I figures dey oughta do is bypass tha middle man and pay us tha fifty million up front. Don't you thank dat would be smart?"

Without so much as a goodbye Councilman Orton turns and heads off the porch. Jesse leans up in his seat, waves and says, "Next time when ya come try tuh stay a little while longer heah."

Ole Pop's starts laughing and his laugh makes me start laughing and it becomes contagious. Mom starts laughing then Nessa starts laughing and we don't stop laughing for a while.

Two days later Ole Pop called me into his room and said.

"Sit down son you and I need to talk."

"What have I done this time?"

"It's time you start handling your weight around here. This situation with the casino owner requires a young man to handle it. Me and Jesse are getting older now. We can't move as fast or think as quick as we used to so when the time comes I want you to do the talking for us."

"C'mon Ole Pop you and I both know that you and Jesse are just as intelligent and quick witted now as you were when I first met you."

"Uh huh, I know that and you know that but not every body believes it. A lot of people think when you get old your brain slows down besides the farm is going to be yours after Jesse and I are gone so it's about time you learn to protect what's yours and protecting what's yours doesn't always mean a physical fight. In fact most of the time a physical fight is what is expected of a black man and that's why we lose so much. This is going to have to be done with your mind. Now tell me what you think is going to happen first?"

"They'll send another person to try and get you and Jesse to sell the land."

"No they won't. The last man we met was the man in charge. If he wasn't, Councilman Orton wouldn't have come. They've made their last offer to us now its time to use the law. It shouldn't be long before our city politicians get in the middle of this. Things are about to get very interesting."

Ole Pop continued to school me as to the way he thought things were going to happen. I was about to get a course in how a man should handle business.

Chapter 17

Three weeks later Ole Pop and Jesse received a letter in the mail from the city government notifying them that the property they owned had been changed from rural zoning to commercial zoning.

The government changed it seemingly overnight. They didn't ask him if Ole Pop and Jesse wanted it changed, they didn't even tell them why they changed it.

That change made their property taxes jump from one thousand dollars a year to twenty thousand a year. The farm was clearing a profit but not enough to cover that big of a property tax increase but it didn't matter to Ole Pop and Jesse. They both were very good with money and some folks say that both of them were probably millionaires but they never talked about it.

The next day we went to the lawyer and told him to fight it. Ole Pop and Jesse knew they were going to lose but they wanted it to be made public what the city had done.

The appeals took several months and just like Ole Pop said, he and Jesse lost. They went to the bank, got a cashier's check and paid the taxes. However by this time the local news had picked up the story.

The local media found out about Councilman Orton's involvement with Wentell Gaming. Then they found out Councilman Orton was one of the sponsors of the bill to raise Jesse and Ole Pop's property taxes. The next day the local paper's headline read, "Farmers lose to casino without placing a bet."

When the news about the casino broke the government the zone change was needed. And that a casino would bring more jobs into the area but once again the news came in and disputed the facts the city government put out. They showed that jobs in other places only rose a few percentage points. Now Councilman Orton was on the defensive.

Several weeks later Ole Pop and Jesse were visited by a Deputy Sheriff. He gave them a writ issued by the court stating they were to appear at a competency hearing the next week.

It seems that Ole Pop and Jesse had both been sent to the base psychologist for an interview just before they were discharged from the army. This was ordered by the post commander for all Vietnam vets on his post. Now the city council, Mr. Brian Adam and his lawyers were playing dirty.

After reading the letter I was as mad as hell.

"How in the hell can they say that about you and Jesse? I don't know anyone saner than the two of you. Somebody needs to knock Councilman Orton out."

Ole Pop looked at me then at Jesse. "Jesse I don't know if he is ready yet. I thought he was ready but he ain't thinking too well right now is he?"

"Naw he ain't Buford. Does he realize he has the answer to this problem in his hands?"

I stand between them wondering what these old men are talking about. I look from one to the other trying to figure out what's going on. Jesse leans over to me and says real quiet.

"Who gets the farm when Buford and I die?"

"I do. But what has that got to do with this?"

Jesse smacks me on the back of the head. "If they are successful in declaring us incompetent then that's as good as being dead and . . . ."

"I get the land. That's why you and Ole Pop were in such a hurry to get the will done."

"Dang Buford did you see dat light come on over his head?"

"Yeah Jesse I did. He was a little slow but he finally got there."

Ole Pop looked at me. "Son there are going to be a lot of trying times in your life. Most of them are going to happen real fast. But if you sit down and think about it most of your bad times will usually come after a warning. When the warning comes get ready for the fight right then so you won't get caught with your guard down and above all always think your way out. Leave the emotion for loving Vanessa and you'll be alright."

Three days later we are in court. Our lawyer argues that all soldiers go through the exam but Brian's lawyers countered by saying the exam gave cause to wonder about Ole Pop and Jesse's competency and the court agreed with Brian and his lawyers. Ole Pop and Jesse were ordered to take the psych exam.

The day after the preliminary competency hearing for Ole Pop and Jesse CNN called our house. It seems someone had called them and told them what was going on in our fair city. It wasn't long before the whole country was interested in what was happening to Ole Pop and Jesse.

In just a few days there were reporters every where. The city council was beginning to look bad as things about the council and the casino owners started to leak to the national press.

A week after CNN came to town the court changed their minds about having Ole Pop and Jesse evaluated. Ole Pop and Jesse were relieved but they weren't happy and the casino owners were about to run into their stubborn side.

Brian's company tried several other legal tactics to get Ole Pop and Jesse's land but were unsuccessful so the company was forced to negotiate with them. But Ole Pop and Jesse wouldn't even talk to Brian's lawyers for several months. When Ole Pop and Jesse finally decided to talk to them it was through me.

The day we met with their lawyers Ole Pop and Jesse wouldn't say a word to them. If there was a need for them to say something they would whisper it to me then sit back and glare across the table.

On the other side of the table was Brian Adams and his lawyers and Councilman Orton. Ole Pop was especially displeased with Councilman Orton. He felt Councilman Orton should have been on our side so he didn't even look at him.

Ole Pop and Jesse's proposal was handed to Brian's lawyers while we sat back and watched. The proposal called for Brian's corporation to lease the land for the sum of forty thousand dollars a month and pay all the property taxes on the land. They would get five hundred acres of land and the rest would be untouched.

Brian's lawyer's were the first to speak.

"Gentlemen, this is completely unacceptable. The casino has so much over head that at this price they wouldn't turn a profit."

As soon he says this Henry picks up his folder, places it in his case and stands up.

"Call us when you decide to come to terms."

Ole Pop, Jesse, Henry and I get up from the table and head for the door. Brian and his team try to get us to come back to the table but Ole Pop and Jesse weren't interested.

Two weeks later the city mailed a letter to Ole Pop stating that some of the land he owned was historic and the city was taking it over. They tried to hide the fact that the bill was sponsored by Councilman Dearing another of the councilmen in councilman Orton's consultant firm but someone on the council leaked it to CNN.

By the time the media got through with our council they were made to look like a bunch of crooks who just wanted to take the land two old men had lived on all their lives. Every day several national news reporters were trying to get interviews with someone on the council or Ole Pop and Jesse.

Ole Pop's lawyer granted an interview to CNN and the reporter followed Ole Pop and Jesse around on the farm all day. When the report aired it showed Ole Pop and Jesse to be war veterans who came home to become hard working farmers trying to survive while the city government tried to take away their land.

Letters started pouring in from all over the country and local activist began protesting in front of the council building. But even then the council refused to leave Ole Pop and Jesse's land alone. It looked like Ole Pop and Jesse were going to lose some of their land but then Thomas Berstein got in the middle of it.

Thomas Berstein was an investigative reporter for one of the major papers in New York. His column was read internationally and he decided he wouldn't focus on our city council. Instead he investigated Brian Adams and Wentell Gaming which was headquartered in New York.

He started digging into their books and business associates. His investigation found that for the last five years Wentell Gaming invested heavily in the campaigns of several of our city councilmen and state Senators. Berstein also found that plans for the casino have been going on in the council for the last five years.

Wentell tried to shut the investigation down but Berstein had too many credible facts and witnesses. Two weeks after the original report Berstein was a guest on "Sixty Minutes" and repeated everything he said in his column. He also produced tapes, bank records and interviews with key officials in Wentell to back his report up.

After his interview the commentator stated that the United States Attorney Generals office was looking into the allegations. If the allegations were true the parties involved would be dealt with according to the law.

Our lawyer had a conversation with some of the council members who were under investigation and convinced them it would be in their interest to drop the motion before the council to take Ole Pop and Jesse's land. The next day the council rescinded the order and The Wentell Corporation was forced to negotiate with us and still Ole Pop and Jesse made them wait.

Three weeks later we were back at the table but Councilman Orton was not present. Brian Adams agreed to the lease but asked that instead of five hundred he could lease one thousand acres. Ole Pop agreed only after the rent was raised to fifty thousand a month. Several days later the contracts were signed and that was that.

We found out later that councilman Orton was paid off and asked to take his consultant firm and go elsewhere. His firm lost a multi million dollar contract and he was pissed. From that moment he tried to stick it to Ole Pop every chance he got.

He sponsored and help get passed an ordinance that didn't allow farm animals within five hundred acres of the casino because it supposedly caused a health hazard. Then he got an ordinance passed that stated all property within several miles of the casino had to be neat with no high bushes or trees.

It cost Ole Pop and Jesse fifty thousand dollars to move the animals to another part of the farm. It cost another ten thousand to bring the property next to the casino up to code.

Ole Pop wasn't happy with the man. But Councilman Orton really tore his butt when he asked for another property tax hike to help increase the police force.

People started asking why they needed to raise the property taxes when the casino was supposed to bring in extra revenue. It didn't matter though. The council raised the taxes anyway. The tax increase is what got the ball started for me to get into the political arena.

After the tax increase people around our city started complaining that councilman Orton needed to go. They even asked Ole Pop if he would run for the office. He turned them down but Councilman Orton heard about it and began slandering Ole Pop's name in the papers.

He was saying things like "Who is making more money than anyone in the city off the casino?" and "Who sold the land that let the casino come into town in the first place."

Finally I got tired of him bad mouthing Ole Pop and decided that the next term I would run against him. Ole Pop advised me against it but I was determined to do it.

When he realized I was serious he sat me down and counseled me.

"Son if you're going to really run against him remember this. There will be compromises you have to make but always make sure it's a compromise your conscious can live with and if it comes down to making a choice between your morals and your political aspirations let the aspirations go."

After hearing that speech and knowing that I carried not only Ole Pops name but my mother and father's name as well I vowed to stick to the issues and let the voters decide. That is the only way I run a campaign.

That fall I graduated from the University of Mississippi and started law school. The next voting term rolled around and I registered my name as a candidate. I had the required amount of signatures but the councilman made the commission count them twice. He wanted to make sure I wasn't cheating.

Then he started the "My opponent doesn't have a clue what he's doing" campaign. You know the kind of campaign I mean. When the councilman talked about me it was always in these terms.

"He's young and ambitious but he can't do the job because he's young and ambitious."

He ran his campaign ads and tried to paint me as a youngster who would mess up things in the district but the polls were showing that the county wasn't agreeing with his assessment of me. That's when things got nasty.

First he attacked me personally. Someone found my juvenile record and accidentally let it slip out. He thought this would knock me out of the campaign.

"How can you trust someone with a record and he's someone from a northern state who doesn't understand people in Mississippi?"

He stressed the part about my being an outsider.

As soon as that happened I went on the radio made a full confession of what happened and also addressed the issue of being from Philadelphia. I stressed that where I'm from is not important. What is important are the facts. Councilman Orton has approved two property tax hikes and the county still has the worse roads and the least money to spend on schools.

The people responded to my radio interview by putting me even further ahead in the polls and Councilman Orton stepped up his attacks. He attacked Ole Pop and Jesse. They just laughed about it but it made me mad.

They weren't the ones who were running against him I was. Ole Pop told me to stand strong and watch because pretty soon the walls of Jericho were going to fall. I didn't understand what he meant at the time but it didn't take long for me to find out.

A week after the radio adds about Ole Pop and Jesse and how they had to take a psych test I received a phone call from Sterling Henson. Sterling was Councilman Orton's campaign manager. He asked if he could have a meeting with me. I told him I didn't want to hear what Councilman Orton had to say. He explained to me that the councilman wouldn't be at this meeting. I asked him to let me call him back.

I found Ole Pop in the barn and talked to him.

"Ole Pop I just got a call from a guy named Sterling Henson. He says he's Councilman Orton's campaign manager and he wants to meet with me alone tomorrow."

"Did he say what he wanted to talk about?"

"No sir. He just said he wanted to meet."

"Then invite him out to the house I would like to hear what he has to say."

I called Mr. Sterling and told him he could come out to the house and he told me he would rather meet some where else. I told him it was either the house or no where. He finally agreed and came to the house the next night.

As soon as he sat down he got right to the point.

"Mr. Wright I want you to know that I personally don't have anything against you but I thought I had better warn you there are certain people around here who want to see you dead. These people have been running illegal operations in this county and they don't want to see Councilman Orton out of office because they have him in their pocket."

Ole Pop looked at Mr. Henson, "Are you telling me that there may be someone out there trying to kill my nephew?"

"Yes sir I am."

"And why are you telling us this? Won't this put you in trouble if they find out?"

"No sir it won't because as soon as I leave here I'm leaving the city for good. I've seen enough illegal activity to last me a lifetime so I'm going to disappear. I just wanted you to know because I would hate to see you get hurt in this campaign."

He stood up, shook both of our hands and walked out the door. Two days later his body is found in a field. It looked like he had been attacked by a wild animal but Ole Pop, Jesse and I knew better.

For the next few weeks Ole Pop was very protective of his family. He wouldn't let me, mom or Nessa go anywhere unless he or Jesse went with me. This was becoming too hard to deal with. I had all but decided to give up the fight when I received something in the mail that changed the political landscape in our county.

I received an envelope with several legal documents in it. These documents were contracts given to certain individuals in the county for construction and utility work. Councilman Orton's name was on them.

There were several other papers with the names of five different construction firm owners on them and their backgrounds. All of these men were known felons and they were the same ones whose name appeared on the contracts beside Councilman Orton's name.

These men weren't even supposed to be considered for city contracts but there they were making millions off the contracts they had with the city and the council members were getting kick backs from them.

I immediately called our lawyer and gave him the papers. He called the FBI and after several weeks of undercover investigations all the men with their names on the contracts were arrested. The FBI was sure there were other Council members involved but only Councilman Orton's name was on the contracts.

CNN somehow found out about it and it was broadcast all over the country. Councilman Orton was charged but after some back room politics he was released. He refused to testify against anyone and every day for a while he was in front of a news camera proclaiming his innocence.

At first Ole Pop was surprised Councilman Orton was still alive. Jesse said he must have some mighty powerful evidence to keep his partners from planting him in the ground. We found out later that Councilman Orton was offered a deal to point out the other Councilmen involved with him but he refused.

With some legal maneuvering Councilman Orton escaped jail but his political career was severely damaged. He tried to convince everyone he lost the election because of the trumped up indictment I started but of course no one believed him. I won the election by a landslide.

After the election was over he wasn't a happy person. No one in the county trusted him anymore. He couldn't even run for dog catcher and win. From that time I became his obsession and he vowed I would hear from him again.

Chapter 18

A week later I was sworn into office and things were working fine. I was in my second year of law school and I was a councilman. A lot of my law professors were proud of my political ambitions and all of them had advice for me but there was one who didn't share their enthusiasm. His name was Dr. Ryan Jackson Mayhew.

Two months before I was elected Dr. Mayhew returned from Japan to become the Dean of our law school. He had been in Japan for the last two years working as the liaison and legal counsel for one of America's biggest computer firms.

He was an older gray haired Irishman who was stubborn and hard to get along with. He was also one of the top corporate lawyers in the world. His motto is, "An unprepared lawyer is a detriment to anyone he represents" and Dr. Mayhew was every bit as serious as Ole Pop and Jesse.

After the election was over Dr. Mayhew called me into his office. When I arrived he was working at his desk. I knocked on the door and without looking up he said, "Come in."

"You wanted to see me Dr. Mayhew."

"Shut the door Mr. Wright and have a seat."

As soon as I sat down he began his lecture.

"Young man I see that you won the election for councilman by default. I would say congratulations but I don't think that is in order considering I don't think you have a clue as to what it means to be a councilman. Do you?"

"I don't understand what you mean Dr. Mayhew."

"Okay let me put it this way. What do you plan to do to help the people of your county?"

"Well first of all I plan on getting the property taxes lowered and then I'm going to get more money for schools and roads."

"And how are you going to do this?"

"I'm going to the council meetings and present a proposal for funding for the roads and Schools."

"And if you rescind the taxes where is this money going to come from?"

"The casino owners."

"How are you going to get the casino owners to pay for the roads?"

"By taking the taxes the council assessed to my county and adding them to the casino owner's assessment."

"That's what I thought. You haven't even bothered to read the legal agreement between the council and the casino owners have you?"

"I didn't know there was an agreement."

"There is always a legal agreement when it comes to money and big business. No one ever does business without something legal on paper. I told your class that fact the first day I met all of you in the lecture hall."

"I remember, but this is a government agreement can't they amend it?"

"Mr. Wright it doesn't matter if it's the government or not a legal agreement is a legal agreement."

"What about those times when the government takes someone's land and calls it imminent domain? There is no agreement there."

"Yes but that law is only used if the government in question feels there is a great need for the land in question. Mr. Wright you are only in your second year of law school you are not qualified to be a councilman."

"I'm as qualified as most of the council members in fact I'm more qualified than most."

"My point exactly. You are just qualified enough to mishandle the business of your county because you're so arrogant that you won't take the time to read the law before you try to bend it. Mr. Wright you cannot bend or break what you don't understand and if you go into your council meetings without the correct knowledge you will do more harm than good. Do you understand what I'm saying to you?"

"Yes sir I do understand and I will do the correct research."

"Good. Now remember one other thing. You cannot help everyone. A lot of people in your county have problems. Your job is to figure out which ones you can help and which ones you can't help."

"Yes sir. Can I ask you a question?"

"Yes Mr. Wright what is it?"

"If I run into anything I can't handle or understand do you mind if I come and ask you some questions about it?"

"That will be fine Mr. Wright and keep in mind I will be watching you."

"Yes sir."

I left his office feeling quite a bit smaller. He was right I had gotten cocky about my election. It was hard not to. I defeated a man who had been councilman for a very long time and not only that I had ended some of the corruption in the council.

I was feeling good about myself until that talk with Dr. Mayhew. Now I wasn't feeling so cocky. He was right also about my not knowing all I needed to know to be an effective council man but I was determined to learn.

I went home and told Ole Pop about the conversation I had with Dr. Mayhew and Ole Pop looked at me and smiled.

"I'm proud of you son. Most young men would have gone off the deep end and argued with the man. You realized he was giving you wise council and you listened and that is what a grown man is supposed to do when he hears wise council. Now listen to me carefully. This man may or may not be your friend that is yet to be determined but it appears that he wants to help you make the right choices in your career. Learn what he has to teach but always make your own decisions and if he turns out to be a good mentor count yourself blessed that the Lord sent him to you."

For the next few weeks while I studied my law assignments I studied the agreement between our city government and Brian Adams. His lawyers were very good and they had sewn up all the loose ends but one.

Ole Pops lawyer had put in an amendment to the contract between Ole Pop, Jesse and Mr. Adams that stated Mr. Adams and his company would pay sixty percent of the expense of taking care of the property. It didn't however specify what property.

When I was sure I had all my facts right I took it to Dr. Mayhew and when he read it he started laughing. When he stopped laughing he patted me on the back and told me to sit down.

"I assume you're thinking of asking your uncle to add the other half of the acreage he owns to the agreement."

"Yes I am. Do you think it will work?"

"It will if you add some new farm equipment, a gas stipend for the equipment, a new barn, veterinarian cost and a state of the art irrigation system to it.

"Ole Pop doesn't need all of that and I don't think he will be willing to ask for it."

"Yes he will. From what you tell me about him he's a smart man and he'll know the more you ask for the more you can compromise on later. They will argue about the cost however after the argument they will be more than happy to compromise and finance the repair of some of the roads in your county."

"Dr. Mayhew would you mind coming to my house and meeting Ole Pop and Jesse?"

"Why would your uncle be interested in meeting me?"

"I think the both of you have some things in common."

"What do we have in common?"

"Well for one thing every time I come into your office I notice that you have blues playing on your CD player."

"Young man there's nothing like a good Delta Blues. It was difficult living in Japan for two years without being able to go to a good blues club."

"Sounds like something Ole Pop and Jesse would say. They even met some of the delta blues players back in the day."

"Is that right? Who did they meet?"

"Well let's see. They met "Mississippi" John Hurt, "Hound dog" Taylor, "Howling Wolf" Burnett and James "Son" House.

"Well I would like to meet anyone who has met some of the old delta blues players."

"Good, how about Sunday dinner?"

"That will be fine. Do I need to bring anything?"

"Just your appetite. My mom is the best cook in Mississippi and when she and Ole Pop get in the kitchen together you can't beat them."

"Sounds good. What time should I be there?"

"We eat at four o'clock on the dot."

I walk out of his office and head back to the farm. As soon as I get home I tell Ole Pop what I have in mind. He and Jesse listen until I get through then read the part of the contract I point out to them and they both start laughing so hard they have to sit down. Ole Pop stops laughing long enough to look at Jesse.

"Well Jesse the boy sure did find a hell of a loop hole didn't he?"

"He sho did Buford. Now I'm glad he's the BOHS round here."

Both of them start laughing again until Ole Pop stops and gets a real serious look on his face.

"Son I still want our lawyer to check this out since he's the one who worked out the deal in the first place."

Then he chuckles again and says, "I know Mr. Adams won't come back to handle this himself because he's too busy trying to get the Federal Government off his butt but I sure would love to see his face when he hears about this."

We all laugh again and then I remember my invitation to Dr. Mayhew.

"Oh by the way I invited Dr. Mayhew to come to Sunday dinner and he accepted I hope that's alright with you."

"Son any friend of yours is welcome in my house anytime. Well I guess we're going to have to put out the real good dinner plates and the big Jelly jars to drink out of. We're going to have a Doctor sitting at our table Sunday."

Both Ole Pop and Jesse fall out laughing. I don't know why but that laugh of theirs always brings a smile to my face.

At exactly three forty five on Sunday a long gray Lincoln pulls into the yard. Ole Pop, Jesse and I watch as it makes a slow approach to a spot in front of Ole Pop's tractor. I can tell Ole Pop is anxious to meet Dr. Mayhew after hearing so much about him.

Dr. Mayhew gets out of the car but doesn't shut the door. He looks around like he's not sure if this is the right place then he looks up at the porch. As soon as he does Ole Pop and Jesse get a good look at his face and they both say at the same time.

"Well I'll be damn."

Dr. Mayhew recognizes them the same time they recognize him and a big broad smile comes across his face.

Ole Pop and Jesse walk down the steps and Ole Pop shakes Dr. Mayhew's hand then hugs him like a long lost brother. Ole Pop almost swallows him up in a massive bear hug.

"Damn if it ain't Sergeant "Make em hurt" Mayhew. I didn't know you were the Mayhew my nephew was talking about and I also didn't know you were the head of the law department."

Dr. Mayhew smiles at Ole Pop. "Master Sergeant "Brick hard" Anderson and Sergeant Ustes "Pushups" Anderson."

Jesse looks at him with a very serious look and says, "That's sir to you Sergeant now drop down and gimme fifty."

Dr. Mayhew quickly comes to attention then snaps a salute and says, "Enlisted men don't get the privilege of being called sir and this old body couldn't do more than two pushups a decade."

All three of them start laughing and Dr. Mayhew shakes Jesse's hand then hugs him.

"I haven't seen you two since we left Nam. Hell I didn't even know if either of you were still alive." How're yall doing?"

Ole Pop lets out one of his booming laughs, "We're fine now that we know you're our nephew's professor. Now c'mon in the house so we can eat."

When they get to the top of the stairs Ole Pop winks at Jesse then looks at Dr. Mayhew.

"You're being kind of hard on my boy aren't you?" Jesse seconds Ole Pop's statement.

"Yeah you been dogging my nephew ain't ya?"

"I have to be hard on him Sarge. He has a lot of potential. He could become a major player in politics if he handles his position correctly. I like to stir up my most promising students to see if they can handle the pressure and he handled himself quite well."

Both Ole Pop and Jesse smile and Jesse adds another two cents worth in.

"Well keep dogging him. He's a little hard headed sometimes but if ya dog him correctly he usually straightens up." Then he winks at me.

We all walk into the house and Ole Pop introduces Dr. Mayhew to mom and then to Nessa. Ole Pops looks at mom, winks then introduces Nessa.

"And this is Vanessa Bell the boys fiancée, he's really sweet on her and she's the boss. If you have any problems out of him just tell her about it and she'll straighten him out for you."

"I see, so he's going to get himself a boss."

Dr. Mayhew turns to Nessa and bows deep at the waist then shakes Nessa's hand.

"Well it's nice to meet you boss lady and I will make sure to talk to you when he gets out of line."

I look at Dr. Mayhew, "I see you have jokes like both of these other old men do."

Dr. Mayhew looks at me with his most serious face and says, "Mr. Wright, are you calling me an old man?"

As soon as I see the look in his eyes I think, "Damn I messed up."

My face drops a little as I try to correct my mistake.

"No sir I was just saying that you like to joke like Ole Pop and Jesse."

Dr. Mayhew cuts his eyes toward Ole Pop then I hear Jesse let out a short snorting laugh. After that Ole Pop, Jesse and Dr. Mayhew all start laughing. Then mom and Nessa laugh to. I've been gotten again.

Now I have three old men cracking jokes on me. As we eat dinner and I look around the table, I realize it's a blessing to make it through life with friends and family to guide you on the journey.

The next day we meet with Mr. McNeal, Ole Pop's lawyer and watch him laugh before giving his okay to the idea. Two days later Mr. McNeal put our plan in effect. As soon as Brian Adam's lawyers got the paper work they were on the phone calling our lawyer.

Mr. McNeal came back with their objections and Ole Pop, Jesse and Dr. Mayhew listened while he explained how the phone calls went.

"Buford you got them boys in New York mad as hell at you. They're threatening to sue you for breach of contract, unethical business practices and anything else they can think of. But I wouldn't worry about it. All you have to do is wait and they'll be ready to bargain soon."

Ole Pop laughed, "I'm not worried. After watching the news and seeing the trouble they're in I don't think they'll put up much of a fight."

Doctor Mayhew started laughing.

"You're right about that. I don't imagine any company with the federal government crawling around in they're business wants to bring any more news people down on themselves right now. They'll settle before long."

Jesse looks at me. "Dang nephew you keep stirring things up and da boss of dat gaming company is gonna come down heah and conversate wit ya." Everybody is laughing as we leave Mr. McNeal's office.

Two months later we are back at the bargaining table with Mr. McNeal and this time I did most of the talking. By the time we get through with the negotiations not only do I get more money for the road but Brian also agrees to put aside fifty thousand dollars a year for our schools.

I was a happy man until I went to the council meetings and found out that once the money gets into the city budget it's controlled by the vote of the council. And a few of the council members have different agendas for the money so all of the money doesn't go where it's supposed to go. Some of it ends up in different projects for the more important council members.

Right there I learned a valuable lesson in politics. Even when you have the best of intentions your work as a politician can be redirected to other projects. There are so many other people involved in policy making with you nothing you do in a political setting is ever done exactly the way you want it done.

For the next two years I learned about law and politics which I found to be two completely different things. Sometimes I would get so mad in council meetings that I wanted to beat the hell out of several of my fellow council members.

Most of the time it wasn't because they were wrong it was because they knew they were wrong and just wanted to be an asshole about it. On those days I could always go to Ole Pop and Jesse and listen to their council or if it was a legal issue to Dr. Mayhew and things would clear up.

The one other area I had problems with was the one Dr. Mayhew had warned me about. He told me I couldn't help every body even though they were going to think that I could and he was right.

After I got the money for the streets and schools people in the city found out and all of a sudden I was the savior of the whole city. I couldn't go anywhere without someone asking for help. One woman wanted me to get her husband out of jail so they could have children. A very close neighbor wanted me to have his property taxes waived or he wouldn't vote for me next time.

Then there was Mr. Charles Hinkle. He was harmless enough but every Monday he would drive to Ole Pop and Jesse's house in his old beat up Ford pickup. And it was the same thing every Monday. He would get out of the truck, walk up on the porch, look at me.

"What are you going to do about those aliens."

Now you would think he was talking about illegal migrant workers from across the border but he wasn't. He was actually talking about aliens from outer space. He claimed there were aliens living in a cave on his property and every night they got up on his roof and tried to communicate with their mother ship.

Every Monday he would come and every Monday I would tell him that I had submitted a request to the council and they were still working on finding a solution for the problem.

I felt bad about lying to the man and I sat down and talked to Ole Pop about it. He gave me something to think about.

"Son I know you don't like to lie to the man and you're right you shouldn't lie to him but don't stop talking to him."

"But I don't have anything I can say to him that would be the truth."

"Yes there is. I know if you think about it you can come up with something to say to him and if not just listen to him."

"Why is it so important that I listen to him?"

"Son have you ever stopped to think that you might be the only thing that is keeping this man alive?"

"What do you mean Ole Pop?"

"Sometimes when a person has nothing to look forward too they have nothing to live for. He's about our age but he has no family and he lives by himself. You have taken an interest in him and he needs that. So let him come by every Monday. Sit down and talk to him and listen to what he has to say and give him a reason to keep on living."

"I never thought of it that way Ole Pop. I'll do that."

"And who knows, you might learn something because every man has something he can teach you."

From that point on when Mr. Hinkle pulled up in the yard I listened patiently and I tried to have at least a logical reason why the council hadn't been to his house to fix the problem yet.

At the end of my second term as a council member I finished law school and passed the bar. Now I was a full fledged lawyer with four years of political experience under my belt. I had learned how to deal with the politics of the city council and I had been in on several pretty important committees. I decided if I was going to be in politics I might as well stop half stepping and get all the way into the game.

That night I informed Ole Pop of my decision to run for the State Senate. He looked me in the eyes for a few seconds before speaking.

"Son you have chosen a very dangerous profession. There are many pitfalls in politics. The temptations are great and they can come from so many different areas from sex to power the temptations are great. I hope you realize that a political career can cost you everything including the love of a good woman. And speaking of good women what are you going to do about Vanessa? Are you going to commute from the State capital to home every day?"

"Ole Pop I'm going to ask her to set a date for the wedding tonight."

"Damn it's about time. You should have married her a year ago. Well son I'll be praying for you"

Ole Pop gets up and hugs me then abruptly turns his back and walks into the kitchen. I suspect he didn't want me to see him cry but I'll never be able to prove it. While he's in the kitchen he tells Jesse about my decision and Jesse comes out and jumps right on me.

"Nephew is ya out ya damn mind? You don't need to go into politics you need to stay right here and run this farm of yours."

"Jesse as much as I like being a farmer I want to help people."

"Then dammit you can become a lawyer or teacher like Nessa. You don't need to leave the farm to help people. Why ya wanna go into a profession where every body is corrupt?"

"Jesse every body can't be corrupt. There has to be some good people in politics."

"I ain't never seed any of em."

"Jesse I just think I will be good at this."

Jesse gets up, walks over and sits down on the arm of the chair I'm sitting in.

"Nephew you'll be good at anything you choose to do and I wish it wasn't politics but if that's your choice then I'm behind you and I'll be praying for you. You gonna need a lot of Jesus where you're going.

Jesse gets up and walks back into the kitchen and I can hear him arguing with Ole Pop.

"Buford I thought we had raised the boy right. Now he don gone out of his mind again. We need to let him go back out there in the woods so dem wolves can finish the job."

Ole Pops starts laughing, "Yeah a good bite in the butt may serve to get his mind back together."

"Dats what I'm talking about. Let old saw tooth hang that other tooth in his butt." They both fall out laughing but I know they're going to miss me.

Chapter 19

Nessa and I talk and she decides that she wants a June wedding. June is only four months away which doesn't leave a lot of time for her and my mother to plan the wedding so needless to say Ole Pop, Jesse and me catch hell during that time.

For the next four months Nessa and mom do everything from ordering dresses and flowers to getting us fitted for tuxedos which Jesse says he's not going to wear.

To quote him, "I ain't never understood why a man has to git dressed in a monkey suit to git himself a bride. Heck all they have to do is jump the broom and dats dat. I ain't gonna wear it and ain't nothin yall can say gonna change my mind."

Of course by the time Nessa and mom get through buttering him up he reluctantly agrees to wear the suit but only if he can wear his own shoes with it.

"My bunions ain't gonna be hurting cause yall is trying to be cute."

In the middle of all the wedding planning I won election to the senate. Right after the honeymoon Nessa and I will have to move to Jackson.

Our wedding day finally arrives and with Jesse as my best man and my best friend Bubba Frakes as my only other groomsman I stand in front of the church remembering what I was when I first got here. It seems like such a far away place and such a distant time.

The music starts and my Nessa makes her grand entrance into the church. I look at her and everything else disappears. Did God send me one of his angels? If he did then I know he must be crying right now because she has got to be the most beautiful one he has.

With Ole Pop by her side waiting to give her away she floats down the isle to me and in front of God and all the people I love we become man and wife for all eternity. I know the vows say till death do us part but the way I feel at this moment not even death could separate us.

We honeymoon in Hawaii. The trip is a present from Ole Pop, mom, and Jesse. Nessa and I have never been to Hawaii and we have good time for the full week we are there. Then we come back to the hard part of being newly married.

We arrive home in time to pack and get ready for our new life. It's hard to leave mom, Ole Pop and Jesse but it's time for us to make our way in the world to see what we can do to make it a better place.

Mom cries when we get ready to leave. I tease her and tell her she's crying because she's losing her daughter and that she doesn't care about losing me.

She smiles and says, "You are my only little boy and I will miss you but you know I always have been partial to Nessa."

"Yeah boy we don't care if you go but you're taking Nessa with you and we care about that."

"Okay I see that you and Jesse have been rehearsing this comedy routine together."

Mom smiles and hugs both of us one last time. I look at Ole Pop.

"Old man thank you for everything you and Jesse did for me. If it hadn't been for the both of you there's no telling where I would be."

"We didn't do anything to improve your life. You're the one who made the right decision and as long as you continue to make the correct decisions you will do all right."

I hug him and Jesse then get into the car and head off to a life with the most precious woman on earth.

This beautiful woman has so much love for life it's hard to picture her as that depressed little girl I first met in high school. She loves me with all her heart and I try to make sure she knows that my love for her will always remain true.

We settle into our new house and start life as man and wife. Nessa finds a teaching position in an elementary school and falls in love with the children and the job. I'm glad she loves her work because being a new State Senator is taking up a lot of my time.

However we do get a chance to talk, kiss, hug and do other things as much as we can which is why I'm not too surprised when I come home one day and Nessa tells me she's pregnant. You should have seen the big smile on my face. Now I'm about to be a father for the first time.

Then it hits me, "I'm about to be a father for the first time."

And suddenly the responsibility of raising a child becomes a scary thought. I need to talk to Ole Pop as soon as possible.

We drive down to Columbia on the weekend and tell mom, Ole Pop and Jesse the good news. Ole Pop looks at Jesse and mom and smiles.

"Well, well, well it looks like my boy is about to see the reaping law first hand."

"I look at Ole Pop. What is the reaping law?"

"Galatians chapter six verse seven says," Be not deceived; God is not mocked: for whatsoever a man soweth, that shall he also reap." And if I remember correctly you was pretty mean when you got here."

Jesse laughed, "Yeah dats right you was a meanun when you first got here and according to Sarah you was pretty mean before you left her which means not only are you going to have to deal with God's law but your mother added to it by putting da curse on ya."

"What curse?"

"You know the one where she said, "I hope when you grow up you have a child dat treats you just like you're treating me right now."

I start laughing and so does Ole Pop. I look at mom. "You did say that to me a couple of times."

"That's because you were working my last nerve. I wanted to knock your head into the next city."

Ole Pop laughed then looked at me with smile.

"From her mouth to God's ears and now son you're in trouble. See, God hears those words from a mother and feels her pain and when you couple that with his own words about sowing and reaping that means you are going to have a child that is as hard headed as you were."

"Yeah dats right. He'll sass ya and git smart and make you have to conversate wit him just like Sarah had to do with you."

I can't help but to laugh, "Why do yall have to bring up the past for."

"We didn't bring it up son, God did. Now you have to deal with it. But you know what Jesse? I believe he's going to handle it just fine."

"He sho is cause he's got a good woman working beside him and that's God's law too. Proverbs chapter thirty one, verses ten and eleven says, "Who can find a virtuous woman for her price is far above rubies. The heart of her husband doth safely trust in her, so that he shall have no need of spoils." And Buford I believe the boy has found his self a virtuous woman."

"I believe you're right Jesse."

I hug Nessa and mom who has been crying all this time and we walk into the house. Mom and Nessa disappear into mom's bed room.

"Vanessa I want you to know that I wouldn't have picked anyone else for my son. I always wished I had a daughter then you came into my life. I hope you and Andre have wonderful children and I hope you stay together forever and come by and let me see my grand children a lot."

"After my mother died I didn't think I would ever have another woman to talk to but you stepped right in and all that changed. Thank you for being the mother I needed during the hard times in my life and you can count on the fact that we will bring your grandchildren to see you."

"So I guess this means you're going to have more than one. How does Andre feel about that?"

"If it were left up to him I would be barefoot and pregnant for the rest of my life."

"Girl don't you let him do that to you. That can be murder on a woman's figure and who's going to take care of all those babies?"

"Oh that's not going to be a problem. We'll just bring all of them to stay with their grandmother for fourteen or fifteen years."

"Uh uh, no, not fourteen years I don't think I could deal with a bunch of teenagers especially if they turn out to be like Andre. Girl that boy was a mess I just wish his father was here to see him now."

"I wish I could have met him."

"He was a good man. He had his faults but he tried to do things right. Now I think we need to go in and start dinner before Jesse starts complaining."

"Mr. Jesse just loves to argue doesn't he?"

"He wouldn't be Jesse if he didn't"

Back in the living room Ole Pop dispenses some of his wisdom to me on how to raise my child. He talks about everything from diaper changing to conversating with the child when he or she gets hard headed. At the end of the weekend we say goodbye again and head back home to work.

I find the level of professionalism in the State Senate isn't much better than the level of the city council. There is still political fighting and personal vendettas between Senators and every one is working for their own cities.

I join several committees including the education committee. I know I had better handle this committee correctly or my wife will have my head. She's always on me about the lack of finance for things the children need and I keep it in mind when I began lobbying for more money.

There is a lot of paper work that has to be read. A lot of it is history which most people have forgotten. I like to read so I manage to read most of the files I receive on school finances and I find something very interesting.

About ten years ago we suffered a bad tornado. It did several million dollars' worth of damage. Federal tax dollars were very slow in coming so there was an emergency law passed to divert some of the money from all school systems budgets to a State emergency fund.

These moneys were used to rebuild houses, factories and schools. However after five years the money was supposed to revert back to the school systems.

After doing some research I found that the money hadn't reverted back to the school system it had been put into an emergency fund for use at a later date. That money was being used for everything from postage stamps for the Senators to plane tickets and hotel rental.

As soon as I found that out I went to work. I lobbied for the release of that money back into the school system so our schools could get some much needed computers. Of course just about every Senator opposed the bill I put before the senate but once again the media came to my defense.

A reporter found out about the bill and began to check on the history of it. He found the public records and did a report about them on his evening news report.

Pretty soon people all around the state began asking questions about the bill and why the money hadn't been given back to the school systems when it was supposed to be. Needless to say when the bill came up for a vote it passed but I made a lot of enemies because of it.

Because of my work on the school bill I was eventually made chairman of the school budget committee. It took a while but with the help of several good people I was able to get the financial books in order.

I made the different county school systems more accountable for their spending. I also managed to get computers for the majority of schools in Mississippi. Of course it helped that Ole Pop and Jesse committed a considerable amount of the money the casino was paying them to my project.

During my year as the chairman of the budget committee I standardized the accounting system used for each school system. Up until now all school systems used their own method of accounting but I sponsored an amendment that made all school systems fall in line with one accounting system.

I soon found out where the excess money was being spent and our committee could tell what was needed and what was not and which school systems needed more money for the next year. During my tenure our state school system rose from forty ninth in the country to eleventh. It is during this time I was approached by several state businessmen who asked if I had thought about running for the U.S. Senate.

At first I told them no and let it go at that. I liked working for my state and had no thoughts of going anywhere else but that was before Dr. Mayhew found out about it. When he found out he told

Ole Pop and Jesse and together they convinced me that I could make a difference in the U.S. Senate so I decided to run for the office.

My opponent was the incumbent U.S. Senator Dick Hilgan. I didn't know Senator Hilgan but he knew and hated me. Senator Hilgan had two reason's to hate me. First, he was one of the Senators instrumental in bringing the casino to our city. Second, during my first term in the city council I opposed a bill sponsored by city councilman Jerry Stone.

Councilman Stone's bill called for money to fund a new convention center and hotel complex in the downtown area to induce tourist to come downtown to shop and see the sights. This complex was going to be funded by money received from a bill Senator Hilgan had managed to get through the senate for our city.

I opposed the bill for the complex because there were plenty of hotels around the casino and most conventions were held in the casino's several banquet halls. I lobbied hard for the money to go to our schools which were in need of new teachers to help ease overcrowding, new computers and general repairs. I didn't know Councilman Stone was only sponsoring the bill because Senator Hilgan wanted the bill passed.

A large construction company had agreed to pay Senator Hilgan one hundred thousand dollars if he could get the city to build the hotel and convention center so they could have the contract. Because of my efforts the plans for the convention center were tabled and the money went to our schools. Right then and there I unknowingly made a powerful enemy and I was about to find out how powerful.

As soon as Senator Hilgan found out I was running against him a meeting took place in a secret meeting place called "the watering hole." It is a room most people don't know about. It sits high in the rafters in the University of Mississippi's basketball stadium. Only certain people are invited to come to this place.

In attendance at this meeting is ex councilman Drake Orton, Senator Dick Hilgan and several key members of the city council. Senator Hilgan and ex Councilman Drake Orton are the ones who called the meeting.

After a couple rounds of drinks Senator Hilgan puts down his glass and looks at Councilman Harry Creighton.

"So you agree that something has to be done about that nigger. If we let him continue the way he's going he'll screw up everything we worked for."

Councilman Creighton takes a sip out of his glass.

"I agree that something needs to be done I'm just not sure this is the way to do it. What if he catches on? If he catches on my career could be over as well as several others in the council."

"He won't catch on. He'll follow this just like a bee to honey. By the time he figures out what is happening his career will be over. Drake here has it all figured out. Drake who are we going to use to pull him in?"

"I know a young lady who is very experienced and very pretty. She will be more than happy to get to him for a price. I want to finish this so we can get on with the business of getting rich."

They all sat back and drink their drinks and Drake Orton smiles. He was finally going to get the nigger who stole his council seat.

The next day I am sitting in the Senate library when Destiny Logan walks in. She is a very pretty woman and most men would love to date her but I already have the lady of my dreams so her presence doesn't affect me.

The library is crowded with a third year political science class doing research for their end of semester papers so she walks over to my table and asks if she can sit down. I say yes without even looking up. She sat down and introduced herself. I look up, tell her my name and she acts like she's really impressed.

"You're the guy who defeated councilman Orton aren't you. It's very nice to meet an honest man." She stuck out her hand and I absent mindedly shook it. "Thank you."

"I'm a graduate student?"

"What is your major?"

"Political Science. I want to be a State Senator like you. If you don't mind I would like to ask you a few questions from time to time."

"That will be fine but keep in mind I have a very busy schedule."

"I promise not to take up much of your time." After our conversations she gets up and leaves.

For the next three weeks where ever I was in the Senate building she always managed to be somewhere in the vicinity. I didn't really notice it. I thought it was just a coincidence until the night we met in the hall outside the library and she told me she thought I was sexy. I told her I had a wife but she didn't care.

The next thing I know she has her arms around my neck and her lips on mine. She caught me off guard. I didn't expect her to do what she did but as soon as I realized what she was trying to do I pushed her away, told her I really wasn't interested and walked away and still she kept showing up.

On one of my calls to Ole Pop I told him about it and he laughed.

"Be careful big boy if Vanessa finds out about this she's liable to whoop your big butt."

Then he got serious, "Seriously son be careful. I don't know why but for some reason I think there may be more to this than meets the eye."

Two days later Dr. Mayhew called me.

"Andre, Buford called me and asked me to check out this young lady who has been hanging around you and I have some information you need to know. She is a professional con artist and her name is Celia Clark but she uses several aliases including Destiny Logan. I understand from my sources that she has been sent to get you involved in a scandal.

"How is she going to do that?"

"Like it is always done. She's probably going to try and get you in bed with her."

"Oh, that's not going to happen. I'm not close to being interested in her like that besides Nessa would break my neck. So what do I do about it?"

"Call this number and ask for detective Steven Shaw."

I call the number and talk to detective Shaw. Dr. Mayhew has already told him what is going on and he explains to me what he wants me to do.

"Wait until you see her again and invite her to the Senate lounge then call me. I will handle the rest. I will be somewhere in the building."

Hours later Destiny finds me in the law library and this time I'm more receptive to her conversation. I invite her to the Senate lounge then excuse myself and go to the bathroom.

I make the call to Detective Shaw and then keep my distance from her. This was very hard because she kept telling me how sexy I was and how much she would like to make love to me. She also kept trying to sit on my lap or wrap her arms round my neck. However I managed to out maneuver her and keep her talking until detective Shaw and several other plain clothes officers arrive.

Destiny tries to convince them that I made her come in the lounge and that I was trying to get her to undress against her will. She even told the police she wanted to press charges for sexual assault.

That's when Detective Shaw shows her the hidden mikes and cameras. He asks her to tell him who put her up to it but she refuses and asks for her attorney. He handcuffs her and leads her out of the lounge.

As soon as I get home I pick up the mail from the dining room table and head for the kitchen so I can tell Nessa what happened. As I walked toward the kitchen I opened an envelope addressed to me. Inside were several pictures of Destiny and me. They showed us talking together and from the angle it looked like we were really close and then there was the picture of her kissing me.

The note said "This is a well known prostitute by the name of Jenny Lewis. If you don't want these pictures to show up in the news send me five thousand dollars."

There was no signature on the letter and no return address. I immediately took out my phone and called Ole Pop and told him about the pictures and what happened in my office.

"Son from this point on you need to be very careful because someone is out to get you. If they are willing to go so far as to hire a con artist there's no telling what they will try next.

After talking to Ole Pop I walked into the kitchen, showed the photos and note to Nessa and explained what happened. Nessa said if this is the way politics is done she would rather I got out. It took me a while to convince her that it would be all right. Secretly I hoped I was right but I wasn't sure. I found out later that Ole Pop was right. Someone was indeed trying to get me.

Several days after Destiny was arrested there is another meeting at the watering hole with the same people as before. Most of the meeting consisted of Drake Orton getting his ass chewed off for botching it up with Destiny.

"Drake I should have known your plan wasn't going to work. Now we're going to do it my way."

"Look Dick I didn't know the nigger wasn't going to fall for the woman. After all most of them have a lot of women hanging around them. I thought this would be easy. Maybe he's a fag or something. How you gonna get to him?

"I'm going to use his friend, Senator Bud Williams."

"How do we know he's going to help us? I hear that he doesn't even like you. Dick sits back in his chair and takes a puff of his cigar.

"I know he doesn't and it really doesn't matter especially since I know his secret."

"What secret

"His wife is wanted in Texas for writing bad checks in Houston, Dallas and San Antonio. She was arrested in San Antonio then posted bail and ran. A year later with another name she married Bud. He didn't find out until the year after that and he kept it quiet. Now he doesn't want his pretty little wife to go to jail in Texas. They don't play down there and besides he would probably go to jail or at least pay a fine for covering it up. So he will play along just to keep me quiet."

The meeting adjourns and Drake makes a phone call to get the plan started.

Chapter 20

On December tenth one day before my birthday I am approached by Bud Williams. Bud and I started in the Senate together and we have become close friends. He asked me to go to lunch with him so we can talk.

During lunch Bud tells me he has a special project for the development of a tire processing plant in his area that would create several thousand new jobs and like politicians do he requested that I throw my support behind this project.

While we were there discussing the dynamics of the project we were joined by a man introduced to me as Jarrett Singler, legal advisor to the governor. After our conversation Jarrett insisted on paying for lunch.

I talked to Ole Pop and Jesse and Dr. Mayhew about it and they all told me to make sure I check it out thoroughly before I committed to it. Dr. Mayhew even did some checking himself and it seemed like it was a project worth backing.

Later in the week I checked on the project and the company and found out in the past they had been sited by the federal government for some illegal dumping. I called Bud and he confirmed what I had found out but he said they had cleaned up their mess and had been cleared by the government.

He faxed me over the paper work to show me they had been cleared by the government. Along with that came paper work that explained what they had done to clean up the area and how many fines they had paid.

After reading all the material I decided that when the time came I would swing my vote his way. The vote wouldn't come up for a month because we were trying to get the state budget passed.

During that time we had several more dinners and we even brought our wives with us. I got to know Jarett and his wife well and so did Nessa so when he invited us to go to Gatlinburg Tennessee with him and his wife we agreed.

He was a pilot so he flew us all there in his little private plane. After arriving at the airport we were taken by private car to the cabin. The cabin was spectacular and I have to admit I was surprised to see such a luxurious cabin out in the middle of nowhere.

The cabin had four bedrooms in it and the most spectacular view of the mountains I had ever seen. Nessa was thrilled about being in Gatlinburg for the first time and we took in all the sights and shows we could that weekend and of course Jarett didn't let me pay for much.

I told him it wasn't fair for us to stay there and not pay anything but he said the cabin belonged to his father and wasn't costing him a thing so Nessa and I enjoyed the whole weekend.

Back in Mississippi, at three o'clock in the morning the phone rings at Dr. Mayhew's house. When he answers it a voice he thinks he recognizes says, "Tell your protégé that he's being set up. He needs to find out who Jarett Singler really is before it's too late."

Dr. Mayhew calls Ole Pop and tells him about the phone call. Nessa and I arrive back home two days later. The phone is ringing as I walk into the house. It's Dr. Mayhew.

"Andre how much do you know about Jarett Singler?"

"He's a legal advisor to the Governor, he and his wife have been married for five years and his father has a cabin in Gatlinburg. Why do you ask?"

"Because I received a call a couple nights ago and the person on the other end told me to tell you to find out who Mr. Singler really is. Since that time Buford, Jesse and I have been trying to find out anything we can about the man and so far we haven't come up with any answers. I think you would be well served if you didn't go anywhere else with him."

"It really wasn't that big a deal. We went to the cabin and some of the shows."

"Who paid for it?"

"He paid for the shows and he told me the cabin belonged to his father."

"Did you talk about anything while you were there?"

"Nothing out of the ordinary and I made sure not to talk about anything political on the trip."

"It doesn't matter if you did or not. If he claims you did that will be enough to cast a shadow on you."

After the conversation with Dr. Mayhew I call Ole Pop and we discuss the whole situation.

"What was I thinking? I should have known this was a set up."

"Son we don't know all the facts yet. This may be a problem then again it may not. Now all you can do is wait and see what comes of it. However I agree with Jackson you need to distance yourself from him until you can find out what he's really all about."

Jesse gets on the phone. "Remember what I told you nephew. Never underestimate someone you've just met."

I hang up the phone and sit in the dark while I thought about what was going on.

A few minutes later Nessa comes in, sits down on the edge of the couch and begins to rub my shoulders.

"Was Ole Pop able to help you figure out what to do next?"

"He said the best thing to do was just wait. How could I have been so stupid as to accept a trip from someone I barely knew?"

"You can't be suspicious of every one baby. Sometimes you're going to be fooled. You just have to keep on going no matter how they try to get to you. You are a good Senator and your mom, Ole Pop, Jesse and I are proud of the work you're doing."

She hugs me and kisses me on the forehead and I'm alright again. She, like no other can soothe my worries and ease my tension and that's why I love her so much.

I decided to make a few phone calls to see if I can find out who Jarrett Singler really is but I get no result. Finally I go to bed puzzled and it takes me a while to get to sleep.

Three o'clock in the morning the phone rings. I pick it up.

"Hello."

"Check your bags there's something in the lining of one of them that you don't know about." Then the line goes dead.

I immediately go to the closet and pull out my bag. I open it up and check the lining carefully and discover a long thin tear I didn't notice before. I open the tear and find a brown envelope with five thousand dollars in one hundred dollar bills. Totally shocked I sit down heavily on the bed waking Nessa.

"What's wrong baby?" I show her the money. "How in the hell did this get in my bag?"

"Where did you find it?"

"In the lining of my bag."

"Someone is trying to make it look like you have taken a bribe."

"Yeah and it was probably Jarrett Singler. I'm going to call the police and take them the money."

But you can't prove he did it. It will be your word against his and you're the one with the money. Why don't you call Ole Pop and Dr. Mayhew in the morning?"

"Yeah I guess you're right."

I put the money in the desk drawer in my office and try to go back to sleep. But sleep wouldn't come and I was glad to see daylight peeking through the window.

At seven in the morning I called Ole Pop and told him what I found in my bag and he told me I needed to come down to the farm so he, Dr. Mayhew, Jesse and I could figure out what our next move should be

Three hours later I walk into the house. Ole Pop and Jesse are waiting on me. Ole Pop explains that Dr. Mayhew would be there after he made a few calls.

I drop the money on the couch beside Ole Pop.

"Ole Pop the caller on the other end didn't identify himself but he told me to check my bag. When I did I found a little tear in the lining and this money. I have no idea who it belongs to or how it got into my bag."

"Well now we know what the trip was all about and whoever called you wanted to make sure you knew they knew about the money. Now it's only a question of what they are going to do with that knowledge."

"So that means we wait again."

Dr. Mayhew knocks on the door and Jesse lets him in. He walks over and sits down beside me.

"Andre I have someone you need to meet. I think she can help you with your problem."

"Who is it Dr. Mayhew?"

"She's an old classmate of mine. She might be able to give you some advice as to how to handle this. I have a meeting I have to go to right now but I want you to meet me at the Shores Hotel in an hour. Buford if you and Jesse aren't busy yall come with Andre."

Jesse gets serious look on his face. "We ain't never too busy for our nephew."

I smile as I hang up the phone. It's good to have strong men behind you.

An hour and a half later we are sitting in one of the best suites in the top hotel in Columbia waiting on Dr. Mayhew's friend. Dr. Mayhew greets us and we sit down to talk for a minute then the bedroom door opens and U.S. Senator Glenora Ann Perkins from Alabama walks into the room.

Senator Perkins is the epitome of an intelligent, strong black woman. She has been in politics for twenty years and she is now one of the more powerful U.S. Senators on capital hill. She is also the role model for thousands of young women.

Time and time again she has proven that not only can women work in the world of politics but they can also excel. My Nessa would have a fit if she knew I was about to meet Senator Perkins. Nessa has been an admirer of hers for a long time.

The Senator is her usual regal self. At the age of fifty seven she has that beauty that can't be removed with time and she still has that radiant smile. She is known for that smile and the hats she wears but this time she doesn't have on one of her hats.

She is never seen out in public without a hat, each one of them different and each one of them a complement to her outfit. This time however she's dressed casual. I never knew her hair was so long. It is dark brown sprinkled with gray and it hangs down to her shoulders. To tell the truth she looks like she could be Nessa's grandmother.

We all stand as she walks into the room and she smiles.

"Well good afternoon gentlemen. Who do I have the pleasure of addressing today?"

Ole Pop looks at me. I am so use to him doing the talking I forget this meeting is with me not him. I offer my hand.

"Hello Senator Perkins my name is Andre Wright and these are my uncles, Buford and Jesse Anderson."

"Have a seat gentlemen, it's nice to meet you."

Senator Perkins sits down first then we sit and she leans toward me.

"Senator Wright let me give you some advice. Political rule number one, when you introduce yourself always say that you are Senator Wright no matter who you are addressing even if it's the President. You are a professional so introduce yourself as one. Now I understand you have a problem that needs addressing."

"Yes ma'am. I believe a person I went on a weekend trip with is trying to frame me for taking a bribe."

"Are you sure you didn't take this bribe?"

"Yes ma'am I am sure. I didn't get into politics to get rich or become corrupt. I found the money in my bag after I received an anonymous call telling me to look in the lining of the bag."

"I see. Do you know who put the money in your bag?"

"I can't actually say I saw him do it but there were only four of us in the cabin so I suspect it was Jarrett Singler. He represented himself to me as a legal advisor to the governor."

"Are you sure he's a legal advisor to the Governor?"

"At this present time Senator Perkins I'm not sure of anything."

Senator Perkins leaned forward and looked me in the eyes.

"Senator Wright political rule number two. If you're going to remain in politics you need to know that unless you have known a person for at least twenty years, you had better check them out before you allow them to get close to you and even then you can't be too careful. Now would you like to know who Jarrett Singler really is?"

"Yes I would."

"Well Senator Wright it seems that your legal advisor to the president is really a highly paid lobbyist from Washington. He has worked with Senator Hilgan when he was trying to get the casino opened in your home state."

"Are you telling me that Senator Hilgan was in on the pay offs with the other councilmen?"

"No that's not what I said. Political rule number three, never say anything you can't prove. What I said was Senator Hilgan and Jarrett Singler worked together to put the casino in Mississippi. Now if you are inferring that he was in on some sort of pay off you may be right but that's not what I said."

"I didn't mean to imply that you said he was in on the payoffs. I was merely making an observation."

"Rule number four. In politics you never make an audible observation that can be quoted by anyone especially the media. Always remember one slip of the tongue can ruin an otherwise promising career. Now let's get down to the business at hand."

Senator Perkins hands me a folder with several pictures in it. I open it and look at the pictures as she talks.

"This is what we already know. First of all Jarrett Singler misrepresented himself to you. Second, He works with Senator Hilgan. Third, you are about to run against Senator Hilgan. Now I'm not going to make any assumptions but I'm pretty sure if it got out you were taking bribes it would ruin your chances of winning the race which means one thing. Senator Hilgan is worried you might win. So what we need to do now is come up with a strategy to help you out of this situation. Do you have any ideas?"

Yes, I'm going to go to the media an expose him for what he is."

"And then you're going to go back to the farm and become one of the best farmers in the world but you won't be working in politics ever again. You have no proof and you're the one with the money. At this time, right or wrong you look guilty."

"Well at the very least Jarrett Singler will go down with me."

"Not necessarily. Jarrett is a very powerful lobbyist. If I were to guess, he's probably paid someone else to say they gave you the money. That person will have a nasty reputation and won't mind the media finding out his past as long as he gets paid. He'll get some press and if he's lucky he'll get a book deal. You on the other hand will only get your reputation shot down."

Now I'm mad mostly at myself. How could I have made such a dumb mistake and why are so many people after me? I have done nothing wrong but my reputation and the work I've done in the Senate is about to be for nothing because someone with a little power wants me out of the way.

This time when I speak my voice has a little edge to it.

"It really doesn't matter does it? They're going to ruin my reputation anyway so why shouldn't I go to the media with this?"

Senator Perkins sits back in her chair, folds her hands in her lap.

"Senator Wright if you're going to become the first rate politician I think you can become then you need to understand that a hot head never wins a political battle. I know it's hard to deal with someone personally attacking your good name but in order to deal with this you have to calm down. Then you need to realize this won't be the first or last time someone attacks your good name. This is the nature of politics and if you can't deal with it maybe you should go back home and be the best farmer you can be."

Right about here Ole Pops leans over to me and says in a quiet voice.

"Son now is the time for you to think like the young man your mother, Jesse and I raised you to be. Hostility is not going to serve you well in this instance. Calm down and listen to wisdom when it's being spoken to you."

He looks me in the eyes and I immediately calm down and apologize.

"I am sorry Senator Perkins."

"That's quite all right Senator Wright I know this is hard. Now I didn't say you shouldn't go to the media. You do need to go to the media with this but if you do it without the proper backup you're going to lose everything you worked for."

Senator Perkins leans back and motions to one of her aides. He walks over and opens a door and a young blonde headed man walks into the room. Senator Perkins introduces him.

"Senator Wright I'd like for you to meet FBI agent Bobby Todd. He has been secretly investigating Jarrett Singler and Senator Hilgan for the last year. He wants you to help set Mr. Singler up in a sting and if we work this right Mr. Todd will get what he wants and you will get what you want."

I shake hands with the agent and he gets right down to business.

"Senator Wright I want you to call Mr. Singler and tell him you know he is the one who put the money in your bag then I want you to send him these pictures."

The agent hands me an envelope. I open the envelope to find pictures of me, Nessa, Jarrett Singler and his wife. They were taken outside and inside the lodge. There's even a picture of Jarrett in the room where Nessa and I stayed. He's standing next to my bags but there is no picture of him actually putting the money in my bag.

There are also several pictures of Senator Hilgan and Jarrett sitting in a restaurant talking. These would be very interesting to the media especially since Senator Hilgan has stated several times that he doesn't know Jarrett Singler and doesn't do business with lobbyist.

The last four pictures are of Senator Hilgan and several members of the Columbia city council most of whom lost their seats in the casino scandal. One picture in particular is of Senator Hilgan, Council members Jerry Dearing and Charley Baker and ex Councilman Drake Orton. Charley Baker is the owner of one of the construction companies caught in the payoff scheme with Drake Orton.

"How did you get these?"

"As Senator Perkins told you I have been on Mr. Singler's tail for a very long time." When he sees these photos he will assume that you have other pictures of him and Senator Hilgan. If you can convince him that you have pictures of him placing the money in your bag we will be in business."

"How is that going to help me?"

"You're going to tell him you will be willing to drop out of the race if he gives you two hundred thousand dollars. If he goes for it then we'll place a wire on you and catch him in the act. If we're lucky we might get him to implicate Senator Hilgan and get the both of them at the same time. After we get what we want I will arrest them and the media will take care of the rest."

"What if he doesn't go for any of this?"

"Then you'll have to deal with it the best way you know how but I will let you have the pictures if they will help."

Jesse leans over and says, "See nephew this is called coaching from the side lines. He's going to give you all the right plays to run but he won't be in the game."

I look at Ole Pop and he nods as if to say, "We've given you all the information you need now it's up to you."

I sit back for a minute and think about it and decide it is the only move I have.

"Okay agent Todd when can we do this?"

"The sooner the better."

We take the rest of the day going over what I need to say and how the operation is going to work.

The next day I mail the pictures to Jarrett Singler with a note that says, "We need to talk." Several days go by and he doesn't call. Agent Todd explains that he's trying to make me sweat it out before he calls and when he calls he'll make it seem that the pictures don't mean anything to him.

However Agent Todd is a seasoned FBI agent and he knows all the tricks. He instructs me not to answer any of Jarrett's calls for two days and not to call him back if he leaves a message.

I do exactly as he asks and after the third call Jarrett stops calling. He doesn't call for the next three days. I believe I have lost my opportunity but Agent Todd tells me to be patient he will call back. Two days later he does and he's none too happy about the pictures.

"Where did you get these pictures?"

"It doesn't matter where I got them all that matters is I have more of them and if you decide to tell the media about the money you put in my bag then I'll have to show them the truth."

"I don't know what you're talking about."

"Really, then I guess these pictures I have of you putting the money in my bag is of no concern to you. By the way that is a nice ring you have on your finger. Did your wife give it to you?"

"You and I both know anyone can see this ring on my finger."

"Yes but I didn't take a close enough look at it to recognize that it is a copy of the presidential Rolex at least that's what the jeweler told me when he looked at the picture. By the way when did you have that mole on the back of your hand removed?" Agent Todd told me about the mole removal then told me to use it as leverage.

Jarrett is silent for several seconds trying to gather his thoughts.

"Okay, if you have the pictures why haven't you gone to the media with them?"

"Because I want to get out of politics and that's where you come in. I want you to tell Senator Hilgan I will drop out of the race and he won't have to deal with me again if he gives me two hundred thousand dollars."

"You must think I'm a fool. Your uncle has enough money for you to live off of the rest of your life. You don't need the money so what's this really about?"

"If you have been watching me and my uncle that closely then you should also know that I haven't received a dime from him even though my idea was the one that got him more money from the owners of the casino. It's as simple as this. I'm tired of dealing with other people's problems I'm ready to leave Mississippi for good and to do that I need money. Now do we have a deal or not?"

"No we do not have a deal. I can't make any deal for senator Hilgan and I certainly wouldn't make any deals with you."

"Then the both of you have a problem. Oh by the way tell the Senator it was very smart to keep his partnership with Drake Orton a secret. But you know how secrets are, they sometimes come out at the most inopportune times."

I hang up the phone before Jarrett has a chance to deny my accusations. Agent Todd is sitting beside me and instructs me not to answer any of Jarrett's calls for the next forty eight hours. He also tells me there will be several agents on the farm just in case. That last statement is very sobering. I hadn't realized that this whole thing could be that dangerous but now I did and I have to admit I am a little scared.

The first thing I do is send Nessa back home to Jackson with several FBI agents watching her. She isn't happy about my decision but she has already missed too many days of teaching time so she doesn't have much choice.

Ole Pop convinces mom to go with her. Mom isn't happy but she knows Ole Pop isn't going to let her stay there without a very serious argument that she will lose so she reluctantly agrees to go with Nessa.

Two days later I receive a text message from Jarrett.

"Meet me at the casino in one hour." I show the text to Agent Todd and he tells me how we're going to work the operation and just before I head to the meeting he gives me a watch that has a wire in it so they can catch our conversation on tape.

I pull into the parking lot and wait for thirty minutes. I've almost decided that Jarrett isn't coming. Finally after ten more minutes I turn on my engine to leave and that's when Jarrett walks over and gets into my car. He points a gun at me.

"Put the car in drive and move." I do what he tells me to do and we head toward the interstate."

"Where are we going?"

Jarrett turns the radio up very loud. "If you open your mouth one more time I won't hesitate to kill you."

Since I'm wired I hope agent Todd heard Jarrett's last statement. I expect the FBI to stop us and get me out of this situation but no one appears so I continue to drive for the next hour until Jarrett tells me to take the next exit off the interstate.

From there I follow his directions. We make several turns and finally end up on a road that leads deep into the Mississippi countryside. We end up on a two lane highway in a part of Mississippi I have never seen before.

Finally Jarrett tells me to slow down. "Pull over in this parking lot and park."

I pull into the parking lot of a small diner advertising country cooking and souvenirs. Jarrett points to a parking space behind the building. I pull into that space and he tells me to get out and don't make a scene or he will kill me.

Before we walk into the restaurant he pushes me up against the car and searches me.

"What the hell are you looking for?"

"Shut up dammit."

Jarrett continues to search me but finds nothing on me. He steps back puts the gun in his pocket and motions for me to walk into the restaurant. Right now the adrenaline is rushing to my heart causing it to pump so fast I can hear it in my ears.

As I walk into the restaurant I can't help but notice that all eyes are on me and the looks I'm getting are very nasty. I also can't help but notice that I am the only black person in the restaurant.

There are some very big men sitting at the bar and various tables in the restaurant and I can tell by the looks I'm getting that if it were not for the fact Jarrett is walking with me I would be a dead man.

Jarrett leads me around the corner to a table in front of the kitchen. To my surprise Senator Hilgan is sitting at the table. He smiles when he sees me and motions for me to sit down in the chair in front of him.

He is just finishing his lunch as I sit down. He takes a last drink from his glass of tea then puts it down and smiles at me. After lighting a cigarette he gets right to the point.

"Son, you are in the wrong place at the wrong time. This restaurant is owned by Caleb Barkley and his family. They're God fearing, good hill people but they've fallen on hard times lately and so has the town. It used to be one of the most popular little towns and restaurants in Mississippi. You could eat here and do a little gambling at the same time. They were making a good living until the casino opened. That's when they lost their regular gambling crowd. Now they are just barely making ends meet and guess what? They know you're the one who brought the casino to our state and they're not very happy with you. Now all I have to do is get up and walk out of this restaurant and I doubt if your family will ever see you again. So this is what you're going to do."

The Senator takes a document out of his pocket and slides it in front of me.

"You're going to sign this paper that says you willfully took a bribe from the person named on the paper then you and Jarrett are going to get up and walk out of this restaurant and I won't ever see you again."

I look at the paper and see a name on it I don't recognize. I look back at Senator Hilgan then put the paper down on the table.

"What about my money?"

"Son, right now is not the time to worry about money. Now is the time to worry about your life. I bet that pretty little wife of yours is expecting you home for dinner."

Senator Hilgan leans up until he's face to face with me. "If you don't sign this paper she will never even see your body again."

I look him square in the eyes and my mind is racing. This is not the way it is supposed to work out. I was supposed to collect the money then the FBI would arrest Jarrett and charge him with trying to a bribe a Senator. Now I'm going to be lucky if I get out of this alive.

Jarrett hands me a pen and I'm just about to sign the paper when all hell breaks lose. Both the front and back doors fly open and several federal agents with guns move into the room surrounding us at the table.

Agent Todd walks in behind them and yells for every one in room to be still. One of the larger men sitting at the corner of the bar reaches for the gun in his waist band but an agent smacks him in the back of the head with the butt of his gun and he goes down. After that everyone else remains calm.

Senator Hilgan tries to snatch the paper out of my hand while everyone's attention is on the big man as he hits the floor but agent Todd is too fast for him. He takes the paper from me then sits down with us at the table.

"Senator Hilgan it's been a long time. How are you doing?"

"Agent Todd I must say I'm a little surprised to see you in this restaurant since you're a New England man. I wouldn't think you would like our southern cooking."

"I'm not here for the cuisine I'm here for the company. Senator Wright here is a good man and he's the reason I'm here. See it's against the law to threaten a citizen of the United States and it's also against the law to try and force him to sign a legal document by threatening his life but I'm sure you know this."

"Actually I don't know what you're talking about but I'm sure my lawyer will."

Agent Todd looks at me. "Senator Wright can I have your wedding band please?"

I take the wedding band off and hand it to agent Todd. Agent places it in an iPad looking device and the conversation between Senator Hilgan and me begins to play.

Agent Todd smiles. "When you tell your lawyer about this meeting make sure you tell him how great you look on video."

Agent Todd looks at Jarrett, "Oh by the way I have a few more pictures of you and this time you're holding a gun."

Agent Todd motions for two of his agents to take Jarrett and Senator Hilgan away.

We return to the downtown FBI offices and I write down my account of what happened. Then in a video-taped interview I answer several questions about my part in the operation. After I finish agent Todd thanks me for my help and I am free to leave.

The next day Nessa and mom arrive from Jackson. Nessa and I decide to stay another couple of days so we can all relax. After that we will head back to Jackson.

The following day we have company at Ole Pop's house. Senator Perkins has decided to pay us an unannounced visit. Its evening time and we're surprised when we see the long black Mercedes drive up and stop. We're even more surprised when Senator Perkins gets out wearing one of her trade mark hats, followed by one of her aides.

I walk down the steps to greet her then offer my hand as we walk back up the stairs to the porch and I offer her a seat. She sits down on the new padded bench Ole Pop bought a few days ago. My mother is sitting on one side of the Senator and Nessa is sitting on the other side.

I introduce my mother to Senator Perkins and they shake hands then she turns and looks at Nessa. Nessa is still in shock at seeing the Senator in person and she's sitting there with her mouth open but she doesn't say anything.

We all know that Senator Perkins is one of Nessa's role models and Jesse, not missing an opportunity at a good joke.

"Close ya mouth Nessa. One of dem horse flies round heah might take up residence in it."

Nessa closes her mouth then drops her head and I introduce her to Senator Perkins.

"Senator this is my wife Vanessa."

Senator Perkins shakes her hand, "Hello Mrs. Wright I understand you have a master's degree in education and you are one of the top teachers at Elmrose Elementary. Are you planning on becoming a principal one day?"

"Yes ma'am I am and I want to say it is an honor to meet you. I have followed your career every since I was in high school."

"Well thank you very much."

Then Senator Perkins leans over and whispers just loud enough for everyone to hear.

"Make sure you keep this young man in line. I believe he's going to be one of the great ones."

Nessa smiles and says, "Yes ma'am I will do just that."

Senator Perkins pats Nessa on the knee. "I wish the two of you all the happiness in the world."

Then she looks at Ole Pop and says, "Mr. Anderson it's good to see you again."

"And it's good to see you again as well but I'm curious. What brings you way out here to our farm?"

"I just stopped by to congratulate Councilman Wright and say that I am glad it worked out for him."

Ole Pop smiled that smile he gets when he's sure someone is trying to put something over on him and he has never been one to bite his tongue. He sits up in his seat looks Senator Perkins in the eyes and says what's on his mind.

"Senator Perkins you will find that I am a pretty smart man and I figure that you have a very full plate. Which means this is a special trip that is taking away from your time else where. You could have congratulated my nephew by phone so what is your real reason for being here?"

Senator Perkins smiles, "Okay Mr. Anderson I'm here for the photo opportunity of being with the man who finally brought down the "Ice King." That's the name Senator Hilgan is known by in the political circles in Washington D.C." He's as cold and slick as ice. A good photo goes a long way in Washington and this one may buy me a few more votes on the next bill I sponsor in the Senate."

"I thought as much. Well I'm sure my nephew won't mind taking some pictures with you and make sure you take a picture with my niece Vanessa I think she would enjoy that."

Senator Perkins turns to Vanessa. "It would be an honor to take a picture with such a gifted and classy young lady."

Then she turns back to Ole Pop. "By the way Mr. Anderson there is also one other thing I need to talk to you about. I understand that you make one of the best chess pies I will ever taste. Is that right?"

Ole Pop smiles, "I do a pretty fair job."

Senator Perkins leans forward and smiles back at Ole Pop but it isn't just a friendly smile. If I didn't know better I would swear she was flirting with Ole Pop.

"Well can a country girl taste a piece of that pie?"

"I don't know Senator Perkins . . .

"Please call me Glenora."

Ole Pop looks at Jesse then back at Senator Perkins and smiles.

"Okay Glenora I might have a slice or two in the kitchen. C'mon in and I'll see if I have any left from yesterdays dinner."

Jesse elbows me and winks then looks at Ole Pop.

"Careful Buford you know that pie has gotten you in trouble with more than a few women."

Ole Pop opens the screen door then steps aside and lets Senator Perkins walk past him. He takes a long slow look at her as she walks into the house and it looks to me like he is looking at things old men shouldn't be looking at.

I'm still not sure of the situation until Ole Pop turns around and winks at Jesse and whispers.

"Shhhhh . . . don't tell all my secrets."

Jesse falls out laughing while mom, Nessa and I sit there with a dumbfounded look on our face.

Jesse stops laughing and looks at us then laughs even harder spitting snuff on his shirt. He wipes his mouth and shirt then looks at us again.

"What's da matter youngins? You didn't think Ole Pop and Jesse still had the hormones in us did ya?" Then he started laughing all over again.

I sit there dumbfounded. I have never heard Ole Pop and Jesse engage in any conversation remotely considered sexual in content but here they are having a joke spiced with sexual innuendos. These old men constantly amaze me.

After Ole Pop and Senator Perkins finish their pie her aide took several photos of us together in the kitchen then she says thank you and explains she has several more stops to make and leaves.

We all sit around talking about her visit and other things but Ole Pop seems to be in another place. I finally ask him what's wrong.

"I don't exactly know but there was something wrong with her explanation of her visit here. I just feel there is more to it than that."

He sits on the porch for the next half hour trying to figure out what he's feeling but eventually he lets the whole thing go and gets back into the conversation. He and Jesse even sing a little blues before we all go to bed. The next day Nessa and I head back to Jackson.

Chapter 21

Three days after we return home the phone rings. It's Dr. Mayhew. He tells me to turn the television on CNN. When I turn on the television a reporter for CNN is doing a news broadcast about Senator Perkins and Senator Hilgan.

"In today's news Senator Glenora Perkins has been asked to appear before the attorney general to help gather facts about recent allegations of alleged bribes given to her by lobbyist Jarrett Singler.

Last night an unnamed source told the attorney general he had witnessed Senator Perkins taking bribes from Mr. Singler. He said the bribes were for a project Senator Perkins is now sponsoring in the Senate.

Ole Pop and Jesse are out on the porch. I open the front door and tell them to come in. The scene on the news has shifted and a new reporter takes over as a picture of Senator Perkins appears on screen.

"We have been told this investigation into Senator Perkins political dealings has been an ongoing investigation. If the rumors are true Senator Perkins political career may be over."

The next scenes are of Senator Perkins walking down the steps in front of the Senate building with several of her aides in front of her while reporters try to interview her about the case and her involvement in it.

She stops to give a brief statement. "Ladies and Gentlemen I can assure you that the accusations are false and the truth will come out in due time. That's all I have to say at this time."

I hear Ole Pop's voice, "I knew something wasn't right with her visit. That's why she never said anything to the media about Senator Hilgan. She's going to use your case to get out of the mess she's in."

"How do we know she's even in any trouble? I mean Senator Hilgan tried to frame me. He probably tried to frame her the same way."

"Son someone has told the attorney general something that was strong enough to cause an investigation. We don't know the source but it had to be credible and I'm pretty sure it came from Senator Hilgan's people."

"That is all the more reason she could be innocent he may be setting her up."

"First of all Senator Hilgan is smart enough and experienced enough to know that false accusations can only come back to hurt him. Second of all remember Senator Perkins own political rule number three. You never say anything in public you can't prove. Whoever is behind this is trying to get rid of Senator Perkins and I believe she knew this was coming. I also believe she knows who is after her which is why she agreed to help you. She needed something she could use to keep the media off her while she negotiated a deal and you're it. She wouldn't have come all the way out here just for some pictures with you. She's going to use your case to make Senator Hilgan's case against her go away."

I still wasn't convinced but I continued to watch the news for the next three days. The more news there was about Senator Perkin's hearing the more it looked like she was guilty. I couldn't understand why she didn't go to the media with the arrest of Senator Hilgan until her hearing started.

When Senator Perkins appeared before the Senate sub committee she explained that Senator Hilgan was trying to frame her because of her involvement in helping to clear my name. She brought along as her proof agent Todd.

Agent Todd explained to the committee Senator Perkins took the bride as part of his investigation into Jarrett Singler's alleged abuse of his lobbyist position. The sub-committee closed the hearings.

I found out later agent Todd didn't tell the whole truth. Senator Perkins only cooperated because she had been caught taking a bribe from Jarrett Singler. Agent Todd used me and her to get Senator Hilgan.

Several months later Senator Hilgan's trial takes place. With my testimony and the tape agent Todd had Senator Hilgan is found guilty of kidnapping and extortion.

In the following months my campaign goes on with several names being added to the race after Senator Hilgan makes his exit. My election certainly wasn't a sure thing but in the end the voters put their trust in me and I win the election. I am now a United States Senator.

At the same time I arrive in Washington, Senator Hilgan is using all of his political clout and calling in every favor owed him to keep himself out of jail. He succeeds but his political career is over and in his mind it's my fault.

Even with the loss of most of his political clout he begins to plan his revenge against me and Senator Perkins. Of course she is first because she was one of his fiercest rivals on the hill. She also beat him at his own game. It would only be a matter of time before he made his presence felt.

After my last campaign stop Nessa and I decide to watch the returns from Ole Pop's house. We get up early in the morning and head home. Nessa's stomach has gotten much bigger now and I am a little apprehensive about going but since it was mom's birthday that weekend Nessa convinced me it would be safe. Of course as soon as Jesse sees Nessa he begins to tease her.

"Dang girl did ya have to eat the whole watermelon couldn't ya have left some for ole Jesse."

"Aw now Mr. Jesse you know you can't wait for your grand nephew. In fact Andre and I have decided that since and you, mom and Ole Pop did such a good job with him we're going to let yall take care of this one too."

"If'n you think I'm gonna be listenin to a squawling baby in da middle of da night you had better think again. And besides yall is the parents I'm just the uncle. My job is to spoil em then give em back to yall and I'm gonna do my part."

Mom laughs, "Jesse's right. We're gonna buy him all the toys he wants and an Ipod so he doesn't have to listen when you and Andre when yall talk to him. He'll be just like Andre was when he was growing up."

Now it was my turn to laugh. "Mom, how are you going to make things hard for us like that?"

"Cause you were hard on my nerves. You made me get old before my time."

"Aw mom I wasn't that bad."

Ole Pop looked at me like he couldn't believe I just said that.

"Boy I can't wait until your son gets to be a teenager. We're gonna let him stay up late and drink some apple wine then we gonna send him back to you."

"Wait a minute now. You can't let him have apple wine. You didn't let me have apple wine."

Jesse starts laughing, "Dats cause you was full of dat other stuff. You didn't need anything else."

Ole Pop's rumbling laugh fills the room. "That's right Jesse. There was a dark cloud around his head suckin up all the oxygen. He couldn't even think straight. He kept doing dumb things. In fact he had to be smoking something the day he decided he would whoop them five wolves."

"See there yall go with the jokes again. We're still going to leave the baby with you."

"Won't make no difference you're still going to have to reap what you sowed and leaving him with us is just going to make the spoilin part easier. When he gets to the point he wants to be hard headed we'll drive to the big city and drop him off."

We all laugh then sit down and watch the election. To my surprise I win by a large margin. I was pretty sure I was going to win but I received three quarters of the votes. That's an impressive margin if I do say so myself.

On our fifth day home Nessa told me she was having pains again. We were both convinced the pains were another false alarm but these pains wouldn't stop. Just in case all of us got in the car and went to the hospital.

To all of our surprise it wasn't a false alarm. Nessa was in labor and for the next fourteen hours I watched my lovely wife go through pain I am sure I couldn't have handled and she handled it like the strong woman she was.

Well actually there were a few times I thought she was going to kill me. Especially at the beginning of her most severe pains when she told me in no uncertain terms that I was never going to touch her again.

She even called me several names right there in front of my mother. And to make matters worse my mother laughed at me. How could the love of my life call me the things she did? I mean after all I was in there with her all the time. I was trying to do my part.

My mother laughed until tears ran down her cheeks and told me not to take it seriously. When I was born she said all the things that Nessa was saying and a few things that were worse than that.

Of course I did the best I could in calming Nessa down including letting her sink her short nails into the palm of my hand as I held her hand during the labor pains. After one particularly hard pain she almost drew blood.

When she let my hand go I showed mom the fingernail marks. She smiled and said, "She wants you be a part of the whole birthing experience including the pain. Now get ready for the next contraction. It's going to be a long night."

At three fifty the next morning my baby boy was born. He was the most beautiful child I have ever seen. Of course the only thing my wife wanted to know was if he had ten fingers and ten toes. Mom told me it was a woman thing and I wouldn't understand.

They washed my son then brought him to Nessa and she called his name for the first time. "Hello Andre Jr. I am your mother and this is your father." He smiled up at us as if to say "I approve of the both of you" and that was it. He had my heart for the rest of his life. I was going to teach him all the things that Mom, Ole Pop and Jesse had taught me.

Thirty minutes later Ole Pop was sitting in the rocker in our room holding his great, great nephew for the first time with Uncle Jesse looking over his shoulder.

When it came time for Jesse to hold him Jesse was all smiles. "Nessa you sho did a good job wit this one. He's going to be a strong boy."

"Hey old man what about me?"

"You didn't carry nothin. Nessa did all the work. You ain't no good for this sort of thing. Only a woman can do as good a job as this."

"Dang I can't get no credit."

"You'll git some credit as long as ya pay the bills on time."

"So all I'm good for is paying bills."

"I don't know." Jesse turns to Nessa, "Does he pay the bills?"

"Yes and he does a good job of it too."

"Did ya hear that Buford. At least he got that much right."

"That's a good thing cause li'l BOHS here is going to need as many positive male role models in life as he can get. I am proud of both of you." For the second time in my life I saw Ole Pop cry. This was one of the more special times of my life.

Chapter 22

One of the first people to visit me as soon as I move into my Washington office is Senator Perkins. I'm not very happy to see her and I let her know it. With a very business like attitude I address her.

"What can I do for you Senator Perkins?"

"Why the formal attitude Senator Wright? When I last saw you everything was just fine. You had gotten your man and your reputation was saved."

"That was before I knew you were only using me to get yourself out of trouble."

"What trouble are we talking about Senator Wright?"

Right about there I remembered Senator Perkins's political rule number three and realized I had no proof. Trying to pin her down about the Senate hearing and her alleged bribe was going to be impossible so I dropped it.

"Look is there something you want to talk to me about?"

"Yes there is. I chair the foreign policy committee and I would like you to be one of my committee members."

"I don't think I'm interested in foreign policy."

You should be. Everything our country is built on now is of global concern. You can't burry your head in the sand and just work for your state. You have to see the big picture."

"If it means I have to lose my integrity I don't think I am interested."

"Senator Wright if there is something you want to say to me please feel free to do so."

"Okay. I don't like being used by people especially people in powerful positions who should be using their power to help their people. To be quite honest I don't like the way you work and I really don't want to have anything to do with you."

"Well at least you don't beat around the bush but let me ask you a question. Do you think you can help the people of your state?"

"If I didn't, I wouldn't have taken the job."

"Do you think a politician owes it to his or her people to be as knowledgeable about his or her job as he or she can?"

"Yes I do."

"Then leave your bruised feelings at the door of the Senate chamber and get on with the business of educating yourself on how to help your state become part of the global community. After educating yourself, if you still feel you can't work with me then at least you made an informed decision."

Senator Perkins gets up, leans over and hands me several books on global economics and just before she walks out says,

"I am sorry this turned out the way it did. I would have liked to be your friend."

I sit in my office thinking about all she said to me and decide that she is right I should at least look at the books and do some research and then make my decision.

For the next week I read the books go online and check out all the information I can. Nessa helps me with my research and we both find out a lot about not only the global economy but our country's economy as well and in the end I decide to join Senator Perkin's committee.

I call Senator Perkins and inform her of my decision and also tell her that I will do all that is in my power not to be used by her or anyone else again. She laughs and wishes me good luck then faxes the agenda for the next meeting to me.

For the next few weeks I find myself immersed in economic issues I hadn't even known existed until now. It was all fascinating and sometimes overwhelming but I kept working and I have to admit Senator Perkins was a great deal of help.

Eventually we have a conversation about her past problems and how she needed me to keep herself out of trouble. She explained that she made a mistake in judgment and a person she thought was a friend turned out to be playing for the other side.

She apologized for using me but also said she gave me as much help as I gave her which was true. If it hadn't been for her I would not be here. Slowly I came to trust her judgment and we became very good friends. She took on the role of another mentor and she was as good a teacher as Ole Pop, Jesse and Dr. Mayhew. She also insisted that Nessa and I call her Glenora and she has become a second grand mother to our children.

During my first term in office I learned several things about foreign and domestic politics. The first thing I learned is nothing is ever as it seems and everything done in Washington as well as abroad has an ulterior motive.

The second thing I learned is no one in politics down to the last janitor makes a move without being sure they are going to gain something either on the front end or the back end. Every one in Washington has a hustle.

It may be a large gain like the ones the big lobbyists get when they spread money around to get a bill passed or killed. Or it may be a small gain like the janitors get when they pass on information to the right reporter but every one in Washington is looking to better their position.

The last thing I learned wasn't as much a learning experience as it was a reinforcement of an old lesson. Absolutely no one is to be trusted unless you do your research on them first.

One of my first task as a member of Senator Perkins's committee was to do research on the poverty levels in certain parts of Africa. After several weeks of research I booked a flight to Africa to look at several cities up close. On this flight I met a man by the name of Omboko Yariehba.

He told me he was on the way back to his home in Luanda Sul where he is a teacher. When he found out who I was and why I was going to Africa he offered to help me with my research.

After spending several days traveling through Africa with a government sponsored tour guide I realized that I wasn't getting the full view of what was really going on and that's when Omboko offered to take me to the places the guide was trying to hide from me. In his words "It is time that the American people come face to face with the real issues facing the poor in Africa."

He came the next day and woke me before dawn. We slipped out of the back of the hotel because the African government had men stationed around the hotel since I was an American dignitary. They explained to me that it was for my own protection when it was actually to make sure I didn't see anything they didn't want me to see.

Omboko took me to several small villages where the people still lived in huts, there was no running water and the living conditions were horrible. He showed me the lack of health care and blamed it on a government more interested in stuffing their own pockets rather than taking care of the people.

Needless to say the government appointed guide was less than pleased when I got back to the hotel. He explained to me that my safety was his concern and he didn't want to go back to his superiors and explain that I was killed while he was my guide.

I think that last speech was given to make sure I would stay with him for the duration of the journey and he was quite surprised when I told him there would be no need to go any further I had seen what I needed to see.

He questioned me as to where I went and who took me there but I didn't give him any answers. Of course before I could leave for America several other government officials asked me the same questions but they got the same stock answers I gave the guide.

When I finally got back to Washington I was ready to give my report to my committee but something about Omboko wasn't fitting right. I couldn't put my finger on it but something kept bothering me.

While we were touring the village Omboko kept trying to impress upon me the virtues of an organization by the name of "Children of Africa." He said over and over that this organization had the right idea as to what really needed to be done for the people of Africa. They even had a school that taught as many of the children of this village as they could.

I had never heard of the organization before and when I got back to the hotel after the tour I tried to look it up on the internet but all I could find was one website with a few lines about the school and that was it. There was no information on what the organization was about or even who founded it.

After puzzling over this for an hour and trying once again to find out anything on the organization I finally called Senator Perkins and told her about my dilemma. She in turn called some people she knew and two hours later called me back.

"Senator Wright Omboko Yariehba is the sole owner of the school you mentioned. He has received money in the amount of several hundred thousand dollars from several Senate sub committees but no one seems to know what he has done with it. How did you run into this person?"

"He was on the plane with me on the way here."

"Then he was on that plane to see if he could get more money from our government. Where did he take you and what did he show you?"

"When I get back I'm going to fax my report over to you after I make a few revisions."

"That will be fine. I'll talk to you tomorrow."

That reinforced the lesson of always know your enemies as well as your friends.

Now I never meet a new person without wondering what angle they are trying to exploit. Nessa tells me that politics is making me too cynical but I explained that it is my job to be thorough and suspicious. She smiled and told me as long as I didn't lose the trusting man she grew up with she was fine.

For the next six years I help pass legislation that not only is good for my state but also helps my country. I have gotten the reputation as a hard working defender of the common man which is a good thing but also a weight on my shoulders.

I quickly find out what is right for some isn't right for all and sometimes the only thing a politician can hope to do is make a decision that will help one set of people while hopefully not destroying another set.

It was a hard thing to deal with knowing that your decision could put people out of work, take their medical benefits from them or cause them to lose their homes but those were the decisions that had to be made.

I did the best I could in making the right decision and casting the right vote I always remembered Ole Pop and Jesse saying, "Never make a decision without consulting the Lord first." I have never cast a vote or made a decision without praying about it first.

After my first term I went through the election process again. I had forgotten how nasty political races could be and this one turned out to be very nasty. My opponent was backed by ex-senator Hilgan.

During Dick's years on the hill he had amassed a considerable fortune. He put a hefty amount of money behind my opponent Brent Shackle. Brent was the banker who handled the money used by ex-Councilman Orton and his committee to put the casino on Ole Pop's land.

Hilgan bought a couple million dollars of advertisement space on the television and radio and they brought up everything from my juvenile record to Nessa's father killing her mother and himself. I thought that was a low blow even for a politician and a lot of voters felt the same.

Dick tried every dirty political trick in the book and I met every trick with the same honesty as I had in the past. When they finally got down to real politics and started questioning my voting record I defended it with honesty and even went on the radio so the voters could ask any questions they liked.

I wasn't confident on Election Day but I won the election by a two to one margin. I reported back to Washington for my second term ready to work. And that's when things got interesting.

First Glenora called me to her office and told me to sit down. "Andre I need to ask you a question. Have you ever thought about moving up to the next level?"

"What is the next level?"

"The white house."

I sort of chuckled. "You and I both know I don't have enough experience to run for President."

"I'm not talking about the Presidency I'm talking about the Vice Presidency."

"I'm not so sure I have the experience for that either."

"Yes you do. You are a good man. You always think things through before reacting and you're honest. Besides this is a good political move for you. It will give you a chance to get the experience you need to run for the Presidency later on."

"There is no way the American voters will view me as anything more than an inexperienced politician who is too young to trust with the White house if something should happen to the President. I'll be more of a hindrance than a help."

"I and several other high profile and powerful Senators and Congressmen disagree and I for one can't think of anyone who is more qualified than you."

"Wait a minute. You mean there are other Senators and Congressmen who feel like you do."

"Yes Andre. There are several Senators, Congressmen and some very powerful people willing to back you if you decide to take the offer. Some of which will be powerful political allies."

"Okay what's the catch?"

"Right now there is no catch. I just think you should consider at least going to a few dinners and finding out what it's all about."

"But I'm just a young Senator from Mississippi."

"You're a thirty four year old Senator with the most integrity I've ever seen on Capitol Hill. I think a lot of Senators, congressmen and women on the hill admire you because you stick to your convictions and never have backed down or compromised for your own gain."

"I don't know Glenora this is a little too much, too fast."

"Actually it's not as fast as you think and it's not too much. The committee likes you but they wouldn't have said a thing if you hadn't gotten re-elected. They knew Hilgan was going to go after you with every thing he had and they wanted to see how you would handle an old veteran like him. You handled yourself well and now they think you are ready for the next step. At least think about it.

After our meeting I drove home thinking about every thing Glenora said. I'm not sure I'm ready to become Vice President. In fact I'm not sure that this is a job I really want. This is going to take some soul searching.

As soon as I get home I sit Nessa down and tell her what Glenora told me and then I told her about my reservations about the whole thing and she had the nerve to get mad at me.

"Andre Wright I have watched you work your way through several political offices and I know you are qualified for the job. I also know you are the most honest and sincere man I have ever met. You are a good, God fearing man and in this day and time that's what this nation needs in its leaders. Someone needs to move this nation to the next level and if not you then who is going to do it?"

"Okay Nessa calm down. I just have a problem with all of this. I didn't get into politics to become Vice President. I got into this to help people."

"And what better way to do that than to go out there and see if this is for real. Find out if this is possible and if it is do what needs to be done. That is what you have done all of your life. What is so different about this situation?"

"This is a lot bigger stage than I've ever been on. If I mess this up I will hurt a lot of people who believe in me especially you, Mom, Ole Pop and Jesse."

"You won't mess this up but if you do we will survive. Just think of what we've survived in our lives so far. I don't think you will make any huge mistakes and even if you do you can't do any worse than some that have come before you."

After a long conversation she kisses me then goes to bed leaving me to think about this whole thing. This is one I need to talk to Ole Pop about. It's about time for a road trip to the farm.

Chapter 23

After returning from the farm with some advice from Ole Pop, Jesse and Mom I was ready for the next step which was meeting the man I would be partnered with if I decided to join the ticket as his running mate. The Meeting was set up at a dinner party given by Glenora and Senator Walter Bowens at his house.

Senator Bowens is the Senate minority leader and one of the men who wanted me on the ticket. He is the one who thought adding me to the ticket would be a "Can't miss" proposition. Still I had to admit I was a bit overwhelmed to be considered for the Vice Presidency with only one term in the senate under my belt. I was a bit shaky as Nessa and I walked into Senator Bowen's house.

After we had dinner and while the other guest drank and talked Senator Bowen asked me to step into his library and he introduced me to the party's candidate for president. I almost turned down the offer and walked away when I found out who the presidential candidate was.

His name is Glenn Worthington. He is the third term Senator from Chicago and we have absolutely nothing in common. There is no way I can see myself on the same ticket with this man. We have opposed each other on several bills. I've found him to be a manipulative person willing to do almost anything to get his bills passed.

He on the other hand thought of me as the naive Senator from Mississippi with a fairy tale look on life. As he explained to some of our colleagues.

"I hope he doesn't hurt himself when he falls off his horse and realizes America doesn't need a knight in shining armor anymore."

He also has a problem with me because of recent events. Several months ago I was instrumental in securing enough votes to kill a bill he backed that would have put another energy plant in his home state.

The bill made absolutely no sense because of the brand new energy plant being constructed in Missouri that would supply the whole region with power. He had counted on the passing of that bill to fill the pockets of some of his already wealthy supporters. Senator Bowens watched us with interest as we reluctantly shook hands. The uneasiness between us was evident.

Senator Bowen was a gracious host. "Gentlemen would you like something to drink?"

Senator Worthington sat down in his chair. "I'd like a scotch on the rocks."

I sat down in a chair across from him. "Nothing for me thanks."

Senator Bowens poured Glenn a drink then sat down in the chair behind his desk.

"Senator Wright I'm sure Senator Perkins explained to you why I wanted you to come tonight. Do you have any thoughts or questions about our idea?"

"I have only one question Senator Bowens. Am I to be the token paraded around by the party to show we are progressive? If so then I respectfully decline."

Glenn chuckled and said, "Is every thing so black and white in your world?"

"If you mean do I see everything as good or bad the answer is yes. The shades black and white keep me from crossing the line and coloring every thing to suit my needs."

My remark hit the target. Glenn glared at me.

"And what's that supposed to mean?"

"It means I may not be right for this position because if I feel any policy the party is backing is wrong then I am going to speak out and there won't be any misunderstanding about it."

At that point I knew I had struck a nerve. Glenn stood up.

"If you have something to say to me why don't you just come out and say it?"

I stood up so that we could talk eye to eye. "I just said what I needed to say."

Senator Bowens stepped between us, "Gentlemen I would appreciate it if both of you would calm down. I'm sure the both of you have your own agendas and that's what we're here to talk about hopefully with as much civility as we can. He motions for both of us to sit down and then he begins his speech.

"Senator Wright I can assure you that you are not our choice simply because of race. If that were true we had our choice of several minority candidates both Congressmen and Senators. Most of these other candidates have more experience than you and would gladly take the vice presidency. However most of them are my age and the party needs good young blood like you and Senator Worthington but we also need a ticket that can win the people over in the next two years. You two young Senators are the top choice of the committee. We think you are a winning combination but it won't happen unless the two of you can work together. So I'm going to leave now and let the two of you work it out. Please try not to destroy my library."

Senator Bowens walks out of the room leaving me and Senator Worthington looking at each other. Glenn gets up, walks over to the bar and refreshes his drink.

"It appears to me that you either don't like me or you don't like the way I do my job."

"I don't know you personally so it would be illogical for me to make a judgment as to whether I like you or not. I do however know your tactics and you are right about the fact that I don't like the way you do your job."

"I don't know about you Senator Wright but the people who voted for me expect me to do everything in my power to provide jobs and financial security for them."

"I understand that and so do the people who voted for me but if it means compromising my values then I would rather let someone else do the job."

"It takes compromise to make things work in politics or are you trying to tell me you never compromised on a bill."

"No I'm not trying to tell you I haven't compromised on several bills. But there is a certain line I won't cross. I have yet to see you draw that line when you are working to get a bill passed."

"Look I'm going to do whatever it takes to get the job done."

"And I'm going to be the one standing in front of you explaining why it is not going to get done that way."

At this point Senator Perkins walks back in and eases the tension. "And that's why we want you to become running mates."

Senator Bowens walks in behind her. "She's right gentlemen. We need a bulldog to be tenacious and handle the business of politics and foreign affairs but we also need someone who can tell the bulldog when not to bite."

Glenn smiled, "So I'm to be the attack dog and he's going to be the trainer."

"It's more like the soldier and the diplomat. You handle the hard line stance of the party and Senator Wright will handle the diplomacy. So what do the two of you think?"

Glenn looks at me, "So do you think you can make sure I don't push the button."

"No actually I think I will hold the keys to the button just in case you decide to push it anyway."

Glenn smiles and holds out his hand. "That's a compromise I can live with. Can you?"

"Yes I can."

We shake hands then sit down and suddenly I remember my past and almost go into panic mode but I hear Ole Pop's voice, "Son now is not the time to panic. Now is the time to think."

I stand up and look directly into Senator Bowen's eyes. "I think there is something you need to know about me. I wasn't exactly an angel when I was young."

Walter smiled and interrupted me. "We already know about your juvenile record and it doesn't matter. You were young then and everyone has a past."

"Yes but don't you think one of my opponents will tell the American people that I once sold marijuana and was arrested for it?"

"Yes I'm pretty sure they will and when they do we'll show them your record since you moved to Mississippi and it will no longer be an issue. In fact if one of your opponents brings up your record by the time we get through with it you will be the model for young men who want to get out of that type of life."

"You mean for young African American men."

Glenora shakes her head, then glares at me and exhales an exasperated breath.

"Andre you need to start seeing yourself as a role model for all the young men of the nation not just the African American ones. Now do you want the job or not?"

"Yes I want the job."

"Good then lets get to work."

The next few months are a blur of work and meetings. First there is the announcement of Glenn running for our party's nomination and a few weeks of media play while the whole country gets acquainted with Glenn. It was decided that I would remain in the background until Glenn won the nomination.

During these meetings and strategy session I got a chance to get to know Glenn. I find out his history is much like mine. In fact he also got himself into trouble trying to make a living the illegal way.

After his last arrest he was sent to his grandmother who lived here in D.C. Without the influence of the bad neighborhoods he was forced to live in because his mother was an addict he turned his life around and graduated from law school. After that he went back to Illinois to practice and eventually got into politics.

He is well equipped to handle the hard ins and outs of politics since he grew up on the streets of Chicago. But hard line negotiation is all he knows. He needed someone with a different perspective he could talk to when his hard line diplomacy didn't work which made us the perfect running mates.

Over the next few months he and I became good friends and he began to actually listen when I pointed out a different perspective on some of the thoughts he had about the direction of the party, politics and life in general. I relayed some of the things I learned from Ole Pop and Jesse to him and he told me he wanted to meet both of them after the campaign was over.

Six months into the pre campaign tour he told me if he became a good president I would be the reason for it. After that we had very little time to talk because the campaign was about to start.

Fortunately for me it would be several months before the convention and Glenn naming me as his choice for vice president. This gives me time to get myself ready for the inevitable rush of media scrutiny and speaking engagements.

It also gave me a lot of time to spend with Nessa which was great considering once the media found out about my being Glenn's choice for vice president our private life would be a distant memory.

During this time Nessa began teaching a fifth grade class of advanced students. After she had been with the class for two months a new student transferred into her class. That in its self is not unusual but her ethnic background would soon become an issue. In fact it would grab the whole country's attention.

Several months later Nessa asked me to come and talk to her class about what I do and how the government works and I meet this child for the first time. Her name is Amira Ala'Aldeen she is nine years old and a native Iraqi and from the start I can see there is something different about her. She asks more questions than any other student in the class and some of her questions are very intense and adult like.

She has a bright beautiful smile but her eyes show a maturity beyond her age and she is very inquisitive about the workings of the government and what I do. She is also very bright for her age.

After class I sit and talk to Nessa about Amira and how bright and inquisitive she is. Nessa explains to me that she's that way every day until her mother comes to get her. She seems to shut down at that time. She stops talking and smiling. In fact when her mother comes to pick her up she picks up her books and walks silently behind her mother without saying one word.

Nessa has tried to talk to her about her home life but every time she approaches the subject Amira shuts down completely and doesn't communicate at all for the rest of the day. Nessa is concerned there may be some abuse going on in the family.

Several weeks later after once again watching the transformation of Amira when her mother picked her up from school Nessa asks me to see if I can find out anything about the little girl and her mother.

"You should talk to the school counselor about this."

"I did three weeks ago."

"What happened?"

"She came back and told me she couldn't find anything out. She also told me that I should let it go for my own sake."

"What did she mean by that?"

"She wouldn't say. But the next day Mrs. Dellion our head principal came to me and told me it would be best if I didn't inquire about Amira's family."

"Did she say why?"

"No she didn't but her secretary told me a man came to see her and looked like one of those official Capital Hill types."

"And you want me to see if I can find out who it is?"

"No, I want you to see if this child needs any help."

"Okay I'll see what I can do."

The next day I begin inquiring about Amira trying to find out where she lived before this or anything I can find out about her and her mother but I am stonewalled at every turn.

After three days of trying I hadn't gotten any more information. Everyone I talked to either shut the conversation down when they heard the name or claimed never to have heard of her. However all of that changed two weeks later with a visit from Glenora.

My secretary always lets me know who is waiting to see me but this time she never said a word allowing Glenora to walk into my office completely unannounced and very quietly shut the door behind her.

When I look up she's standing in front of my desk. She puts her finger to her lips to tell me not to say anything then she motions for me to follow her.

We walk in silence out of the building and around the corner to a little park just down the street from my office building. We sit on one of the benches beside a fountain and Glenora gives me a look of concern.

"Andre I need to warn you about your inquiry into Amira Ala'Aldeen's family. Do yourself a favor and leave this alone."

"My wife got the same warning from her counselor. Why is everyone trying to conceal this little girl's family?"

"There are things here that you don't understand and in not understanding you could ruin your chances of becoming the vice president. I've seen my share of young Senators find themselves on the wrong side of the state department and that is not somewhere you want to be?"

"Why would I be on the wrong side of the state department just because I'm trying to find out about a little girl?"

"I can't answer that. All I know is someone in the state department wants you to leave her and her family alone. Now I know that does not sit well with you so I'm going to put it to you like this. If you keep inquiring about the little girl she's going to be pulled from your wife's school and neither of you will ever see her again. If you care for the little girl let this go."

Glenora stands up and walks away without saying another word. Now I'm not only concerned about the little girl I'm concerned about how she can cause this much concern from a major Senate member like Glenora.

As I walk back to my building I decide that maybe it would be best just to let this be. When I get home I sit Nessa down and tell her what Glenora told me.

"Well maybe Glenora is hiding something from you like she did the first time."

"I don't think she would lie to me and you don't either. I believe she's telling the truth this time and I think it would be in Amira's best interest if I drop this."

"Well if you think this is best okay but if she ever shows any signs of abuse I will call the police."

"That sounds like the right thing to do."

After that I drop the whole matter and get back to the job of being a Senator. I have just about forgotten the whole thing until a late night phone call forces me to begin my inquiries again.

It's three o'clock in the morning when the phone rings. Nessa turns over and picks it up.

"Hello."

After just a few words Nessa sits up in the bed. "What's wrong Amira?"

Nessa listens for a few minutes then hands me the phone.

"Hello."

"Senator Wright this is Farrah Ala'Aldeen. I know you don't know me but I need your help. Is it alright that my daughter and I come over to your house?"

"Yes it is. We will be waiting on you."

"Thank you Senator Wright."

Fifteen minutes later a dark sedan pulls into the driveway. Amira's mother gets out of the car and knocks on my door. When I open it she whispers, "Don't talk" then motions for Nessa and I to follow her to her car.

When we get in the car Amira is sitting in the back seat. We can see she has been crying. Nessa gets in beside her and Amira immediately wraps her arms around Nessa's neck. I get in the front seat beside Amira's mother and she looks at me.

"Senator Wright I am sorry we have to meet this way but I don't know if your house has been compromised with listening devices."

"What is this all about?"

"I don't know Senator Wright. All I know is there are listening devices in our house and men have been following us for the last month. I want you to know that helping us could prove very dangerous for you and your wife. If you want to leave now I will understand."

"First tell me what this is all about and then I will let you know what I'm going to do."

"My daughter and I are from a small village near Hafar al batin. I worked on a military base not far from where I lived. There were several top secret projects being handled on that base. After the projects were over your government agreed to allow anyone working on the base safe passage to this country and citizenship when we got here. My daughter and I took advantage of the offer but now it looks like we will be deported back to our village. If that happens we will be put to death."

"Why are they deporting you and why would you be put to death?"

"I have heard that it is because of my brother but I don't understand what they mean."

"Who is your brother?"

"El Amir Aljarah."

"Where is he now?"

"Back home in Iraq."

"I've heard that name before. Isn't he part of the men who are carrying out the suicide bombings?"

"He would never be apart of anything like that. Can you help us?"

"What about my other question? Why would you be put to death if you return to your village?"

Amira's mother holds her head down. "Because I left my husband behind. He was abusive to me and Amira and I decided to take the opportunity to escape."

"But why would that cause you to be put to death?"

"In my village the husband has the last word on everything including what his wife can do, say or wear. If a wife disobeys her husband he can beat her until she learns her lesson. If she disgraces him by trying to run away he can have her put to death."

"Okay, what do you want me to do?"

"Please see if you can keep your government from sending us back to our village."

"I will do what I can?"

Nessa and I get out of the car and just before I shut the door I lean in. "Can I contact you at the number you called me from?"

"Yes."

I watch as Amira's mother drives off. As she turns the corner the lights of a dark vehicle parked two blocks down from my house come on. I watch as it pulls out and turns the curve behind her.

The next day as soon as I walk into the reception area of my office my secretary informs me that someone from NSA is in my office waiting on me. I walk into my office and he introduces himself.

"Hello Senator Wright my name is Charles Crafton. I'm the assistant director of NSA."

"I know who you are what I don't know is what you want."

"Senator Wright we are concerned about your relationship with Miss Farrah Ala'Adeen."

"Who is this we, you are talking about?"

"I can't get into that but I need for you to understand that you are getting into an area that you are not qualified to handle."

"And what area is that?"

"There are certain things you need to know about Miss Ala'Adeen. She is at the center of a group we have been after for the last two years."

"And what group is that?"

"A terrorist cell named "Final days" led by El Amir Aljarah. El Amir is Miss Ala'Adeen's brother."

"So you think she is part of this group."

"Yes we do."

"Then why haven't you arrested her yet?"

"For security reasons."

"What exactly does that mean?"

Mr. Crafton gets up, picks up his coat and turns toward the door. Over his shoulder just before he walks out he says, "Senator Wright do yourself a favor and let this rest. It will cost you more than you want to pay."

"Is that a threat?"

The door shuts behind him before he has a chance to answer and it didn't matter he had already made his point. He really didn't need to answer the question.

An hour later I have another visitor to my office. Suddenly I am becoming the most popular man on Capital hill. Senator Bowens walks in and sits down in front of me. He looked like he has had a long day that was only going to get longer.

"Andre I hear that you are challenging NSA on the subject of national security."

"No, actually I'm trying to make sure that an American citizen doesn't have her rights trampled on."

"Andre I advise you to leave this alone. It can only hurt your career. You don't need this hanging around your neck."

"What you mean is the party doesn't need me hanging around it's neck if I choose to pursue this."

"Okay if we're going to get down to the truth. You are right the party doesn't need this to turn into a scandal."

"Then why don't I make it easy for you Walter? Tell the party to find someone else to run with Glenn."

"We are not prepared to find someone else. You and Glenn are the super team we have been grooming to win this election. We still want you as the vice president but if this turns into a scandal we will let you go."

"I understand as long as you understand I won't let this go until it is concluded."

Walter gets up slowly and looks me in the eyes then shakes his head and lets out a long exasperated breath.

"I just hope you don't ruin your career or even worse end up in federal prison." Then he turns and walks out the door.

I sit down in my chair to think about this. This is only my second term in office and I'm in a political situation that could ruin my career. I needed to make sure the next move I made was the right one.

Fortunately the next move was made for me when I received a folder with information in it that told me everything I needed to know. As soon as I read the material in the folder I left my office and headed for Mr. Crafton's office. I was going to get some answers.

I walked into his office and told his receptionist who I was. She explained he was out for the rest of the day. I handed her a piece of paper with an omega insignia on it and walked out of the office. Before I could get to the elevator Mr. Crafton catches up with me.

"Where did you get this?"

"I think you and I need to talk somewhere more private."

He turned and walked back to his office and I followed. As soon as he shut the door behind us he asked the question again. I handed him the folder with copies of the material that was in it. He sat down and read the material then looked at me.

"This material is classified. How did you get it?"

"That doesn't matter. What matters is you know that Farrah Ala'Adeen is not a terrorist and you are using her as bait for her brother. She and her daughter are legal American Citizens at least that's what the papers you have in your hands say. So why are you harassing this woman and her daughter?"

"We don't know that she's not a terrorist. We have to keep her under surveillance for the security of the country."

"I'm not questioning your surveillance I'm questioning her deportation. It is not legal especially since she is a legal United States Citizen. Are you hoping that she will break down and tell you where her brother is?"

"Senator Wright I think you had better go."

"No problem, I can leave but don't be surprised if CNN and the civil liberties union should somehow find out about this. Now I know you have enough power to censure me and probably get me run out of Washington but you need to know that I'm not going to give this up."

I turn around to walk out and over my shoulder I say, "By the way you can keep the papers you have in your hand I have the originals."

Several days later I'm in a conference meeting with Glenora and our committee when NSA agents walk in.

"Senator Wright we need you to come with us."

"What is this all about?"

"All will be explained to you after you come with us."

I look at Glenora and she tries to hide the distressed look on her face but she doesn't do a very good job of it. I get up and the agent's escort me out of the building.

After walking two blocks down the street they direct me into the justice building. They make a great show of letting the other people in the building know that I am being escorted by NSA agents. Now the gossip on the hill will be "Why was the new Senator from Mississippi being escorted into the justice building by NSA agents?"

We take the elevator up to the fifth floor and when the doors open I am standing directly in front of the door to the office of the director of NSA.

Chapter 24

When I walk into the office Mr. Crafton is sitting in a chair in front of a desk and behind that desk is Adam Crawford head of NSA. He motions to the seat beside Mr. Crafton.

"Please have a seat Senator Wright."

Even though I'm boiling inside I remain calm and sit down. Now its time to use all of the intelligence Ole Pop and Jesse instilled in me and realize that this fight isn't going to be won with my fist but with my brain.

"Senator Wright I asked you here to tell you that you are about to get into National Security issues that could compromise several of our positions in the Middle East."

"Are you actually trying to tell me that Amira and her mother are that big a security risk?"

"No I'm not. What I am telling you is their little problem is not worth compromising three years of work for."

"Do you know what will happen to Farrah and possibly Amira if you send them back home?"

"That is not my concern. My concern is that our country is safe and that should be your concern as well Senator Wright."

"My concern is that you are trying to send two U.S. citizens back home illegally. We're sworn to protect all of our citizens and that includes you as well Mr. Crawford."

"So I can not convince you to drop this."

"No sir you can't."

"Well it is your decision. However I do have one other question, where did you get your information?"

At that point I decide it is time or me to leave. I stand up and begin walking toward the door.

"I don't think I'll answer that question. Now unless you're planning on keeping me here under lock and key I have work to do."

I walk right past several NSA agents, out the door and back to my meeting.

After the meeting is over I return to my office. For some reason the papers that I received anonymously are stuck in my mind. I walk over to my desk, unlock the top drawer with my key and find that the papers are gone. I should have known this would happen.

I walk out to my receptionist. "Miss Lakely did you let anyone in my office while I was gone?"

"No Senator Wright. No one has been in the office at all today."

"Did you leave the area for any time?"

"Well yes sir I had to go to the ladies room."

I walk back into my office going over several scenarios in my head including thinking that Miss Lakely could have been the one who took the papers. I finally conclude that is a silly notion. Miss Lakely is sixty years old I doubt if she would be in the spy business.

Now I had no papers to prove Farrah and Amira's deportation was a cover up so they could be used as bait. It is now my word against NSA and without proof all I have is rumors.

I sit down in my chair to think the situation over and my desk phone rings.

"Hello."

"Senator Wright would you like to know the whole story?"

"Who is this?"

"Washington monument, half hour."

The phone goes dead. I grab my hat and head out the door. A half an hour isn't a long time to get to a tourist attraction.

Half an hour later I am sitting on a bench in front of the Washington monument. I sit there for almost an hour before I realize the person isn't going to show. Someone is playing games with me and I'm tiring of it quickly.

When I get back into my car there is a very small and thin case containing a DVD sitting on the front passenger's seat. Written on the outside of the case are the words, "Slide this into your pocket and don't let anyone see you do it."

After looking around to see who was watching me I put my car in gear and drive home.

When I get there Nessa is in the kitchen preparing dinner for Andre Jr. I kiss her and pick up Andre then walk into my den. I place the DVD in my player and sit down in front of my television. The next thing I see is Paul Trice and investigative reporter for CNN.

"Senator Wright I think you should know the information you are about to see may get you and your family in trouble. It may even get you killed so I suggest you get rid of this DVD after you see it."

I sit and watch as the DVD shows intelligence info on how Farrah's brother El Amir Aljarah has been accused of several bombings in the Middle East and Europe and how it is believed he has risen to the top of the organization known as "Final Days." NSA knows this group is planning on doing something really big but they don't know what it is.

In order to stop this plot they are planning on sending Farrah and Amira back to their village knowing that El Amir knows she will be put to death and will send someone to try and stop it. NSA will then hopefully follow whoever he sends back to him and a black opts unit will kill everyone in his organization.

Thousands of miles away in Iraq El Amir is talking to one of his relatives. For the last three months he has been hiding out with his relatives and in several of the caves in the area. He has made a habit of moving every two days keeping him one step ahead of his government.

"Our operative says it is likely that Farrah and her daughter will be sent back to Hafar al Batin. If it were not for the actions of a Senator Wright she would have already been sent back.

"This Senator Wright, Who does he work for?"

"As far as I can tell he works for no one but he is trying to keep Farrah in the United States and NSA has already flagged him as a security risk."

"Why is he ready to put himself in harms way for someone he doesn't even know?"

"I do not know but he is fighting very hard for Farrah and Amira."

"Find out all you can about this man. I want to know his background, education and family."

"Yes El Amir."

The next day when I walk into my office Miss Lakely looks nervously at me then at my office. I know by her look that someone is in my office and that someone has her scared to death.

I open my door and am not too surprised to see Adam Crawford is sitting in the chair in front of my desk. I walk in, put my coat and brief case down and sit down behind my desk.

"It is customary for people wanting to see me to wait in the reception area."

"I don't have time for formalities. I know you have received some information from CNN reporter Paul Trice. I need to know what that information is."

"How do you know I have any information? Never mind answering that question. I know you have me and my family under surveillance and I also know you can probably make me and my family go away. That doesn't change the fact that you are planning on using a woman and her child as bait. They will probably get killed in the process and you will go on with your life as usual."

"Senator Wright no matter what you think of me, it is people like me who keep this country safe."

"Safe from what! You don't even know who you're looking for. I am not going to give you the information and if you don't mind I have work to do."

As Adam Crawford gets up to leave my office he gives me one last warning.

"Senator I am going to do my job even if it means a few good people get hurt in the process."

"I take it when you say good people you are talking about me or my family."

I stand up and walk around my desk so that I can get face to face with Mr. Crawford.

"Let me explain something to you. If it takes the death of an innocent woman and child to do your job then I suggest you find some other way to do it. I'm not going anywhere and I will not let this drop. Now you do what you have to do."

Mr. Crawford walks out of my office. He's not happy but he doesn't say another word. As soon as he is gone I use my cell phone to call my wife.

"Nessa I need for you to pack some clothes I'm taking you and the children home to Ole Pop."

"Andre what's wrong?"

"I'll tell you when I get home."

When I get home and tell Nessa why I want her and Andre Jr. to leave we have a major argument. She understands sending Andre Jr. to Ole Pops but she is bound and determined not to go. I am just as determined that she is going. It takes a lot of convincing but eventually she agrees to go but only because of the news she gives me when we both finally calm down.

"What did you say?"

"I said I'm pregnant again."

"We're going to have another baby!"

"Yes Andre we are going to have another baby."

I am so overjoyed I pick up Andre Jr. and run around the room in a circle but then it hits me. I have the head of NSA and who knows who else mad at me because I'm causing problems with their plans. I look at Nessa and she has never looked so beautiful and I'm even more determined now to get her out of D.C.

Thank God its summer and school ended a week ago or I would never have been able to convince Nessa to go to Ole Pops. While we're in flight back to Mississippi Nessa goes to sleep on my shoulder. I love her so much it would kill me if I thought I had brought any harm to her.

When we finally make it to Ole Pop's I sit down with him and explain the whole situation and then I do something I struggled with doing all the way home. I give him a copy of the DVD I received from Paul Trice.

"Ole Pop if anything happens to me see that this gets to the right people."

"Okay son but why hasn't the reporter put it on his news cast?"

"He is missing. I think he's afraid that he might be put in jail if the NSA can find him and he knows it's a lot harder to get rid of a Senator than a newsman."

Jesse rushes into the room, "Buford, Andre you need to come into the living room."

We follow Jesse into the room where Nessa and mom are already gathered around the television. CNN is reporting that the terrorist group known as "Final Days" has taken over the American Embassy in Pakistan.

The news cameras outside the compound show several men in the windows and doors of the building. Each of them has a vest of explosives around their chests. The reporter explains that they've just gotten word that El Amir Aljarah is indeed in the building. He is also strapped with an explosive device.

The Reporter pauses for a moment then says, "Ladies and gentlemen we're going to cut to Washington and a special report from Adam Crawford head of NSA.

Adam comes on screen. "Ladies and gentlemen all we know at this time is that this is the work of a group called "Final days." They demand the release of Desir Amouud. The explosive devices they have on their bodies are connected to heart monitoring devices. If their heart stops the bombs on their chest will explode. That is all the information we can give at this time."

Adam turns and walks off the podium while a large group of reporters shout questions to him. He walks back into the oval office and shuts the doors.

I immediately get up, kiss Nessa and my mom and walk out to the porch with Ole Pop and Jesse. Ole Pops looks at me.

"Son be careful you are dealing with some very powerful people and right now they're not very happy with you."

Jesse puts his hand on my shoulder and looks me in the eyes, "I told you never to underestimate any one you meet for the first time. The other part of that is, don't show em everything you know the first time you meet em. They know everything about you but your heart and your heart is good. Don't let them bring you down to their level."

Three hours later I am back in my office. The first person to call me is Glenora.

"Andre I know you've seen the news so you know what is going on. There are some people on capital hill who would love nothing better than to end your political career right now. Be careful who you talk to."

Fifteen minutes later my cell phone rings again.

"Hello."

"Senator Wright its Farrah Ala'Adeen."

"Are you and Amira alright?"

"Yes we are thanks to you. They picked us up and we were headed to the airport but suddenly they took us back home."

"Have you seen the news?"

"No I haven't. I try not to look at the news much."

"There are some things we need to discuss. I'm headed to your house. I should be there in forty minutes."

"No Senator Wright that would not be a good idea. There are several news trucks and an army of reporters in front of my house. I will try to get out of the house quietly later and call you."

After the phone call it is hard to concentrate on work. I make several phone calls to a few colleagues I hope I can trust but none of them have any information I can use. Finally I sit in my office running everything I know through my head but it doesn't help. After another half hour I close my brief case, grab my coat and head for home.

As I pull out of the underground parking lot a black sedan with two men in it pull out behind me. Several miles later it is still with me. I don't know if they are there for my protection or waiting to find a good spot to kill me. Right at this moment I am scared as hell but I have to do what I think is right.

Thirty minutes later I arrive at my house and watch the black sedan park several houses down from me. I expect to have visitors but they don't get out of the car.

It is dusk dark outside when I walk into my living room and turn on the lights. I am startled to see Farrah Ala'Adeen sitting on my couch with a gun in her hand. I shut the door and stand right in front of it.

"Senator Wright are you alone?"

"First put down the gun and then we'll talk."

"Not until I find out if you are still willing to help me."

"I gave you my word."

"A person's word doesn't count or much in this city."

"Okay then let me answer your first question. No I am not alone. There are two men in a brown car parked down the block. I assume they are NSA agents. They followed me from my office. I also assume if they hear that gun go off they will be in here without a moment's hesitation. Now would you mind lowering the gun?"

She lowers the gun and I sit down beside her. "Senator Wright there are several things I haven't told you about me."

"Before you say what you have to say did you know that your brother and his group have taken over the American Embassy in Pakistan?"

"He told me he had nothing to do with this group."

"The news has shown pictures of him standing with in a room full of hostages. He is holding a gun."

"If I could just see him maybe I could persuade him to give up."

"I don't think the NSA is going to allow you into Pakistan."

"Then maybe they will allow you to go. If you go give this to him. If he is still the brother I grew up with he will understand."

Farrah takes the necklace from her neck with some kind of insignia on it and hands it to me.

"Give it to him and say "I know your heart. Please don't make me and Amira lose it."

I look at the necklace then back in her eyes and suddenly the light goes on in my brain.

"El Amir isn't your brother is he?"

Farrah hesitate for a minute then lowers her head.

"No Senator Wright he's Amira's father. I purposely got pregnant before I got married. I never loved my husband we were put together by my father. I love Amir."

"And that's why your husband would have put you to death."

"Yes. Senator please save Amir. He is a good man. Make him see that he doesn't have to do this."

"I will see what I can do."

From behind me I hear a sound and turn just in time to see four strangers walk into my living room. Three of these men have guns but the fourth one on the left is the one who speaks to me in perfect English with a Middle Eastern accent.

"Senator Wright it will not be necessary for you to give me the necklace. Please give it back to Farrah."

I turn and hand Farrah the necklace. Farrah's face is usually a blank stare with little emotion but now the shock shows readily on her face.

"Amir, what are you doing here? The news . . . ."

"Is wrong."

Amir turns to me, "Hello Senator Wright it is good to meet you."

For the first time I see the man who has caused all of the secrecy, questions and threats from NSA. I have to admit I am a little shocked. He looks nothing like the man CNN says is El Amir Aljarah. He also doesn't look anything like the terrorist he has been portrayed as.

The pictures of El Amir all over the news are the typical pictures American's see of Middle Eastern terrorist. The El Amir in the picture has a long beard with a turban and the native wardrobe of his country. He also has a gun belt around his shoulders and he's holding an assault rifle.

However standing in front of me now is a clean shaven man dressed in a Harvard tweed suit with a fine leather attaché case in his hand. He presents an image any corporate lawyer would envy.

Before I can say anything Farrah runs past me and hugs El Amir. He returns her hug with the warmth and affection a husband would give his wife after being away from her for so long. Not the type of emotion you would expect from the leader of a terrorist cell.

"Amir I have missed you so much."

"And I have missed you also. When you opened the back door and slipped into the house I wanted to hold you then but I couldn't chance it until the Senator came home. Where is Amira?"

"She is in a safe house in Tennessee. I have relatives there who are taking care of her. How did you get here?"

Paul Trice the CNN reporter who started me on this journey walks into my living room.

"He's here because of me. Senator Wright I am sorry for taking you and your family through this but the country needs to know about this and you are the only one on capital hill I remotely trust with this information."

"What is it you think the country needs to know?"

He hands me a large brown envelope and sits down beside me. "I think you need to read this while I explain what is really going on here."

Chapter 25

As I look through the folder there are charts and graphs with chemical symbols on them. The charts and symbols are written in English but the reports are written in Arabic. I don't understand the majority of it. However I do understand the words "fuel cost" and "rising gas prices."

"Okay Mr. Trice what am I looking at?"

"What you are looking at are charts, graphs and chemical equations that outline a new strain of grain. This grain when combined with a new synthetic oil product will make a viable source of fuel. You are also looking at communications about world gas prices as well as the Middle Eastern oil supply. In the next year gas is going to go up by two dollars all over the world.

"Well according to what I've learned about gas prices we're at the mercy of the OPEC nations since they control the majority of oil in the world."

"That is correct and the oil companies and OPEC nations have been causing the oil prices to steadily go up since the late nineteen nineties."

"I'm pretty sure every one in the nation either knows that or suspects it."

"Yes but every one in the nation doesn't know the reason for it."

"Good old fashioned greed is the reason for it. They own the biggest oil supply so they make every one pay whatever they want them to pay."

"Once again you are right but did you know the oil reserves will soon be depleted?

"Of course just like any natural resource it either has to be replenished or simply disappear from the planet and since it can't be replenished it will have to be replaced which is why every country in the world including the U.S is gradually going to gasohol."

"So far you are up to speed but here is the part you and the rest of the world does not know. The oil companies have been paying American lobbyist for the last ten years to convince congress to make laws that govern the making and distribution of gasohol. They are also doing the same thing in other countries. Their excuse is they want to make sure the gasohol used in cars is emissions free. They claim they are afraid if all countries go to a form of Alcohol based fuel then what you Americans call bootleggers will flood the market with gasohol that has all types of impurities in it."

"I can understand their caution but how does this help them?"

"Oil lobbyists and some of our politicians have convinced Congress and our president to create a new Energy Commission. This commission will be responsible for regulating the new fuel supply. The president and Congress will only sanction fuel that has been approved by them."

"I didn't know about this commission but why is that a bad thing? Fuel should have been regulated thirty years ago."

"Half the people on the commission are either retired oil men or retired Senators and congressmen who are being paid by the oil companies."

"That is a problem however you are a reporter one good report from you and the world will find out and all of this and it will be stopped."

"You are right a good reporter could stop it but if the report came out and people started investigating it they would also find out about this report in front of you. It shows why this energy commission is so important to OPEC and the oil companies. Also it shows the real reason why they have been raising oil prices so high."

"And why is that?"

"Do you remember a few years back when four genetic scientists died in a mysterious fire at a science conference in Bahrain?"

"Yes I do. What does that have to do with oil?"

"Those scientist did not die they were kidnapped. The fire was set as a diversion to kidnap three of the best genetic scientist in the world. They were taken to Kabul and forced to work on creating a genetic grain to be used as gasohol. The profit from OPEC's high gas prices was put into this research."

"Okay but grain for gasohol can be grown anywhere."

"Yes but this particular strain yields a high quality type of alcohol that will make a fuel that burns ninety nine percent clean. It can also produce an oil that when combined with other chemicals will produce a high grade synthetic motor oil. And lastly because it has been genetically altered it cannot be used for food. The OPEC nations do not have to share it with anyone. That makes this strain of grain perfect."

"I'm sure OPEC is not the only ones working on the grain problem. Someone else will come up with another alternative."

"There have been several teams doing the same research. Of those teams only two were as close as OPEC is to finding the answer. Both of those teams mysteriously lost their best scientist. One team lost its top scientists in a lab accident and the other lost two top scientist in a car accident. Both of these accidents were suspicious."

"Are you telling me that the OPEC nations are killing anyone who is successful with their research?"

"Yes I am."

"Do you have proof of this?"

"Amir provided me with several pictures of scientist being killed."

"Then we should get these to the proper authorities."

"Who are the proper authorities? If we give these pictures to the wrong people all of us including you will end up dead. Senator Wright we are talking about trillions of dollars. When the world finds out about the benefits of this grain the commission will very easily make it the only type of grain sanctioned to make gasohol by the world governments. OPEC will continue to dominate the world's fuel supply. This information is the reason El Amir is being branded a terrorist. However the papers in front of you will prove that El Amir isn't a terrorist he's just trying to do the right thing."

El Amir places his arm around Farrah and looks at me.

"I accidentally found out about this plan a year ago. I told my supervisor about it then found out he was part of the plan. That is when they tried to kill me and that is when I vanished.

Unfortunately I couldn't take Farrah and Amira with me. Senator Wright if you do not help us I am afraid Farrah, my daughter and I will perish."

I turn and look at Paul. "Why didn't you just put all of this on your news program?"

"Before I could do that Amir's government convinced our government he was a terrorist. As soon as they did there was no way anyone would believe his story even with the report."

Amir shakes his head and I can see in his eyes that he is very tired. "Now you know why I am on the run."

"Is our government in on this conspiracy?"

"No. They are being used by my government. Not even your oil companies know about this."

"Did you know the group you're supposed to be the leader of has taken over a U.S. embassy and the news is reporting that you are there with them?"

"Yes, which is why I'm hoping I can get you to talk your government into taking my family and I prisoners in a very public display. Our government will have to allow the U.S government to keep us here especially if a U.S Senator is the negotiator."

"I guess that's where I come in?"

"Yes. If you are willing to accept the job and I hope you do. With your help and the facts in this report hopefully I can negotiate for our freedom. If you do not help us I will be killed along with Farrah, my child and anyone they suspect may know about this."

"I have one question. Why did you pick me?"

"Paul and I went to college together at the University of Maryland. I trust his judgment implicitly. He is adamant about the fact that you are an honest politician and I believe him. Now will you help me or not?"

"I will see what I can do however there are a few things I need to know. The first thing that I need to know is how the both of you got into my house without being followed."

"The people who are following you have no reason to watch your house since your wife and child are not here. It was easy to slip in while you were away as did my Farrah."

"But if they have the house bugged as I am sure they do, they know you're here now."

"We have placed jamming devices all over your home. They have fooled the listening devices into believing there is no one here. However now that you are home it won't take them long to figure out their devices are not working. We need to move to a safer place."

"How are you going to do that with the two agents that followed me sitting outside?"

"Get into your car and drive away. When they follow you we will leave."

El Amir hands me a phone. "Take this phone and don't let it out of your site. It has internet capabilities. Go to www.jamsyte.com, type in "Sugargasandoil" the password is Calaadthirtyfive. There will be an email there for you. That is the only way we can communicate until we can figure out how to get out of this mess. And make no mistake, if my government finds out you know where I am they will torture you first then kill you."

Before I leave I head to my den to use my copy machine to make a copy of all the information in Amir's report. After making the copy I put it in a manila envelope and place it in my brief case along with the original report.

Right now I need to find out if the information I have in this report is accurate or if Amir is trying to use me. Is he really who he says he is or is he really a terrorist?

Five minutes later I am in my car driving pass the men who have been assigned to watch me. I turn the corner and watch my rear view mirror. A minute later their car turns onto the street behind me. I head out of the area wondering how in the world I got myself in this situation.

Ole Pop told me a long time ago that if a man has any faith in God at all he'll never make an important decision without consulting the father about it first. So as I drive, the Lord and I have a talk.

"Father I don't have a clue as to what I'm doing but you do. I need your guidance in this matter. Guide my feet to the right path and allow me to do whatever is your will. I trust in you to give me the wisdom to handle this situation and I thank you for that guidance. In your darling son Jesus name I pray Amen."

After my conversation with the Lord I feel better. As Jesse says all the time "Take your burden, lay it in the Lord's lap then step aside and watch the Lord be the Lord."

I smile as I drive and say to myself. "Okay Lord it's you and me, mostly you."

I take out the phone Amir gave me to call Bruce Carlin an old friend of mine from college. Bruce is typical computer geek he's also a Bio Engineer with a PHD and several years experience in the field. He can tell me if the data El Amir supplied me is the real thing.

I explain to him what I need then I impress upon him how fast I need him to get this information back to me.

"I will get it to you as fast as I can."

"Thank you Bruce I owe you one."

I hang up the cell phone then open the folder Amir gave me and take pictures of the pages that have scientific formulas on them. After sending them to Bruce all I can do is wait.

As I head for my office the black sedan keeps its distance but makes no moves to hide. My cell phone rings and almost scares me to death. I didn't know I was this keyed up. I need to somehow calm down if I'm going to handle this situation.

I take my phone out then look around as if someone is driving beside me peeking into my window. After seeing only my reflection I think to myself, "Look at this little country boy. He's keyed up and paranoid. Who would have thought he would be in this situation."

I let out a nervous chuckle and answer the phone. "Hello."

"Senator Wright this is Adam Crawford. I need to see you in my office as soon as possible."

"Why don't you have your men pick me up? They've been following me all day."

"I don't have anyone following you."

"Look I may not be a super spy but I know when I'm being followed. Besides your men aren't trying to be discreet about it they've been in plain sight all day."

"Did you get a good look at these men?"

"Yes I did pretty much."

"Did one of them have black hair?"

"Yes."

"Was the other one bald?"

"Yes. Why are you asking me these questions? They're your men."

"As I said at first they are not my men but I know who they are and I need you to follow my instructions."

"I guess I need to be concerned now because you claim these men don't belong to you."

"Senator Wright what street are you on and find a cross street so I can reference your position."

"What is going on? Why do you need to know that?"

"I'm going to tell you once again those are not my men following you and I don't know what they think you know but if they get to you, you may end up dead. Now what street are you on?"

"Interstate ninety five. I'm coming up on mile marker one thirty eight."

"Good keep driving until my men get to you."

"And then what?"

"When they find you they will tell you what to do."

"And how do I know I can trust you?"

"Senator Wright we are both here to serve our country. I'm only trying to do my job."

The muffled sound of Amir's phone ringing in my pocket once again jangles my nerves.

"Mr. Crawford someone else is trying to call me I'm going to put you on hold."

"Senator don't put me on . . . ."

I lay his phone down on the seat and open Amir's phone.

"Hello."

"Andre this is Bruce. Where did you get this formula?"

"I can't tell you that. What kind of formula is it?"

"It appears to be a new strain of grain. It will grow very fast although It looks to be totally useless."

"What do you mean?"

"It's not good for consumption."

"What if I told you that it's going to be used to make gasohol?"

"That would make sense especially since it can't be used for food. And since it grows so fast it would make a limitless supply of fuel. This could potentially revolutionize the fuel industry and make someone very rich."

"Thanks Bruce that's all I want to know."

I close Amir's phone, put it back in my pocket and pick up my cell phone.

"Mr. Crawford are you still on the line?"

"Yes I am."

"Okay I'm going to come in. What do you need me to do?"

"Nothing it's about to be taken care of."

Crawford hangs up the phone and seemingly from out of nowhere several cars surround me and the car behind me and pull us over. I don't get a chance to do anything before my door is opened and I'm pulled from my car and placed in another car which drives off at a high rate of speed.

"Senator Wright I'm agent Kellum. I'm going to take you to the director."

"Was it necessary to drag me out of my car?"

"The director will explain every thing to you when you get to his office."

From that moment on we sit in the car in silence as we head for downtown D.C.

As soon as we get to Adam's building I'm put in his private elevator and rushed directly to his office.

"Senator Wright, please have a seat we need to talk."

"Before we start I need to know what you intend to do about Farrah and Amira?"

"They are no longer my concern, you are."

"Why am I your concern?"

"Because I suspect that you have been in contact with El Amir and if that is true your life is in danger."

"Why would my life be in danger? According to the news reports El Amir is in Iraq occupying a U.S. embassy."

"Senator I know you don't believe that because you have been in contact with him."

"And why would I do that?"

"Senator Wright we don't have time to play this game. There are things you don't know about El Amir."

"Then why don't you enlighten me."

"I can't. All I can tell you is that it's crucial that we find him as soon as we can because his life is in danger."

"Okay then let me speculate. Would this have anything to do with a report on oil?"

"So you have been in communication with him. I must warn that any U.S. citizen who harbors a terrorist can be charge with treason and put to death."

"Okay now who's playing games? You have no proof that I'm harboring anyone so the threats won't work. Now why don't you just tell me the truth then maybe I will cooperate."

Adam walks around his desk and sits down on the edge of it in front of me.

"Senator I don't want to tell you anymore about this because it will put not only you but your family in danger as well."

"I've already been told that once tonight. Tell me something I don't know."

Adam holds his head down and exhales an exasperated breath.

"Okay Senator Wright but remember you put your self in harms way. El Amir is an accountant for OPEC. Somehow he came into possession of some very sensitive materials about OPEC and a few of our oil companies. If this information comes out it will cause a huge global disturbance it could even result in a major war. We need to find him before that information comes out."

"What you mean is you need to find him so you can send him back to his country to be killed. Then you will bury the information and business will go on as usual."

A chuckle escapes Adam's lips. "Senator you have been looking at too many conspiracy movies. We don't want to kill El Amir. We simply can not allow the information he has to come out. The consequences could be terrible."

"So OPEC will corner the fuel market again and our country will still be in the same shape."

"So you know what the information is?"

"Yes I do and you are right I have been in contact with El Amir and before you ask no I will not turn him over to you. Quite frankly I don't trust you."

"Senator Wright if his country gets to him before we do what you don't want to happen will happen. However if we can secure him we can force the OPEC nations to go by the rules and the oil companies involved will be punished with severe sanctions and fines."

"Really, and what about the new energy commission our government is about to create?"

"We already know which people are in the pockets of the oil companies and they have already been removed from the list of candidates to sit on the commission."

"And how do I know what you are saying is true?"

"Because the head of the new commission is going to be Senator Perkins. If you like I will call Senator Perkins so you can talk to her."

"I already have her number I can call her myself. Now am I a prisoner here or can I leave?"

"I would prefer that you stay in the building. There are foreign agents outside this building who would like to get their hands on you."

"Fine, give me a room I can use. I know there is surveillance equipment in them but at least let me think I have some privacy."

Adam leads me to a room down the hall from his and I sit down and call Glenora.

"Hello Andre."

In my most formal voice I speak to Glenora. "Senator Perkins is it true that you are going to head the new energy commission?"

"Andre are you all right? You sound like you are under some stress."

"Senator Perkins you have no idea but I will explain if you will answer my question."

Glenora's voice immediately takes on a professional tone.

"Yes Senator Wright I just found out that I'm going to head up the new commission."

"Thank you Senator Perkins now you and I need to talk."

I quickly tell Glenora where I am and tell her I need her advice. Thirty minutes later she is sitting beside me while I explain what I know. Shortly after that she and I are sitting in front of Director Crawford.

Glenora is not her usual gracious self. She starts the meeting with a point blank question to Mr. Crawford.

"Mr. Crawford I would like to know exactly what your agency is planning on doing with El Amir if you should find him?"

"My agency isn't going to do anything with him. You will have to ask the justice department about that. Now I can't answer any more of your questions. I have instructions to deliver you downtown."

With a puzzled look on our face Glenora and I follow Mr. Crawford out to the garage and several waiting cars. We get in and the driver pulls out of the garage headed toward Capitol Hill.

Chapter 26

Rajeeb Al Batal is as mad as he has ever been and that is saying a lot. In the past he has been mad enough to kill whole families if things didn't go his way. He is not a man you want to have as an enemy. His rage knows no boundaries and his reach is global. He is the man in charge of security for one of the wealthiest sheiks in Arabia and he's not happy that his people are the ones who let El Amir Aljarah get away.

His second in command is Jaamir Hassan Fadel and at this moment he's as afraid as he has ever been in his life. He has seen what Rajeeb is capable of and he knows that at any moment he could lie dead on the floor.

Rajeeb walks up until he is face to face with Jaamir. "How did Amir get out of the country?"

"He had help from an American reporter."

"How did an American reporter get away with the most wanted man in the country?"

"We don't know yet Rajeeb but our men are looking into it."

"I want the men who let Amir escape killed and I want Amir found and killed. Is that understood?"

"Yes Rajeeb." Hassan walks out and Rajeeb sits down behind his desk and picks up his phone. Somewhere in a hotel suite in D.C. a cell phone rings. The owner of the phone is in a very important meeting but after seeing who is on the phone he gets up and quietly exits the meeting. When he gets to the hallway he answers it.

"Hello."

"Do you have the answer I seek?"

"No but we have been following one who may have the answer. Unfortunately he has not led us to it yet. I will call you and tell you when the question has been answered."

"You need to make it quickly we are running out of time."

Rajeeb hangs up his phone and sits back to look out of the window of his office.

Fifteen minutes after Rajeeb's conversation Glenora and I are escorted into Simon Blakely's office.

"Glenora it's good to see you and Senator Wright." Glenora shakes his hand. "I wish I could say the same. Why have we been brought here?"

"We need to talk about our national security. By now I'm sure you have heard about El Amir Aljarah taking over the American embassy in Hafar Al batin and I know you know that is a lie. However what you don't know is the embassy has actually been taken over but by a man named Abu Kareem Sawar. He is the leader of a tribe of people who own the land next to El Shazir. El Shazir is the second richest sheik in the Middle East and the head of the OPEC council. This group along with one of our oil companies is
· trying to take over the world's next fuel supply. We have known this for some time now and our agents have been trying to put together enough information to stop them."

I sit up in my seat. "If you know this why are you still trying to send Farrah and Amira back to him?"

"How do you know we're trying to send them back to him Senator Wright?"

"You already know I've talked to El Amir so let's drop the secrecy act. Now why would you send Farrah and Amira back to El Shazir?"

"What makes you think it's El Shazir who wants them back?"

"Because he is Amira's husband. He was the one they ran away from in the first place. So why are you trying to send her back to this man when you know he will kill her."

"If he wanted to kill her, his agents in this country could have done that long ago."

"Then why not protect her?"

"We kept her under surveillance to make sure they didn't get the chance to take her out of the country."

Then why not put her in one of your safe houses?"

"We needed her out in the open to see if El Shazir really wanted her."

Glenora leaned forward and looked directly in Simon's eyes. "What you mean is you used her for bait."

"Not bait. She was the bargaining chip. We were going to use her to force Amir to bring us his information. However now that he is in the country she no longer matters. That is why we need Senator Wright to tell us where he is."

"How do you know I know where he is?"

Simon turns on a small tape recorder on his desk and we can hear Amir's voice followed by mine and Farrah. Glenora looks at me then back at Simon.

"If you knew he was in Senator Wright's home why didn't you pick him up?"

"This wasn't done with our surveillance equipment. It was taken off the lap top of one of the men in the car that was following you Senator Wright. I'm pretty sure they didn't receive it until you had already left your house otherwise they would have stormed in and killed everyone.

They were following you waiting on orders to kidnap you and take you somewhere private so they could torture you. We intercepted you before they could do that. Unfortunately the same agents who emailed this to them also emailed it to Rajeeb Al Batal. Now we have a bigger problem."

"What problem is that?"

"We just received communication from Rajeeb. He wants Amir delivered to him in the next twenty four hours or he will begin killing hostages."

"So we're supposed to send this man back to his death."

"No, what we're going to do is negotiate for the release of the hostages but we need to know where Amir is."

"What's to guarantee that you won't send him to Rajeeb as soon as you find him?"

"We don't want Rajeeb to have him. We need the information he has to force the sheiks to negotiate a settlement. We don't want them to have control of the next fuel supply for the world."

I look at Glenora and she says, "The next move is up to you."

Shaking my head I sit back to think about the situation. If I give Amir up they may very well send him back however if I don't a lot of Americans could be killed in the embassy. After a few minutes I make my decision.

———

Across town in the lobby of a seedy hotel a young lady checks in and receives her key. She is a beautiful blonde with a very attractive figure. Her name is Emily Carson but that's not the name she uses for her profession. Her professional name is Candy and she is what some would call a lady of the evening.

She walks out the door, across the pavement to her room. After unlocking the door she looks around before entering and shutting the door behind her.

Fifteen minutes later a nondescript blue midsize car pulls into the parking lot and parks in front of the room. A tall, thin man with a medium build gets out of the car. He has on a long coat with the collar pulled up to cover his face and a hat pulled down over his eyes. He quickly walks to the door and knocks.

Candy cracks the door to see who it is then opens it to let the gentleman in. He smiles, takes off his coat before kissing her and walking over to the bed. They have been meeting like this for a year and a half.

After they are finished he hands Candy her payment. She smiles as she takes five one hundred dollar bills out of his hand. She folds them and places them in her secret place between her breasts then walks out the door blowing a kiss at him just before the door shuts. He sits up in the bed, lights a cigarette, pours himself a drink and smiles.

To him she is well worth the price he has to pay for her. He gets a thrill not only from the young woman but also from the sneaking around. Now he can go to work feeling relaxed and calm. He had to do some maneuvering to get to the hotel unseen but it was worth it. No one knows about this meeting not even his wife but you know what is said about things like this. Things done in the dark will soon come to the light.

As the young lady gets into her car the steady click and buzz of a camera can be heard in a car across the street from the hotel. The man with the camera is a reporter for the Washington Post. He has been following this young lady for the last three months and he is getting close to breaking the news story of the year, maybe even the decade.

The reporter has to wait for almost an hour before the other occupant of the hotel room cracks open the door and peaks. Before stepping out of the room he makes sure no one is around.

Out of habit he pulls the collar of his coat up even though it is already where he wants it to be and he pulls the hat down lower. But as he turns to walk toward his car the reporter gets several good shots of his face.

After the man gets into his car and pulls out into the street the reporter starts his car and pulls out behind him. Since the reporter already knows where the man is going he steps on the gas and passes him without even looking his way.

———

Across town Senator Bowens is having a meeting with Thomas Yardley. Thomas is the head of the committee ready to back Senator Worthington's run for the democratic nomination.

"Walter I still think we should drop Senator Wright. He's involved in something that could potentially blow up in his face."

"It might and it might not. I still think he's the one for the job in fact you already know that if it was left up to me he would be the presidential nominee instead of Glenn. I just don't think Glenn is the one we need."

"What you mean is you don't think he's clean enough. He doesn't have to be squeaky clean besides you and I both know that conservative white voters still won't vote for and African American President."

"I think you underestimate where the country is now."

"And I think you are naive to think that race isn't going to play a part in this election."

"I know race is going to play a role in this election but I also know that Senator Wright is an honest politician and a good man and I think America will recognize that."

"If this Middle Eastern thing blows up in his face he won't get a chance at the Vice Presidency. I just hope the media doesn't find out that he's our choice for vice president until this mess with Amir is concluded."

———

An hour later I am in CIA headquarters and Simon is waiting on me to make the hardest phone call of my life. I have decided to ask Amir to come in and trust our government to protect him. I take out the cell phone he gave me, open it up and connect to the internet.

After reaching the jamsyte web page I type in the word "Sugargasandoil" and the prompt ask me for a password. I key in Calaadthirtyfive then type the words "Amir are you there?"

Minutes later my screen lights up with the words "Is it safe for us to talk?" I key in the word "Yes" and for the next few minutes we text each other.

"What news do you have for me?"

"I have been in touch with the CIA and they have explained to me the situation with Rajeeb Al Batal."

"What lies have they told you?"

"They told me that he is trying to have you killed. They also told me they would protect you if you come in."

"How am I supposed to trust them when they are the ones in league with my government? How am I to know they won't kill me themselves?"

"They already know about the fuel scheme and our government doesn't want them to corner the fuel market. They have been trying to find evidence they can show the UN to get world opinion against them but they need your help."

"And if I help them what happens next."

"They will provide a new identity for you, Farrah and Amira so that you can start your life together without having to look over your shoulder for the rest of your life."

"Do you give me your word that is what they will do?"

For the first time I hesitate. One of the things I learned from Ole Pop and Jesse is never give your word unless you are sure you can live up to it. I'm not sure that I believe Simon so how can I give my word on this? Finally I decide if I'm going to commit to this it's going to be all the way. If I'm wrong I'll deal with it later.

"Yes you have my word."

"Give me an hour and I will let you know where you can find me."

Down in the basement of the building an agent hits a switch and closes his lap top.

"The texts were encrypted and the call was bounced to several computers. I didn't have enough time to trace it."

Upstairs I close the phone. "He will call me back in an hour and let me know where we can meet."

Then I lean forward in my chair. Mr. Blakely I hope you are being honest with me about this because I have just given this man my word that he won't be harmed. I don't give my word lightly. I don't want Amir, Farrah or Amira harmed in any way."

"Senator Wright I will do all that is in my power to protect them."

The phone rings in Senator Bowen's office and even though he's busy trying to write a speech to support the bill he is sponsoring in the senate he finally picks up the phone. Besides if he didn't pick it up whoever it was, was just going to keep calling like they have been for the last ten minutes.

"Hello."

"Walter this is Thomas did you know that Senator Perkins and Senator Wright are both meeting with Simon Blakely right now?"

"No I didn't. Should I?"

"You mean you don't know what they are meeting about?"

"Once again should I?"

"If it has something to do with the mess Senator Wright has gotten himself into you should."

"And how do you know he's in a mess?"

"You and I both know that Simon wouldn't have them come to his office if they weren't in trouble."

"Actually their going to his office is not a problem."

"How can you say that?"

"If they have done something wrong they would be under arrest instead of in his office. If he has them in his office it's because he needs their cooperation."

"Well I still think we should drop Senator Wright before it's too late."

"Of course you do especially since you didn't want him on the ticket in the first place. Look Thomas, I still think he's the best man for the job and I still think he's going to come out of this smelling like a rose so just relax and we'll see how it goes okay."

"Okay but if this turns into a scandal the committee is going to want your head."

"And I would expect no less. Goodbye Thomas."

Thomas hangs up the phone and sits back in his chair. There is no way he is going to be able to tell one of the most influential men in Washington that the committee is still backing Senator Wright for the vice presidency.

The phone rings interrupting Thomas's thoughts. He looks at the phone and grimaces. This is not going to be a pleasant conversation.

"Hello."

"Did you tell Walter what I told you to tell him?"

"Yes I did."

"And what did he say?"

"He is still backing Senator Wright."

"How in the hell can he still back the man? Doesn't he know this kind of scandal can ruin the party?"

"He doesn't think Senator Wright is in any trouble."

"Not in any trouble? What in the hell is Walter using for brains. If I were still in the senate I would call a meeting of the council and I would take over the leadership. Walter is an incompetent fool."

"Well right now there is nothing we can do about it but wait."

"We don't have time to wait. Our party needs strong leadership and we need it now. A scandal could ruin the whole party for years to come."

"I understand but Walter doesn't and as long as he is the Senate Minority Leader Senator Wright is the party's choice."

Ex Senator Dick Hilgan closes his cell phone without bothering to say goodbye to Thomas then slams it on the desk in front of him.

The sound bounces off the mahogany walls all around his office. He sits back in his chair with a nasty expression on his face.

He still has an office near Capitol Hill and he's still one of the most influential and powerful men in Washington even after losing his senate seat. His only thoughts are of Senator Wright and the vice presidency.

There is no way he is going to let Senator Wright get into office as the vice president of the United States of America. As long as Dick lives and works in Washington Senator Wright will not be the vice president.

Dick decides it's time for the nation to meet the party's choice for vice president. He smiles, turns on his lap top and begins to type a memo to Senator Bowens.

Senator Bowens

I have been informed about the party's choice of Senator Andre Wright for vice president and quite frankly I'm concerned that he is not experienced enough to handle the job. While I agree the party needs fresh young leadership there are other Senators who would handle the position a great deal better. I would appreciate a face to face with you so that we can discuss this.

Dick Hilgan

Dick places the signed letter on his desk then once again sits back but this time he smiles. He has long known there is a leak in his organization and he knows who the leak is. He has used that leak from time to time to alert the media and get them on his side of an issue. Every politician knows that leaks are bad unless the leak can be controlled and used in your favor.

All he has to do is write a memo and leave it on his desk before he leaves for the day. After office hours Mary Justin the custodian for his floor will come upon it while cleaning his office.

After reading it Mary will make a copy of it then call Gerald King the Washington Post reporter and alert him. Somehow that memo will end up in Gerald's hands and Mary's bank account will swell. Sometimes a little or sometimes a lot depending on what the information is. This time her bank account will grow a lot.

At six o'clock that evening Gerald answers his phone and Mary tells him about the information she has.

"Are you sure this was written by him?"

"It's got his signature on it. Now how much is it worth to you?"

"We'll discuss that when I see the memo."

"Uh uh I don't think so. No money, no memo."

"How am supposed to know that it's the real thing?"

"I haven't passed you a bad tip yet now how much?"

"If it's the real deal I'll give you five hundred for it."

"As big as this information is you must be out of your mind. I'll take three thousand dollars and not a penny less. Your news paper will make a hundred times that when you break this story."

"Now who is out of their mind. I can't pay you that much."

"Then I guess I'm going to have to find someone who will."

"Hold on now. Give me an hour to see what I can do."

Gerald hangs up the phone and calls several of his other sources but none of them have any information so he calls Thomas Yardley at home.

"Hello."

"Mr. Yardley this is Gerald King of the Washington Post. I have a report that Senator Wright is going to be Senator Worthington's running mate is this true?"

"Where did you hear that?"

"I'm sorry I can't reveal my sources to you."

"Well you need to choose you sources better."

Thomas hangs up the phone before Gerald can ask another question. Now Gerald is sure of the information.

He calls Mary back. "If I'm going to pay you three thousand dollars then I'm going to need the original memo."

"I can't do that. You're going to get me fired."

"If you want the three thousand I need the original memo."

"Damn! Let me call you back."

Mary hangs up the phone and shakes her head then from behind her she hears Dick Hilgan's voice.

"What does he want?"

She turns around to see Dick Hilgan standing in his doorway with two security guards and before she can speak Dick interrupts.

"Before you say anything I want you to know, I know you are the one who has been leaking information to the media. Now before you deny it you need to know there is a camera in this office and I have you on tape stealing memos that may contain sensitive government issues. This is punishable by ten years in federal prison. However I am willing to forgive all of this if you tell me what Mr. King wants."

Mary doesn't have much choice. She's standing there with the memo in her hands and Dick and the security guards probably heard the whole conversation. She has to cooperate.

"He wants the original memo."

"Is that right? And how much is he willing to pay for it?"

"Three thousand dollars."

Dick walks over to his desk, sits down and lights a cigar.

"Is that all? My dear you can most certainly do better than that. Call him back and tell him you will give him the memo but it's going to cost him five thousand dollars."

"I'm not about to call him back. I know what you're trying to do. I'm not going to call him back so you can trap me."

"Mary I want you to look at the screen across the room."

Dick hits a button and Mary sees herself on the screen. First she picks up a memo off Dick's desk. Then she makes her call to Gerald King. After which she makes a copy of the memo and places it back on Dick's desk then the screen goes blank.

"My dear I don't have to trap you. I already have enough evidence to put you away for a long time. However if you do something for me, you will make five thousand dollars and I will have you transferred to another building without you losing your job or your benefits. So what's it going to be?"

Mary makes the call and even though Gerald tries to argue about the amount eventually he agrees to pay five thousand dollars for the original memo. An hour later Mary delivers the memo to him and after he drives off she walks around the block, gets in Dick's limo and is driven home.

Back across town in a very exclusive Washington suburb Candy is once again entertaining a client. After an hour he walks into the kitchen to get a beer but finds that Candy has finished the last beer. He walks back into the room Candy is in, hands her some money and tells her to go to the store. She's not happy but she takes the money, puts on her clothes and heads for the local store.

The reporter who has been following her is perched in a tree outside the rock wall that surrounds large grounds and house. With a telephoto lens he has been snapping pictures of Candy, the house and hopefully the occupant if he comes out. He snaps pictures until she's out of sight then he returns his focus to the house.

Candy's client opens his back door and walks across his patio to the pool and jumps in. After swimming several laps he gets out of the pool dries off then walks over to a lounge chair and sits down.

The reporter is still taking pictures and waiting, hoping Candy might come back and join the man at poolside so he can get a picture of them together. Thirty minutes later his patience is rewarded when Candy drives up, parks her car and heads for the pool area. Her client is lying on a lounge chair by the pool and she leans down, kisses him and hands him a cold beer.

After drinking a few beers Candy and her client become intimate by the pool. The reporter shakes his head as he snaps picture after picture of them by the pool. Who would have thought that pro basketball player Theo Suggs would have a need to hire a professional girl like Candy especially since he just got married three weeks ago.

The reporter uses two rolls of film on the couple. Now all he needs is a few comments from Candy and her boss and this story can be put to bed. It's going to cause huge scandal and in the process put him in the national spotlight. If he's lucky he may even get a book deal out of this

Chapter 27

"I am telling you Amir this man can not be trusted. He is just like all Americans. He thinks he is privileged and he is a part of a corrupt government. He is leading you into a trap."

There are six men in this room but only one of them thinks Amir should trust Senator Wright and even he's not sure what will happened if Amir turns himself in but he's sure of one thing. If Amir continues to stay in America without some kind of protection, his own government will eventually find him and kill him.

"Look Amir I can't tell you what the government will do with you once they have you but you won't be safe without some kind of protection. Senator Wright has done the right thing so far I think you should trust him to do the right thing now."

"No Amir it would be a mistake to trust this man. His country only understands one thing, money. He will sell you to the highest bidder."

"Enough! I have made my decision. Paul where is the safest place for me to meet Senator Wright?"

"The safest place is right in front of the CIA building but not before I make some arrangements and call Senator Wright."

———

An hour after my first call Paul sends a message to me.

"Amir is ready to come in but before he does I need you to do something for me."

I read the message then look at Simon. "Amir is ready to come in but he wants you to call Joshua Utley and tell him what is going on. After Amir sees the news cameras you will see him."

"You don't really think I'm going to call the head of CNN and invite him into my building do you?"

"I didn't say invite him into your building. His people can stay outside they just need to be here."

"I'm sorry but if I call Mr. Utley every news crew in Washington will show up. I will not have that many news crew staked out in front of the building."

"Either the cameras are there or Amir won't come in. So you need to make a decision."

Simon grimaces and shakes his head but he really has no choice in the matter. He's been monitoring Andre's phone and his people have been able to isolate the call. But so far they haven't been able to break the code and they can't trace the call. Every trace they've run so far has been bounced all over the country. Simon picks up the phone and dials.

As soon as Simon is done I open my phone and send a message back to Paul.

"The meeting has been arranged. You can come in now."

I receive a return message, "Are you sure CNN will be there?"

"Yes, along with every news crew in Washington. If you are watching they should show up in a few minutes."

"We are watching CNN. As soon as Amir sees the news report he will come in."

I shut the phone and look at Simon. "Do you really think this is going to work?"

"Yes it will and whoever thought of it should be working for me."

"I have to ask this one more time. Are you going to honor your part of this deal?"

"You have my word on this Senator Wright."

"Then I guess I'm going to have to trust you."

———————

Thomas Yardley is sitting in his chair behind his desk. He has just hung up the phone to keep from answering any more of Gerald

King's questions and he's as worried as he can be. Finally he makes a frantic call to Walter's home.

"Hello."

"Walter, Gerald King of the Washington Post just called me. He found out about Senator Wright and the vice presidency. What are we going to do?"

"We're not going to do anything."

"Are you out of your mind? By tomorrow it will be all over the news along with the mess he's gotten himself into in the Middle East."

"By tomorrow there will be no mess in the Middle East and as far as the media is concerned they would have found out anyway so there's really only one problem. How did Mr. King find out about Senator Wright?"

"I don't know."

"Come on Thomas. You and I both know the only real opposition to Senator Wright being the vice president is Dick Hilgan and we both know that leaking information is one of the things he does best. I'm willing to bet if we look into this deeply enough we'll find his signature behind it."

"You're wrong about that. He wouldn't do anything to hurt the party."

"Really? And trying to black mail Senator Wright out of the senate race wasn't something he would do either was it?"

"Look Walter I have some pressing business I need to attend to I will talk to you later."

Walter hangs up the phone. There is only one reason Andre is having such a hard time winning the full committee's support and he needs to get rid of that reason so the committee can move forward.

―――――

Several hours later news crews having heard about CNN gathering in front of the CIA building are now trying to get in the best position to make their report. They have no idea what is getting ready to happen but if CNN is here then they are going to stay and find out.

Two security guards find Paul Trice before he can talk to any of his colleagues and escort him inside the building to a conference room and tell him to wait there. Outside the building several CIA agents are walking through the crowd looking for anyone they think might be an assassin or suicide bomber.

Moments later Simon, Glenora and I walk into the room. I shake Paul's hand. "I'm glad you made it."

"I'll be happier when this is over. Is every thing ready?"

"Yes. We have security all around the area and Simon has set up a conference call to Rajeeb. We can hook up this phone to the call so Amir can talk as well. When is he coming in?"

"As soon as he talks to Rajeeb."

"Why would he possibly want to talk to Rajeeb?"

"Amir has something to offer him that will make Rajeeb release the hostages and hopefully stop chasing Amir and Farrah forever."

"Okay let's get this started."

———

Across the world in Riyadh, Saudi Arabia's capitol city Rajeeb Al Batal receives a call from Simon.

"Why is the head of America's security calling me? What do you want?"

"We need to talk about Kallah El Shazir."

"Who is this El Shazir?"

"I really don't have time to waste on this so can we dispense with the misinformation and get on with it."

"I have no idea of what you are talking about."

"Really then I guess this book I have with the Golden Roman numeral II on it just above Kalleh El Shazir's name doesn't concern you. I am sorry for wasting your time. Goodbye."

"Wait a minute. What is in this book you have?"

"Like I said I don't have time for this so either acknowledge that you know what I'm talking about or hang up the phone."

"Suppose I do know what you are referring to? What happens next?"

"We start negotiation for the hostages as well as the problem your employer and his friends are trying to cause with the world's fuel supply."

"I don't know anything about this fuel problem of which you speak but I can negotiate the hostage problem. However I will not do anything until I have Amir back in this country where he belongs."

"I'm afraid I can't do that."

"Then this conversation is over."

"Actually before you hang up the phone I have someone you need to talk to."

Amir takes over the conversation. "Hello Rajeeb."

"You infidel dog, you will die a long and painful death when I bring you back home."

"It's good to hear from you too my friend. However before you decide which of your many painful ways you want to kill me you had better let Kallah know I want to talk to him."

"He will not talk to you."

"Yes I think he will. He knows I have the oil plans and his account books. Tell him I will give them to the Americans. Those books might end up in the hands of the other OPEC partners. After they find out how much money Kallah has been taking off the top I will be the least of his problems."

"I don't believe you dog."

"Tell him I am giving one of his American bank account numbers to the American intelligence agency. By the time he tries to withdraw his money the Americans will have seized the account. He will lose eighty million dollars. I will wait for his call."

"I will find you and cut your tongue out."

"That will be fine but I think you had better ask your master for permission first."

Amir hangs up the phone and sits back as the car he's riding in speeds down the interstate.

Rajeeb hangs up the phone abruptly ending the conference call. Andre, Glenora and Paul all look at each other and Simon is already on the phone with one of his agents.

Glenora and I have several questions for Paul and I ask the first one.

"Paul did you know about this?"

"No I didn't. I thought the books he gave me were all the information he has."

Glenora ask the next question. "Do you think El Shazir will go along with Amir's plan?"

"I hope so. I would hate the fact that Amir would have to hide for the rest of his life."

"With security so tight around Amir how did he get all of that information out of the country?"

"With a little help from some people I know who are good at smuggling things."

"How did he get El Shazir's books?"

"Amir wasn't just a book keeper he was El Shazir's head accountant. There was nothing that went on in Shazir's business that Amir didn't know about."

Simon hangs up the phone and I look directly at him as he takes a glance at his watch.

"Did you find the account?"

Simon picks up his cup of coffee and smiles. "Yes we did and it is now frozen."

"And now all you need is Shazir's books to get the hostages back and stop their plan to continue monopolizing the world's fuel supply."

"Hopefully your friend Amir will supply them."

"And in what part of Utah or Arizona or Oklahoma will witness protection place him and his family in? Or will he be hid right here in Washington so you can keep a close eye on him."

"You are very insightful no wonder your party wants you as it's vice presidential candidate."

Paul's eyes light up. "The party chose you? This has got to be my lucky day. I've got two of the biggest exclusives on the biggest news stories this country has seen in a long time."

"I'm afraid you are too late on this last piece of news. Your friend Gerald King is about to beat you to this story."

I look at Simon. "How did he find out about it?"

"Senator Wright you have some powerful enemies on Capitol Hill or should I say you have a powerful enemy on the hill."

Glenora looks at me and we both say at the same time. "Dick Hilgan."

The phone rings before we can start a conversation about Dick. Simon picks it up.

"Hello."

"This is Kallah El Shazir. I want to speak to Amir."

"I'm going to have to put you on hold for a minute. He's out of the room right now."

Simon places the call on hold and Paul uses the same phone to call Amir.

"Hello."

"Amir, Kallah El Shazir is on the phone."

Simon connects them. "Hello Kallah how are you doing?"

Kallah says something in Arabic that only he, Amir and Simon understand. Simon is fluent in several Middle Eastern dialects it's his job. Amir interrupts Kallah.

"Speak English Kallah I want everyone in the room to understand you."

"You son of a dog I will see you dead before I give into your demands and the death of the American hostages will be on your head as well."

"Kallah I have your books and I know the numbers to all your bank accounts, especially the accounts here in America. The Americans have found and frozen the small account and after this call I will give them the large account number. Both accounts will be frozen but that is not your biggest problem. I will send a copy of your books to the council. When the rest of the council finds out what you were doing your death will be as glorious as mine. Now we can compromise and make this work for the both of us or we can die together."

"What do you want?"

"I want you to denounce Farrah as your wife then forget about us completely. Then I want you to release the hostages into American custody. I want Senator Wright to be the one to fly over and secure their release. Then I will give your property back to you. You will agree to this with the understanding that these negotiations are being recorded and I will keep a copy of the recording. As far as the money goes you are going to have to negotiate with the Americans about that. Do we have an agreement?"

"How do I know you will fulfill your part of the bargain?"

"Senator Wright will have the books with him when he gets off the plane. However if you try to do anything foolish a copy of this conversation along with the copy I still have of your books will be sent to everyone on the OPEC council. Now do we have a deal?"

"Yes we have a deal".

"Good. You can make arrangements with the Americans to get your property back." Amir hangs up on his end and Kallah talks to Simon about how they are going to make the exchange.

Once again my phone startles me as I try to listen in on Simon's conversation.

"Hello."

"Senator Wright I want to thank you for taking care of Farrah and Amira. I hope we can meet again under better circumstances. If all goes well I will no longer be hunted by anyone. I also want to thank you for that."

"I was doing what I was supposed to do."

"Yes but many people would have chosen not to do so. Will you please put Paul on the phone?"

I hand Paul the phone and Amir tells him where to find the original books and also thanks him for his help. Paul hangs up the phone and waits until Simon finishes negotiations with Kallah then they all walk to the basement, get into several cars with agents surrounding them and head for the post office.

Outside the front of the Simon's building Dorothy Lockland, the White House media liason is reading a prepared statement to the press.

"Ladies and gentlemen we have been in constant contact with El Amir Aljarah and we have reached what we hope will be a peaceful ending to the hostage situation in Hafar al batin. We have agreed to bring Desir Amouud here to talk to El Amir Aljarah. As per the request of Mr. Amouud we are letting the media know he is coming here. Amouud hopes this will keep any harm from him. We hope to have him here at any time now. That is all that I have at this time."

All the reporters shout questions the same time but to no avail. Miss Lockland has already left the podium and disappeared into the building. Reporters begin looking around for anyone who can provide more information but there is no one to be found.

As the car containing Simon, Glenora, Paul and I head towards the post office Simon calls the president.

"Good evening Mr. President. Negotiations with Kallah El Shazir have concluded."

"Were you able to secure an agreement with him?"

"Yes sir he has agreed to talk to the OPEC council and convince them to share the grain information. He also supplied the name of the oil company executives who helped with the gas price hikes."

"So this matter is closed then?"

"It will be as soon as Senator Wright flies to Riyadh and delivers the information to him."

"Why Senator Wright? Don't we have experienced agents who can do that?"

"Amir will not come in and seal the deal if Senator Wright is not the one delivering the information."

"Fine. Let me know when this is finished."

"Yes sir."

Simon hangs up the phone just as they arrive at the post office. One of his agents walks into the building and a few minutes later hands the package to Simon. He opens it and as promised Kallah's account books are in it. The motorcade turns around and heads back to Simon's office.

Half an hour later Dorothy Lockland steps up to the podium again and addresses the media.

"Ladies and gentleman I have just received word that Desir Amouud will be here in a few minutes. He will make a short statement then he will move into the building. There will be no questions."

Fifteen minutes pass before Jafar Calid Mahmoud one of Amir's bodyguards walks out of the front door and steps up on the podium. Several agents are in front of him as well as behind him.

He is dressed in traditional Middle Eastern attire but his English is impeccable as he addresses the media. The media moves in as close as they can to listen to the person they think is Desir Amouud.

"I am here to speak to El Amir Aljarah and his people. El Amir I too want the Americans out of our country and peace for our children but this is not the way to do it and I am not worth dying for. It is time now to let the diplomats handle the problem. It is clear that war is not working. Please I beg you, let the Americans go and let the diplomats do their job."

Mahmoud turns and steps from the podium and is hustled into the building before the reporters can ask him any questions. Dorothy steps up on the podium and again reads from a prepared speech.

"Ladies and gentlemen we are hoping that with the help of Mr. Amouud we can bring this hostage situation to a peaceful end. We will let you know when we have made progress in this matter."

Once again she steps off the podium and is gone before the reporters have a chance to ask any questions.

The next day I am on a plane to Riyadh. Last night I studied the customs of the middle East and the CIA provided me with several experts in the field to pepper me with questions. Now that I am in the air all I want to do is catch up on my sleep but there is still more I need to know about this diplomatic visit and release of the American hostages. I try to remember everything but it is a lot to absorb.

We land in Riyadh with a host of the world's media waiting on us. However they are several hundred yards away as our plane hits the runway. As soon as our feet hit the ground we are put in a waiting limousine and driven directly to Kalleh El Shazir's estate to make the exchange.

Chapter 28

At six the next morning CNN broadcast the news of Senator Wright being Glenn's running mate. Dick Hilgan is sitting in his office with his morning cup of coffee, listening to the news and smiling.

"Now let's see how they handle this. Glenn is going to drop like a rock in the polls and by the end of the week Senator Wright will be a distant memory."

The media is a live with this new development. Political pundits from both sides explain why it will or will not work. By the evening several news agencies have taken straw polls. These polls range from ninety percent to ninety percent against.

America is not sure about Senator Wright. Most of America doesn't even know Senator Wright but all of that is about to change.

At seven o'clock Dick Hilgan receives a very unpleasant phone call from Thomas Yardley.

"Dick I just found out that Senator Wright is headed to Riyadh to secure the release of the prisoners."

"How in the hell did that happen?"

"I don't know. All I know is he left three hours ago."

"What are the chances of him pulling it off?"

"According to my source it's almost a done deal. All he has to do is show up and El Amir Aljarah will hand the hostages over to him."

"Who in the hell decided to send his ass over there?"

"My source couldn't tell me that."

"Damn! If he pulls this off it's not going to be easy to get rid of him but I damn sure am not going to let him be the next vice president of the United States."

Dick Hilgan closes his phone and sits back to think. He has to come up with some way to end Senator Wright's career.

The information Dick and Thomas just talked about on the phone is considered a part of national security. Not only are they not supposed to talk about it on unsecured communication equipment they aren't even supposed to know about it.

There are going to be serious repercussions when the right people hear about this. Dick has just gotten caught in his own game and he's about to take Thomas down with him.

Our convoy arrives at Kallah El Shazir's palace and we are escorted into a sitting room. It is a magnificent place with marble floors, twenty foot ceilings, beautiful high arched windows that overlook what I can only describe as the most breath taking patio I've ever seen. This is the type of place I would love to bring Nessa for a vacation.

Not long after we are escorted into this room, One of Kallah El Shazir's assistants arrives to take me to his office. When I get there I meet Rajeeb Al Batal for the first and last time if I'm lucky.

He is not a pleasant man and he makes it known that if it were left up to him there would be no compromise and Amir would be found and killed. He's about to go on a tirade on how America has treated his country but El Shazir walks in.

"That will be all Rajeeb."

"But Kallah how can you negotiate with these dogs?"

"I said that will be all Rajeeb!"

Rajeeb walks out but he is still steaming. El Shazir sits down behind his desk.

"Senator Wright I apologize for Rajeeb. He is very intense especially about our country. Now let us get down to business. Do you have my books?"

I open my briefcase, take out the books and hand them to him. He looks through the books then looks at me.

"You do understand that if any of this comes out in the media I will make Amir and you wish you had never heard of me."

"Mr. Shazir until last night I didn't know you existed so forgetting you will be very easy. Now if you are satisfied with the books can we get on with the business of freeing the hostages?"

"I need to make certain arrangements before we can leave and it is going to take us at least three hours to get there. We will leave later this evening. In the meantime you and your people will be my guest. Your rooms are already prepared."

Shazir makes a phone call and his assistant walks in and takes me back to our waiting room. Thirty minutes later we are headed to the embassy in one of Shazir's limousines.

Back in Mississippi Ole Pop, Jesse, Sarah and Nessa are glued to the television screen. The morning I left CNN broke the news of my being our party's nominee for vice president if Senator Worthington should win the nomination.

An hour after that CNN again got the scoop on every one else by broadcasting the fact that I was the Senator who was sent to Riyadh to negotiate for the hostages. Now the whole country is watching and waiting.

After the latest report Nessa looks at Ole Pop. "Ole Pop do you think he's going to be able to get the hostages?"

"I don't know Nessa. This is a very delicate situation. Things have to be worked out just right."

"I just want him to come home."

Ole Pop wraps his arm around Nessa. "I know you do Nessa but this is one of those times you have to take it to the Lord and leave it there and let him handle it."

"Dats right Nessa. Tha Lord has never failed you and Andre yet and he won't forsake yall in this hour of need. Now I believe it's your turn to wash dem dishes ain't it?"

"Uncle Jesse I know you're not going to make me leave the television when my husband is across seas and they might report on him at any time."

"What dat gotta do wit anything? The dishes still needs washing don't dey"

"C'mon Uncle Jesse you can wash the dishes this time and I'll wash them next time."

Nessa slides across the couch, wraps her arms around Jesse and kisses him on the cheek. "Wuuuvv you."

Jesse half heartedly tries to elbow her off of him. "Gone now I don't need all that slobba on me."

Nessa kisses him again and squeezes a little harder and Jesse gives her a half smile.

"Okay I'm gonna wash those dishes this time but look heah missy. You can just leave dat "wuuuvv you" mess off. I ain't buying none of it."

Ole Pop looks at Sarah. "Sarah if he's not buying it then why is he getting up to do the dishes?"

"Cause he loves the attention Nessa and I give him. Isn't that right Jesse?"

As Jesse heads for the kitchen over his shoulder he says, "Sarah Mae Ann Wright, don't you start working on my nerve!"

"Ooooooooo not the whole name. Uncle Jesse, guess what, Wuuuvv you."

Jesse turns around and glares at Sarah. "Now cut that out!"

Ole Pop, Sarah and Nessa laugh and continue to talk while they wait on news about Andre.

It is ten o'clock in the morning when Candy checks into the penthouse suite of one of the best hotels in Miami. The penthouse is already paid for and she was flown down there by one of her clients to spend the weekend with him. She doesn't know what time he's coming and she really doesn't care. All she cares about is going out shopping then coming back and eating lobster for lunch.

As she walks in and out of shops on the beach the reporter keeps snapping pictures. He followed her to Miami hoping to actually catch her with her client. It's only a hunch but there can't be too many other reasons she's down here. If the reporter is right all he has to do is wait and if he's lucky he will get some of the best pictures he's ever gotten.

Candy finally walks back into her suite at five in the evening. At six there is a knock on her door. When she answers it he walks in, pulls her into his arms, gives her a long kiss and shuts the door behind him.

On the roof of the building across the street the reporter opens his dinner. Its one of those cellophane wrapped sandwiches you can buy from any small store. He has a bag full of them because he doesn't know how long he's going to have to stay up there.

The penthouse suite Candy is staying in has an outdoor pool. If the reporter is lucky he'll get a shot of her client and that will make staying on this rooftop and paying the airfare to Miami worth it. Just one picture and he goes from the small time to the big time.

At one o'clock in the morning the reporter finally gives up and lies down in his sleeping bag to get some sleep. Ten minutes later Candy runs out of the penthouse to the pool area in the buff followed by her client who is also in the buff.

The reporter almost sleeps through the whole thing but it begins to rain and he wakes up just in time to see Candy and her client getting out of the pool. He quickly aims his telephoto lens at them as they both run to the door and catches several good shots of them including one of them kissing just before closing the door.

Back in Hafan Al Batin it has been two hours since the meeting with Shazir. I've had time to shower and change clothes which is a good thing since it is so oppressively hot in this country.

It is finally time for us to make the eighty mile journey to the American embassy. That is when Rajeeb walks to my room and explains to me that only I will be allowed to make the trip.

I try to explain to him that some of the people with me were diplomats but I didn't get to finish my sentence before he interrupted me.

"Either you go alone or you don't go at all."

"What does Shazir have to say about this?"

"It is his order that I am obeying?"

I walk into the room where my diplomatic escorts are and tell them and as I suspected they weren't going for it. They all said I didn't have the experience to deal with the situation. They needed to be there if something changed about the deal.

I didn't find out until much later that the members of the diplomatic team were black opts. Their mission was to bring me back alive or dead. No matter what happened inside the embassy complex I was to be brought back home. The president was not going to let a Senator be captured by terrorist.

The team argues with me for several minutes until I finally say I'm going alone. They don't like it and neither do I but we really don't have a choice in the matter. If we cause any problems in Shazir's home it will spark a major international incident so my team lets me go.

We head out of Shazir's complex with Shazir and me seated in the middle car with several cars in front of us and several cars behind us. His driveway is a mile long and paved but as soon as we pass the gates we hit sand. For the next several miles men can be seen on the hills and in mini encampments by the side of the road and all of these men are armed.

"Shazir who are the men in the encampments we are passing?"

"They are loyal men of my country who are willing to die for their beliefs."

"But why are they encamped by the side of the road?"

"That is just a precautionary measure. I assure you it has nothing to do with you."

I sat back and watch the road but something about this whole thing just didn't sit well with me. Is it possible I was being set up to be some sort of fall guy? I hoped not because this is not where I wanted my life to end."

It takes us an hour and a half to reach our destination and as soon as we get within a half mile of the city we begin to see reporters and camera crews from several different countries.

When we get to the embassy there appears to be a whole army of Saudi soldiers standing guard out front. The confusing part is I don't know if they mean to keep any other terrorists out or to keep the Americans in. This was becoming a little to unsettling for my taste.

We are stopped right in front of the fifteen foot tall iron gates as an officer walks up to the car. Our driver rolls down the window and the officer immediately salutes then turns and says a few words in Arabic.

Our driver closes his window as the gates slowly begin to open. We move into the compound and for the first time I am afraid. I mean more afraid than I have ever been in my life.

There are men standing on the walkway that juts out from the wall all the way around the building. All of them have vest on with what looks like dynamite in the pockets. Every one of them is carrying an assault rifle and every one of them has the same intense look in their eyes.

We pull up in front of the embassy and get out of the car only to immediately be placed against the car and checked for weapons. It was bad enough when they searched me and the driver but when they searched Shazir I knew something was wrong. I was beginning to realize that this was not going to be as cut and dried as I was led to believe.

After the search we are led into the embassy where I see the hostages. There are nine men, five women and a little girl. All of them were sitting on the floor in the front hall and all except the little girl have gags over their mouths and their hands tied together. There are almost as many guards as prisoners. This is not a good situation.

I looked at Shazir. "I need to talk to them to make sure everyone is alright."

Shazir turns and speaks to one of the armed guards who then walks down the hall and disappears into one of the end rooms. Several minutes later a very tall man comes out of the room and walks toward me.

Something about the way he carried himself immediately let me know he was the leader. He walks right up to Shazir and says something in Arabic. I don't know what he said but I could tell by the tone it wasn't good.

They both walked down the hall leaving me with the hostages and guards. They stop in front of the door the tall man had just walked out of and continued their conversation there. They are still speaking Arabic so I have no idea what's going on and no idea what to do to get these people out of here.

I take a few steps toward the hostages and one of the guards turns his gun toward me. The leader speaks a few rapid words to the guard and the guard backs off. Then the leader speaks to me and Shazir translates. "He says it's alright if you check on your people but they can not move from their spots on the floor."

Shazir and the leader began to talk again and I walk through the hall checking on the hostages. I stop in front of one of the ladies who appears to have been crying.

"It's going to be alright." She takes my hand, squeezes it and smiles.

I continue to check on the hostages until I come to the end of the hall. As I turn around to walk back I feel a little hand slip into mine. I look down to see a pretty little girl with blue eyes and blonde hair smiling up at me. She looks to be about eight or nine years old.

Her mother looks frantic. She tries to stand up and reach for her daughter but the guard next to her shoves her back to the floor. I look at him expecting him to take the little girls hand from mine and push her back to her mother but he doesn't seem to be too concerned.

She squeezes my hand and I look down again and she motions for me to bend down then she whispers, "They don't know I can speak their language. My mother taught me when I was real young. The tall man's name is Abu Kareem Sawar and he is not happy about the deal the other man has made with you. He says his people should be receiving their fair share of the money from the oil being taken from their land. The man who came with you doesn't want to tell you this. He has told the man that the American's won't pay any more money."

Shazir and Abu Sawar abruptly turn and walk toward us. Shazir has a very unpleasant look on his face. When he reaches me he takes me by the arm, spins me around and begins leading me toward the door.

"He won't negotiate with us. He says if his brother Shamir Kasaan is not released from prison the Americans will all be killed."

I stop in my tracks and turn to look at Shazir. "I would appreciate it if you tell me the truth. If you don't then Amir will release the copies he has and I understand the other members of the OPEC council will not be very forgiving."

"I am telling you the truth."

"Really, what about the money you owe this man and his tribe for the oil you have taken from their land."

Shazir stammers then recovers, "I don't know what you're talking about."

Right about here he and I are at a stalemate and since he speaks the language I don't think it's going to turn out to my advantage but the little girl says something to Abu Sawar and he begins to walk our way.

Shazir turns and walks toward the girl but I am faster. I quickly walk back to her and gather her in my arms. The guards raise their guns with every intention of killing me and the little girl but Sawar speaks and they all lower their guns.

Sawar walks over and looks at me then says something to the little girl. After she answers him he looks directly at me as he says his next words. The little girl translates for me.

"He wants to know if you are willing to pay them for their oil?"

"Tell him we have already paid Shazir for the oil but if he will give me a minute I will talk to Shazir." She tells him what I said and he nods.

Still holding the girl I walk away from Abu Sawar and look at Shazir as I walk pass him away from the hostages. He doesn't like it but he follows me to the door.

"Okay this is the way this is going to work. You are going to get this man the money you owe him or you are going to end up a dead man when Amir sends his copy of the books to your OPEC partners."

"I will do no such thing and you had better watch your tongue before you are the one who ends up dead."

I turn and begin to walk back toward Abu Sawar. As I walk I look at the little girl and loud enough for Shazir to hear I say, "Tell Mr. Sawar what Mr. Shazir just said."

From behind me I hear "Wait. Okay I will do as you ask."

"I need you to do it now. He is not going to let the hostages go until you do."

"It will take some time to get that much money here."

"How long will it take?"

"As long as it takes for your government to release my money."

"Then we both will stay here until the deal is worked out. Now tell Mr. Sawar what you are going to do. Don't whisper and don't make a mistake because my friend here will tell me if you do.

Shazir tells Abu Sawar what has been said and after he finishes the little girl smiles at me and holds up her thumb. I give her a big hug.

"What is your name?"

"Crystal Ashton. What is yours?"

"Andre Wright. Crystal you are a very smart and brave girl."

She leans down and whispers in my ear. "No I'm not I just like to talk a lot."

I put her down and she runs to her mom and hugs her. Her mother has tears running down her cheeks. I walk over to her mother, stoop down and remove the tape from her mouth.

"Hello my name is . . . .

"Senator Andre Wright from Mississippi. I voted for you last term. I am Carolyn Ashton and you've already met Crystal. We're from Corinth Mississippi."

"Well it is a blessing to meet you and your daughter. Without her I don't know if this would have gone our way."

"Do you think they are going to release us?"

"I don't know but thanks to Crystal it looks better than it did ten minutes ago."

We all settle in to wait. We're still in the hall surrounded by guards and it could become a volatile situation at any time but I have faith that it's going to be alright and he's never failed me yet.

Dick Hilgan is sitting in his study and just like all of America he is glued to the television only for a completely different reason. If he's lucky Senator Wright will make the wrong move and get the hostages or himself killed. If not it's going to take a lot of time and money to keep him from getting the vice presidency.

He watches as the pictures of the inside of the compound flash across the screen. It is not looking good. Those fanatics will kill him and that will be the end of the whole thing. Then Dick can get back to having Glenora Perkins removed from office.

"They thought they could bring down the most powerful man in Washington and not have to pay for it. I'm going to ruin both of them then I can move on to help my candidate win the presidency."

Back at Ole Pops house reports are coming that Andre has just been driven into the embassy compound. The reporters report on the terrorist that can be seen on the walls as large iron gates open to allow Andre's car through.

The cameramen get a few quick shots of the inside of the compound before the gates close and the shots are frightening. All of America is sitting in front of their television hoping and praying the hostages will be alright.

Ole Pop eases out of his chair to one knee and drops his head.

"Lord this is your child speaking to you."

As soon as he begins to pray Sarah, Jesse and Nessa bow their heads and take each other's hands

"Father we know you have everything in charge and we know that nothing will happen to Andre without your consent. Lord we ask that you watch over your child while he does what he has to do. And father if it be thy will allow the hostages to come back safe to their families because somewhere a child is missing a father and somewhere a mother is missing a daughter and somewhere a wife is missing a husband Lord. Allow these families to be reunited. In your blessed son Jesus name I pray. Amen."

Sarah, Jesse and Nessa all say amen behind Ole Pop then they all turn back to the television. All over America people are sending up prayers for the hostages. Some churches even have prayer vigils and the country waits for the hostages to come back home.

Chapter 29

It is now twelve noon in Saudi Arabia and it has been a difficult twenty four hours. During the negotiations I had to make a call to Simon and ask him to move twenty million dollars to Abu Sawar's account.

Before he would move the money he insisted that one of my diplomats be allowed to come in and check me and the hostages. He wanted to make sure everything was alright. Mason Trison, the lead diplomat was put in a car and driven to the embassy.

Mason is a Navy Seal with ten years experienced. He is the most experienced member and leader of our diplomatic team. He's been trained to get out of situations normal men wouldn't even think about. He is also a very patient and intelligent man.

It takes several hours to get him there then another hour for him to make a thorough search of the facility. He has been told if he gets a chance to kill as many of the terrorist as he can and rescue as many of the hostages as he could. However after talking to me and checking out the building he makes the call to Simon and the money is transferred.

After the transfer the hostages are allowed to pack their bags then we are all led out to the embassy yard. We're all placed in a large truck and driven out of the embassy.

As we are driven out of the compound I know the reporters are out there waiting to take pictures so I try to sit as far back in the truck as I can. I wanted the cameras to capture the hostages. They were the really brave people in this ordeal.

But as Ole Pop says, "Sometimes when you do your best you can't hide it."

Just before we got to the gates Crystal moved away from her mother and sat in my lap. She whispered to me.

"Thank you for getting us out of there."

I put my left arm around her to make sure she did not fall then whispered.

"You are the one who got us out."

We pass through the gate while cameras of every sort snap hundreds of pictures and I'm sure that I am the least one on them but just as we pass a tree a quarter mile from the compound with a CNN cameraman in it. He begins filming and he focuses on me holding Crystal.

The shot is run on CNN with the caption, "Senator Wright negotiates the release of the hostages." That shot is seen all over the world.

We arrive at the airport where we meet up with the rest of my diplomatic core and after a short meeting with Saudi Arabian officials we are put on a Marine transport plane and flown to Kuwait.

When we get to Kuwait we board a large commercial jet with no one on board but the passengers and our diplomatic group. Hours later we arrive at Andrews Air force base and after several hours of debriefing we are taken to the White House to meet the president.

Back in Saudi Arabia in Kalleh El Shazir's office Rajeeb Al Batin is listening to his leader rant and rave about the misfortunes he suffered at the hands of Amir.

"I want Amir, Farrah and their child found and I want them killed."

"I told you, you should have killed him when you found out he was the father of Farrah's daughter."

"And I should have listened. The dog cost me two hundred million dollars and a share of the profits from any future drilling on Abu Sawar's tribal lands."

"And what do you want me to do about the American Senator?"

"Leave him alone. It will serve us no purpose to make the Americans angry over his death."

Rajeeb turns and walks out of the office leaving Shazir standing in the window looking out at the pool.

As soon as our plane lands at Andrews a prearranged senate committee begins an investigation into the illegal business dealings of one our country's oil companies.

The CIA agreed not to talk about Shazir's part in the fuel scheme however that deal did not extend to any American company or citizens involved in it.

In the next month several high ranking officials of one of the richest oil companies in America are fired then put in jail. Someone had to take the fall especially after CNN did an expose on the conspiracy.

After our meeting with the president and an hour of photos several NSA agents drive me to Simon's office for a brief meeting. Glenora and Paul are there also.

"Senator Wright you'll be happy to know that Amir has been reunited with Farrah and Amira and are being flown to a safe place to start their new lives together."

"I thought they would be here when I got back."

"We thought it would be wise to move them while you were negotiating with Kalleh El Shazir."

"What you mean is you needed to be able to send them back if you needed to."

"No actually I meant what I said. If we had tried to move them now Kalleh El Shazir might have tried to kill them anyway. Amir stole his wife and made him lose a large sum of money so I'm sure he's not a happy man so I think we did the right thing. By the way here is a note from Amir."

I take the note and open it.

Senator Wright

There are no words to describe how indebted to you I am. If it had not been for you Farrah and Amira would possibly be dead by now. I want to thank you for the life of my wife as well as my daughter and if you ever need anything from me, let me know and I will give it to you.

Amir

Back across town Dick Hilgan is sitting in his study at home with a Jack on the rocks in his hands. CNN has his undivided attention as they report the release of the hostages and show the picture of Senator Wright with the little girl in his lap leaving the embassy compound.

This picture is going to be seen all over America and the world. Americans every where are going to celebrate the release of the hostages without any gunfire or loss of life.

As the report goes on Dick can't take it anymore and launches his drink across the room where it slams into the wall then shatters into pieces of ice and glass.

"Sombitch! How in the hell did he pull this off. This has got to be staged. There is no way that sombitch could do this."

Dick picks up the remote, turns off the television then slams the remote down on the table. Andre Wright is becoming a big pain in the ass and he's going to have to deal with him and it's going to have to be quick before the son of a bitch can use this to his advantage.

Back in Mississippi Sarah and Nessa are dancing in the middle of the floor and Ole Pop and Jesse shake each other's hands and pat each other on the back then once again Ole Pop gets down on one knee and begins to pray.

"Lord it's me again. I just want to tell you that you did a good job. Jesse speaks up, "Yes sir Lord a mighty fine job."

"Father we want to thank you for bringing Andre as well as all the hostages home safe. We know we're not worthy but once again you have proved that you are God and God all by yourself. Thank you Lord. In your darling son Jesus name I pray. Amen."

Amen's resound around the room and Sarah and Jesse head into the kitchen to cook dinner. As they walk to the kitchen Jesse begins working Sarah's nerve.

"You means ta tell me that I'm gonna have tuh eat yo cookin tonight."

"And what's wrong with my cooking?"

"Nothin cept you puts too much grease in da skillet when ya fries dat chicken."

"Don't tell me how much grease to cook my chicken in."

"Look uh heah missy I'm da one who taught you how to cook. I remember when you got here you didn't know a skillet from a stew pot."

"Well, I know what a skillet is now so don't make me have to use it on you."

Jesse turns around and walks back to the chair Ole Pop is sitting in.

"Buford you gonna let dat girl sass me like dat. Go out there and get a switch and come in here and conversate wit her for a while."

Ole Pop lets out one of his booming laughs, "Jesse you and I both know we're too old to be trying to conversate with anybody. Besides Sarah is a grown woman now. She might go out there and get a switch and conversate with us."

Jesse's eyes open real wide then he lowers his voice, steps closer so Ole Pop and Nessa are the only ones who can hear him but he speaks just loud enough for Sarah to hear.

"You know you might be right bout dat. I guess I'd better hush up then."

Sarah has been listening to every word and leans out the kitchen door.

"Jesse you're not the only one who can swing a switch now come on in here so we can get finished."

Jesse reaches back and covers his butt with both hands like a child trying to keep a parent from whoopin him. Then he walks back into the kitchen.

"Yes'm Miss Wright mam I'm comin."

Nessa starts laughing then Ole Pop laughs and from in the kitchen they can hear Jesse and Sarah laughing. Andre is back home safe and the spirit of life and happiness is all over the house.

It's twelve thirty when the election caravan of Senator Worthington arrives back at the Vanderbilt Plaza hotel in Nashville. Glenn is sitting in his suite relaxing. He has just finished giving a speech at Vanderbilt University and it was well received.

This is one of his opponent's key states. If he can make a dent here it will go a long way in helping him win the Democratic nomination.

Of course after the speech there is the usual political hand shaking and meeting the people time which made for a long night but now he's back in his room watching CNN. Andre has completed his mission successfully and now it looks like Glenn's ticket is going to be hard to beat in November.

Glenn is just about to turn the television off and get in the bed for some long needed sleep when his secretary knocks on his door.

"Come in."

"Senator Worthington I'm sorry to bother you but there is a reporter on the phone who insists on talking to you. He said to tell you he needs to talk to you about someone by the name of Candy. I told him you don't know anyone by that name but he insist that you do."

With the mention of the name Candy all the blood drains out of Glenn's face leaving him white as a sheet. Without saying a word he gets up and walks into the next room to take the call.

"Hello."

"Senator this is Quentin King. I wanted to give you a chance to respond to the fact that you have been seen with a known prostitute Emily Carson better known as Candy. Would you like to make a comment?"

"I have no idea what you're talking about and please don't call here again."

Glenn hangs up the phone and sits down on the couch beside it. How much does this reporter know and how did he find out? And what if there are pictures? Glenn hangs his head. If there are pictures then his career as well as his marriage is as good as over.

Five minutes after the call to Senator Worthington, Thomas Yardley receives a call from Quinten King.

"Mr. Yardley as the head of the selection committee that chose Senator Worthington to run for the democratic nomination I wanted to know what your thoughts were on the fact that he has been seen in the company of a known prostitute?"

"I don't have time to deal with rumors."

"I can assure you sir this is not a rumor. We have pictures of him coming out of several hotels with a prostitute by the name of Candy."

"Before I can make any comments I need to see the pictures."

"You will see them tomorrow in the Washington Post. I just wanted to give you the opportunity to explain his actions."

"I have no comments."

After Thomas Yardley hangs up the phone he immediately calls Senator Bowens.

"Walter I just received a call from a reporter. He says that he has pictures of Glenn with a prostitute by the name of Candy."

"I already know about it. Glenn just called me."

"What did he say? Is it true?"

"According to him it only happened two times but he didn't know they had pictures of it."

"This is bad. This is really bad."

"Before we go off the deep end let me find out what I can and I'll call you back."

Walter hangs up the phone and calls Larry Paulson. Larry is one of the layout men for the Washington Post. He lays out the stories in the order they'll be placed in the paper just before they go to print. He's also on Senator Bowen's payroll.

"Larry this is Walter."

"Let me call you back in fifteen minutes."

Twelve minutes later Walter's phone rings.

"Hello."

"You got a major problem on your hands. We're about to run an expose on a Washington madam and one of her girls is your candidates favorite playmate."

"Are there pictures of this?"

"Yes and two of them are going to blow your candidate out of the water. One of them is of him kissing the woman and they're both naked."

"Damn! Thank you Larry."

"Just make sure I get something extra. This is the biggest story of the year."

"You'll get a generous bonus for this one.

Walter hangs up the phone and calls Thomas back. "It's even worse than we thought."

"What do you mean? How can it be worse?"

"They have a picture of Glenn and this Candy woman in the nude embracing."

"Damn! You're kidding."

"They're running it right now as we speak."

"Damn! This can't get any worse. We can't win an election with this kind of scandal. What are we going to do?"

"We replace him with another candidate."

"Who can we replace him with that will wash the stink of this away from the party."

"Senator Wright."

"Are you out of your damn mind! Our opposition will chew him up and spit him out."

"Have you been looking at the news lately? After what Senator Wright did in Saudi Arabia and the photo ops he got he makes a very impressive candidate."

"Well I won't back him."

"Fine then tell me who can replace him and win."

I don't know but there has got to be a better choice."

"Call me back when you find them and don't forget you have less than six hours because the pictures will be in the morning paper."

Walter hangs up the phone leaving Thomas to think about the situation. Walter knows that Andre is the best if not the only choice to replace Glenn. Now all he has to do is wait until Thomas figures it out. He fixes himself a drink and sits down behind his desk to wait on the call from Thomas.

Thomas sits down on his couch after fixing himself a drink. As much as he hates to admit it he knows Senator Wright is the best and only answer for the party if they are planning on winning the election. He's still absolutely sure that conservative white Americans will not vote for Senator Wright but he also knows the committee doesn't have another choice.

Fifteen minutes later the phone rings and Walter picks it up.

"Hello Thomas."

"Okay you're right. We don't have a choice in the matter but do you think he will take it under these circumstances?"

"Yes I do. I think he knows he should have been the choice all along."

"How can you say that? All of America will look at him as a last minute replacement."

"Then it will be up to us to change that perspective. The people of America deserve intelligent, strong leadership and I believe they will find out that Andre is intelligent, honest and will make a good leader. I believe they will vote for him."

"I hope you're right but it's going to be a hard sell."

"We'll see. Now come over here so we can plan a press release."

"How are you going to plan a press release when you don't know if he's going to take the position?"

"I'm going to call him and Senator Perkins right now. We need to have this meeting and get this settled before the news breaks in the morning."

It's been a long week and after all the meetings and debriefings I finally get a chance to call Nessa and when she answers the first thing I say is "I love you."

"I love you too. Now tell me everything that happened."

"Nessa you know I was working as a diplomatic agent for our government. I can't give you any of the details of what happened."

"You're right. I'm sorry I forgot and I really don't care as long as you are home safe. Oh and by the way you looked really good on the news with the little girl in your lap."

"I tried my best to keep that from happening but it happened anyway."

"That's the same thing Ole Pop said you were trying to do. Then he said "Sometimes when you do right you can't hide it.""

"He said that to me several years ago. I don't know how that old man does it but most of the time he's right."

After I talk to Nessa I talk to mom, Ole Pop and Jesse and it's twelve o'clock before I can get off the phone and go take a long hot shower.

I thought the shower would give me a little energy but it didn't. I can just barely lift my feet to walk to the bedroom. I miss Nessa and Andre Jr. But I'm so tired I need to get some rest before I fly to Mississippi to pick them up.

Just as I settle into bed and find that spot where I can pass out and sleep for the next eight hours my cell phone rings. I want to pick it up and toss it across the room but instead I pick it up and look at the display.

It's Glenora. Now why is she calling me at this time of night?

"Hello."

"Andre I know you're probably in the bed but you need to get dressed and come to Walter's home as soon as possible."

"Why? What's going on?"

"Just get dressed and get there as quick as you can."

I look at the phone for a minute then shake my head and put it back to my ear. "What is so important that it needs to be done tonight?"

"Andre Wright I don't have time to argue with you. Now stop being hard headed and go to Walter's house. I'll explain it all to you then."

I hear the steady buzz after she hangs up and after shaking my head and chuckling and talking to myself. "You're the one who asked for this job." I put the phone down, get up and begin putting on my clothes.

Chapter 30

The large iron gates open and I drive up Walter's drive to the front of his house. His driveway is already full of cars including Glenora's long, black Lincoln and that surprises me. Now I really want to know what is so important that all these people are here at one o'clock in the morning.

I'm greeted at the door by Walter's butler and led into his study. There are several people I know in his study including several people I am surprised to see there. Avion Shoemaker, Terri Hernden, Mark Goldstein, Bill Guterez and Thomas Yardley are all in attendance at this meeting.

All these people are members of the selection committee who chose Glenn to run against Congressman Dalwin. Two of which I am sure are not my biggest supporters. What is going on here? Walter motions me over to a seat next to Glenora.

"Andre we have a major problem. Glenn has gotten himself into something we can't fix."

"What kind of something?"

"There are some compromising pictures of him and a young lady about to be published by the Washington Post."

"Okay I can see where that might be a problem but politicians have survived this kind of scandal before. There is a long way to November we can just ride it out."

"First of all riding it out only works if you are already in office and second, the young lady is a prostitute and she works for a madam. This madam is the one who is being investigated but when

305

the public finds out that Glenn has been hiring prostitutes his candidacy will be over and that's where you come in."

"Where I come in?"

"We want you to take his place."

I stand up and look Walter in the eyes. "You're kidding right?"

"No we're not. Andre you are the perfect choice."

"To do what get beat by a land slide? You and I both know that when this comes out we're going to lose at least a quarter of our support and when you tell them Glenn's being replaced by a Black man. We'll lose some white votes because I'm Black. We'll also lose some black votes because I'll be looked at as the token you had to put in because you didn't have anyone else to take it."

"No they won't Andre. They will respect you for taking over in the middle of the campaign and don't forget there are an awful lot of white voters out there who will vote for you simply because of the job you did in Saudi Arabia."

"So what you're telling me is we're going to base our campaign on Saudi Arabia."

"No we're going to base our campaign on you. You are a good, God fearing, intelligent man and I think if we market you that way the American people will get the message and vote for you."

"I appreciate the compliment but there is none good but the Lord. I'm just an average every day man . . . ."

"And that's what we're going to market. We're going to use your average everyday image, your strong work in the Senate and the images of you in that truck coming out of the U.S. Embassy with those American hostages safe and secure."

Glenora stands up and walks to me. "Andre you got into politics because you didn't like the way politicians treated regular people like Ole Pop. Now here is your chance to help a nation full of people like him. It's a good idea and it is the right time. All you have to do is keep doing what you have been doing since you became a politician and that is help the people. And if you call Ole Pop he will tell you I'm right."

I sat down in my seat and shaking my head. This is all too much too fast then a question forms in my head. I look up, find Thomas Yardley and look him in the eyes.

"Are all of you in agreement on this?"

Thomas raises his glass, drains it walks over to the bar pours another quarter glass full then walks over and sits down beside me.

"Andre I agree with you. I don't think voters will vote for you. I think they will look at you as a last minute choice. However Walter thinks you are the best choice so I will go along with him."

"Thank you for being honest with me. Look I appreciate all of you being willing to put me on the ticket but this is a lot to take in. I need some time to think about this."

"Well that's another problem. We don't have any time. The paper will come out at six this morning and we need to be ready with a statement by twelve noon. We need your answer now."

"I need to make a call first."

I walk out to my car, get in and take out my cell phone and dial Ole Pop's number. In just a few moments I hear Nessa's sleepy voice.

"Andre what's wrong?"

"There is nothing wrong but I need to tell you something you're not going to believe then I need to talk to Ole Pop."

"What is it Andre?"

"I've been asked to take over the campaign for Glenn. If I take it I'll be campaigning against Congressman Dalwin for the democratic Presidential nomination."

Nessa is instantly wide awake. "What! How did that happen? I mean what happened to Glenn?"

"It's a long story. The short of it is he was caught with another woman."

"Oh no! I bet Carolyn is devastated."

"I don't think she knows yet."

"Well someone needs to tell her."

"By six o'clock she'll hear about it on the news."

"That's just wrong. No woman should have to hear something like that from the news media instead of her husband."

"I know Nessa, I know. But right now I need to talk to Ole Pop."

I hear Nessa get out of the bed, walk down the hall and knock on Ole Pops door. A few moments later I hear Ole Pop's voice and know I'm about to get some good advice.

"Son Nessa told me that you are being asked to replace Senator Worthington as the committee's choice for president."

"Yeah Ole Pop and they need an answer right away so they can have a news conference this afternoon."

"Why so fast?"

"The committee doesn't want the bad taste of what Glenn got himself into to stay on the public's mind for too long."

"What did the young man get into?"

"Glenn was caught with a prostitute. A reporter has pictures of Glenn and a woman named "Candy" in a very compromising position. The head of the committee says we need to be ready in the morning when the news comes out."

"Is the announcement going to be made by Glenn or someone else?"

"I don't know we never discussed it and Glenn wasn't a part of this meeting."

"Then how do you know if Glenn knows about this or not?"

"Glenn knows about the reporter because he received a call from him. Right after that call he called Walter to confirm the reporter was telling the truth."

"Yes but does he know about this announcement?"

"I don't know. I haven't talked to Glenn."

"Then I think before you give the committee an answer you need to find out how Glenn feels about this. If he doesn't have a problem with it then decide what you are going to do. However if it isn't alright with him then you'll have to make this decision without the blessing of the man who was the party's first choice and your friend."

"Thanks Ole Pop. You always give me something different to think about."

"That's alright son just make sure to call us back and tell us what decision you made."

I hang up the phone and immediately call Glenn. It takes him a few minutes to answer and when he does his speech is slightly slurred.

"Hello."

"Glenn this is Andre. We need to talk."

Glenn's speech was slurred. "Damn Andre I made uh mistake."

"Glenn are you alright?"

"I'm drunk Andre cause I just screwed up my life. I should have left Candy alone. I tried to leave her alone but I was weak."

"Glenn don't say that over the phone. You never know who is listening. Now where are you?"

"I'm on the plane headed home. I should've known better. I did know better and I did it anyway. Did I tell you the reporter called and talked to Carolyn?"

I shake my head and exhale slowly. I was hoping Glenn was at least going to be the one to break it to Carolyn but that can't happen now. Hearing about this from a reporter had to be hard for Carolyn. Glenn may not even get the benefit trying to put his marriage back together.

"How do you know they called her?"

"She called me and asked me if it was true. I couldn't lie to her anymore. I told her the whole story. She told me she never wanted to see me again then hung up."

"You'll work it out Glenn but first put the drink down you need to be sober when you get off the plane to meet the press."

"Yeah you're right. Would you do me a favor and meet me at the airport?"

"I'll be there when you land."

"Thank you Andre. You should have been the one running for president."

"They picked the right man. You're human and you made a mistake."

"Yeah and this one is going to cost me my marriage."

The phone goes dead leaving me with a decision.

I walk back into Walters den knowing the decision I make is not going to sit well with him or anyone else in the room but it is a decision I can live with.

"I appreciate your confidence but I won't make this decision without first asking Glenn how he feels. I don't think it would be right to agree to this without first meeting with him."

"Andre I understand your loyalty but we don't have a large window of opportunity for this. We need to have an answer ready when the Washington Post comes out this morning."

"I'm sorry I won't make this decision before I speak with Glenn in private. He has asked me to meet him at the airport and I am going to be there to support him. If that is going to be a problem for you then maybe I'm not the right man for the job."

"You realize the media will be all over him as soon as he touches down. And by meeting him at the airport you will also be put under scrutiny. The media is going to want to know if you used the same madam."

"They can look under all the rocks they want to I'm still going to meet Glenn at the airport."

I get up, walk out of the office and head for my car. It is now four o'clock. I have time to go home, shower and shave before I go meet Glenn at the airport.

After I leave Walter's office Thomas takes over the meeting.

"Okay Walter now what? If he meets Glenn at the airport He's as good as dead to us. We need to come up with another candidate."

"Fine I'm going to say to you what I said on the phone. If you can find someone to replace him at this point in the campaign I will back them."

Glenora looks at Thomas. "So you're just going to give up on Andre?"

"Senator Perkins I know he is your protégé and all . . . ."

"That doesn't change the fact that he's the best candidate for the job. He's honest, loyal, smart and he just got the hostages released from Saudi Arabia. He's not a boy scout but let the media check into his background. I can assure you they won't find anything and after they get through he'll come out on the other side clean. Then let America decide if he is or isn't presidential material."

Mark Goldstein gets up, walks over to the table next to Thomas and picks up the coffee carafe, refreshes his cup then takes a seat beside Thomas.

"I agree with Senator Perkins. From what I can see he's not only our party's best choice he may be America's best choice. Hold the announcement until Senator Wright is ready and let's see how this plays out. If it doesn't work we can always pick someone else."

Avion Drake, Terri Hernden and Bill Guterez all agree with Mark's statement leaving Thomas standing by himself again. Walter stands up and looks at Thomas,

"So we're all in agreement. We'll put out a press release stating that we will make a decision about his replacement on Thursday. That will give Andre plenty of time to talk to Glenn and make his decision."

Thomas looks at the other people in the room and realizes that he is in the minority in this situation then shakes his head in resignation to the majority. He doesn't think it will work but he as no choice at this time.

The meeting breaks up and Thomas drives home. Dick Hilgan is going to go completely out of his mind when he finds out Senator Wright is going to be the committee's new presidential nominee.

Thomas thinks about it on the way home and decides not to call Dick until later in the day. He pulls his cell phone out and turns it off. Now he doesn't have to deal with Dick until he's ready.

Thomas pulls into his driveway, gets out and walks into the house. It has been a long night and he needs some sleep but as he steps into the house his home phone rings. He already knows who it is so he ignores it.

It stops ringing for a few seconds then begins ringing again with a new call. This is repeated several more times before Thomas turns off the ringer and climbs into bed.

It's six o'clock in the morning when Glenn's plane lands at the airport. The media is out in force. They can smell a good scandal and they want to bring their readers and viewers a blow by blow description of it.

Fortunately airport security has roped off the area Glenn has to pass through to get to his car and the secret service agents keep the reporters from getting close to Glenn. However he is close enough to hear the questions shouted at him and I could see by the look on his face the questions bothered him a lot.

Cameras are flashing in his eyes as he tries to avoid as many pictures as he can without looking like he is trying to hide. I sat in the car watching him walk toward me. He has the look of a desperate and tired man and later that evening his tired and desperate look will be broadcast all over the country.

It seems to take hours for him to get to the car when it actually takes only a minute and a half. When he gets to the car a secret service agent opens the door and a few of the reporters see me and they fire several questions at me before the door closes.

Glenn slides in the car and after the door is shut the driver pulls off. He's usually sharp in his appearance with every hair in place and tailor made suits but not at this moment. He looks like he hasn't shaved in the last two days, his coat is wrinkled his hair looks like it hasn't been combed.

He turns and looks at me and manages a small smile but his eyes give away his true sadness.

"Well do you think I could screw up any better than this?"

"Glenn you can make it through this. You're the bull dog remember."

"You don't really believe that and neither do I. The media is going to do a hatchet job on me and I have no defense. I'm guilty as charged and the whole nation is going to know it including my wife and her mother and father and my children."

"Look Glenn you need to go home and talk to Carolyn and see if you can work this out. The nation can wait your marriage can't."

"What marriage? I no longer have a marriage thanks to my stupidity. Carolyn told me by the time I got home she and the kids wouldn't be there."

"Then you need to find her and try to work it out."

"It won't do any good she hates my guts now."

There is a mini bar in the back of the car and Glenn picks up a glass, adds some ice and begins to fill it with Vodka. This isn't the Glenn Worthington I have come to know and respect. This is a beaten man and I need to do something to see if I can get a friend back on his feet again.

"Put that damn glass down. This is not the time to bury yourself in a bottle."

"Leave me alone. I need a stiff drink."

"Dammit Glenn do you love Carolyn?"

"Yes I do but . . . ."

"Shut up dammit and listen! The Glenn Worthington I know would go after her and work it out not bury himself in a bottle. If you love your wife then work it out."

I take the glass out of his hand and put it back on the bar.

"Now go home and get yourself together then find your wife and work things out."

When we pull up in front of Glenn's house reporters are already there waiting on him. Police officers have roped off his driveway so the car can pull in and go directly to his garage. After the garage door closes Glenn gets out and before he walks away he looks at me.

"If anybody should be president of the United States it should be you."

"I'm not sure I'm ready for the position."

"Well you better get ready. It's going to be yours and you had better handle it right or I will be one of the Senators who will give you hell."

"If it were to happen I bet you would."

"It's going to happen. The committee doesn't have a choice about it and when it is offered to you take it. If I can't have it I don't want anyone else but you to get it."

Glenn walks off and I sat back as the driver backs out of the garage. I'm still not sure I want to take the nomination over. There are too many things that can go wrong and I still don't think the white American public will vote for me. Little did I know I wasn't going to be given the chance to make the decision.

By mid afternoon the whole nation knows about Glenn and the prostitute named Candy. They also know about the Washington madam and some of her more famous clientele including a professional basketball player by the name of Theo Suggs.

After Theo's wife found out about him and Candy the police had to be called to the house to stop and argument that escalated into an all out fight. It seems that his wife wasn't happy about being embarrassed on national television and she wasn't willing to walk away from Mr. Suggs quietly.

By late evening the media had interviewed anyone remotely involved with the madam Adrienne Stone. Her lawyer was denying everything while privately threatening some of the more prominent Senators and congressmen on the hill. By the next morning they all knew about her accounting books with her client list and cell phone numbers in it.

After watching the news report Dick calls Thomas again. He has been calling Thomas cell and home phones non stop since early this morning but Thomas wasn't answering. It is now late evening and Thomas finally answers the phone.

"Where the hell have you been? I've been calling you all day."

"Hello Dick. I've been working."

"What the hell is the committee going to do about replacing Senator Worthington?"

"We're going to wait until this dies down then make a decision."

"Do you have someone in mind?"

"Yes we do."

"Who is it?"

"Before I tell you I think you need to know that it was a unanimous decision."

"Dammit who is it?"

"Senator Wright."

"Are you out of your damn mind? There is no way we can win the nomination with him. White voters are not going to vote for him. You go back and tell Walter I said if they go through with this I'm going to withdraw my support and so will my friends."

"I don't think that's going to change their minds and quite frankly it won't change mine either."

"Don't tell me you're backing this nigger too."

"That was uncalled for Dick. His race has nothing to do with the fact that he is a good man and I think he's the right man for the job."

"Well you and the committee can all go to hell as far as I'm concerned."

Chapter 31

Dick slams the phone down and sits back in his chair. There is no way Senator Wright is going to occupy the most powerful chair in the United States. Dick Hilgan is not going to let that happen.

After pouring himself another drink he turns the sound of the television up just in time to hear a CNN report on Adrienne Stone. Sources have told the reporter that Ms. Stone has been threatening several prominent Senators and congressmen with exposure. It is reported she will give the media her books if they don't find a way to get her out of the mess she is in. That triggers a thought in Dick's brain.

He's absolutely sure his name is in the book but it doesn't matter to him. He's divorced and has already been disgraced and run off the hill but if he can get Adrienne to put Senator Wright's name in her books then he can get rid of him.

Dick checks his rolodex, finds her number and calls it. After a few rings she answers.

"Hello Dick what can I do for you?"

"I understand that you need a little help getting out of some trouble you're in. I can help you if you help me."

"How can you help me? You don't have any pull on the hill anymore?"

"I have enough to get you out of this mess and I also have a hundred thousand dollars for your trouble."

"Are you sure you can help me?"

"Have I ever let you down before?"

"No you haven't. Okay what do you want me to do?"

"I want you to add Senator Andre Wright's name to your books then let the media have them."

"I'll add his name but I won't let the media have them until you get me out of this mess. They are talking about giving me ten to twenty years. I don't want to do any time."

"I can do that for you."

"As soon as you do I will turn my books over to the media."

"Give me two days."

Dick hangs up the phone and sits back in his chair. Two blocks from his house two CIA agents sit in front of a lap top and listen to the replay of Dick's conversation then get on the phone and call Simon Blakely.

Thirty minutes later Simon is listening to the replay. He listens to the conversation then has his agents make a copy which he emails to Senator Bowens with a note.

Walter

> Senator Wright handled his diplomatic mission well. I believe he will make a good president I know you feel the same. Here is something you will be interested in. You will know what to do with it.

There is no signature on the letter but Walter knows who it comes from and he does indeed know what to do with it. He makes a call to Bobby Todd who, after the successful completion of Dick Hilgan's case has been promoted. He now heads the conspiracy section of the bureau and he also is in charge of Adrienne Stone's case.

Walter arranges a meeting with Bobby and at that meeting Walter hands a CD over to him. An hour later Adrienne is sitting in agent Todd's office with her lawyer.

"I want to know why you have dragged my client down to your office."

"You're client is about to do thirty years in jail if she doesn't give me the right answers."

"You're on a fishing expedition. You're not going to arrest her. Some very powerful people will be extremely mad if you do."

Agent Todd doesn't bother to answer instead he turns on the CD player then sits back in his chair. As soon as Adrienne hears Dick's voice she knows she's in trouble.

After listening to the CD in its entirety Adrienne's lawyer stands up.

"If that's all you have then we'll be leaving now. This and all the other evidence in this case will never be released. There are too many people who will be harmed if my client is charged with anything."

Agent Todd ignores the lawyer. "Miss Stone this CD will prove that you are involved in a conspiracy with Dick Hilgan to frame Senator Wright for something he didn't do. And since Senator Wright has been involved in some very sensitive work for the government not to mention the fact that he is running for Vice President you are in very big trouble."

Adrienne's lawyer smiles and sits down. "As I have just stated my client doesn't have to worry. That CD will never see the light of day and even if it does I will claim entrapment. You could have put ex Senator Hilgan up to this."

Todd moves forward, leans on his desk and looks Adrienne directly in the eyes.

"Your lawyer's theory would be correct if it weren't for the fact that I am the agent who got Dick Hilgan thrown out of the senate and almost thrown in jail. There is no way your lawyer could convince a jury Dick Hilgan and I would team up to entrap you."

Agent Todd leans back, opens his folder, takes out a court order and slides it to Adrienne's lawyer.

"That is a legal order from the justice department. It says that the information we have is from a legal wire tap so it will be admissible in court."

Agent Todd turns back to Adrienne. "After the CD is admitted every piece of evidence your lawyer brings into court will be questioned by the Justice Department lawyers. Your case will be left with your word against Senator Wrights. Now who do you think the court is going to believe, you or a squeaky clean Senator freshly returned from freeing the hostages in Saudi Arabia?"

Agent Todd leans back in his seat and smiles.

"Oh by the way when this CD comes out all of the people you have in your little black book will scream entrapment. They will claim you are trying to frame them the same way you were trying to

frame Senator Wright. Unfortunately for you most of them will get
away with it leaving you without a bargaining chip. You're going to
be surprised how fast your influential friends leave you when you
have no leverage."

Agent Todd closes his folder and removes the CD. Adrienne
looks at her lawyer and with a grim look on his face he shakes his
head letting her know she no longer has a choice in the matter.
Finally she looks at agent Todd.

"What do you want me to do?"

"I want your books and any copies you have and I want you to
testify against Dick Hilgan. We have the CD but I want to make sure
he doesn't get away like he did the last time."

"Will it get me out of going to prison?"

"No but it can get you a nice country club prison and some easy
time."

"Okay."

"Now let me make myself perfectly clear. If you do not give me
the books and all the copies I will send you to the worse federal
prison in America. Do you understand?"

"Yes I do."

At nine the next morning all the networks have interrupted their
regularly scheduled programming for a special news report. The
network cameras roll and the newspaper cameras snap picture after
picture of Glenn as he steps to the mikes in front of his house.

All the committee members are at home without a clue as to
what Glenn is doing and Walter is the only one watching television.
As soon as he finds out Glenn is about to hold a press conference
he calls the other committee members and they all turn on their
televisions.

As Glenn prepares to make his statement the members of the
committee look on in shock. Not even Andre knows what he is about
to say.

"Ladies and Gentlemen I have called this press conference to let
the American people know that I am sorry for the mistakes I have
made. I didn't mean to do anything that would embarrass my family
or my country. Unfortunately that is exactly what I have done and
for that I sincerely apologize. If I had it to do over again I would have
done things differently but it is too late for that. So it is with sadness

that I not seek the democratic nomination for president. However before I go I would like to take this time to ask the American public not to hold what I have done against Senator Wright. He is a good man, a good Senator and I think he would be an excellent president. That is all I have to say. Thank you."

Glenn turns around amid a symphony of reporters shouting questions at him and walks back into his house leaving many questions unanswered. The one question he didn't leave unanswered was who he thought should be his replacement.

As soon as the press conference is over Walter calls me. He needs an answer from me and he needs it now. Unfortunately he gets my answering service because I'm on the phone with Ole Pop.

"Ole Pop did you see the press conference?"

"We're sitting here looking at it now. Did you talk to Glenn before he did this?"

"Yes I did but I didn't know he was going to have this press conference and neither did the committee."

"What did he say to you?"

"The same thing he said at the press conference."

"So he told you to take the committee's backing and seek the presidential nomination?"

"Yes he did. He said he couldn't think of anyone else he wanted to replace him."

"Can you do the job?"

"I don't know Ole Pop this is a lot of responsibility there will be a lot riding on how I handle this."

"I didn't ask you about that I asked you if you can do the job."

"Yes I think I can."

"No son! I think I can is not good enough for this nation. We need someone who knows they can run this country. So one more time, can you do the job!"

As per usual Ole Pop's words inspire me. "Yes I can do the job."

"Well son it's not my decision to make. What is your decision?"

"I'm going to run for the nomination."

"Then take it and give it all you've got."

I hang up the phone and sit there for a minute. This is going to be one of the hardest things I've ever done and I still have my doubts. Can I actually win the nomination and if so can I actually win the presidency?

My phone rings and interrupts my thoughts. It's Glenn calling.

"Glenn why didn't you tell me you were going to give a news conference?"

"Because I knew you would be there to stand with me and I didn't want my scandal to affect you. I know you're sitting there with your doubts about taking the nomination. Don't doubt it do something about it. That is the advice you gave me about my marriage and I have talked to Carolyn. She's still mad at me but she is willing to talk about it. At least I'm not like Theo Suggs. His wife hit him with the living room lamp."

He and I both laugh at the thought of a big strong basketball player being hit by his wife.

"Yeah I saw that. But I'm still unsure about this nomination Glenn."

"Listen to me damn you. Take the damn nomination and run this country like I know you can."

The phone goes dead before I can say anything and before I can gather my thoughts it rings again. This time it's Walter.

"Andre did you see the press conference?"

"Yes I did."

"Andre I need your answer and I need it now."

"I'm going to run."

"Good now we can go to work."

The first thing I do is call Nessa and tell her she has to be here for the press conference announcing my accepting the committee's nomination to run for the presidency. She tells me she loves me but isn't all that happy to be at the press conference. She hadn't given much thought to what her role would be. I told her she would be fine and hung up the phone to prepare my speech.

An hour later Nessa's flight takes off. She didn't want to come back to Washington without Andre Jr. But mom convinced her to leave him with her for the first press conference and she could take him on the next one.

That didn't keep her from being anxious about being introduced as the nominee's wife. Ole Pop told her she was going to make a beautiful first lady. Then Jesse told her to leave the house before he got a switch and conversated with her and she reluctantly left.

My cell phone rings as I'm driving to the airport to pick up Nessa. Glenora is on the other end.

"Andre, Walter called me and told me that you are taking the nomination is that right?"

"Yes it is Glenora. I'm going to give it my best shot."

"Well then I would like to be your campaign manager."

"You already have a job as one of the best Senators in Washington besides who is going to chair the new energy commission?"

"Andre I have been on the job for longer than I want to. I have been planning on retiring for the last four years. My term will be up after the election and it will be my last."

"But Glenora the people still need you."

"No, actually they need you and that's why I want to be your campaign manager."

"Okay I tell you what. You can have the job if you will take a job in my cabinet if I win."

"You mean when you win, and you have a deal."

I hang up the phone and smile. Ole Pop always told me what God had for me was for me. I don't know if this is what God wants but it sure is lining up really quick and easy. This is going to be a very interesting race.

The next day at precisely five o'clock Eastern time I walked up on the podium for the first time as the committee's nominee for the presidency. I have to admit I was shaky but with Nessa by my side as well as Glenora and Walter I began.

My speech lasted thirty minutes and in that time I outlined the plan I had for taking the country into the future. I was surprised at how many things I wanted to do. I guess I had been sub consciously thinking about what I would do if I were in charge of the country.

Before I made the speech I told Walter I would only run on a platform I believed in and I had to argue with the committee to get some of my proposals through but in the end we came up with a compromise I could live with.

After our quick meeting to set a platform Thomas walked over to me and shook my hand.

"I didn't realize you had given any thought to a platform but I must admit you have some good ideas and I like the way you stick to your guns. Now all you have to do is stay this way all the way to the White House."

After the speech we all rushed back to Walter's home to watch the news reports and Glenn called me.

"Mr. President you looked good on your first outing. One thing though try not to sound so "Holier than thou" when outlining or defending your views. That attitude will turn potential voters off."

"I can't help who I am and what I believe."

"I didn't ask you to change who you are what I'm suggesting is that you pull back the judgmental part of your personality just a bit. People don't like to be judged. Now where are you headed to next?"

"I'm headed home to make a speech at The University of Mississippi."

"Well good luck."

"Wait a minute. How are you and Carolyn doing?"

"We're still in the talking stage but I think we're going to do alright."

"That's good to hear. I'll call you after I leave Mississippi."

"You don't have to do that. You're going to be busy."

"Not too busy for a friend."

I hang up the phone and for the next two hours we sit and watch the news for the reaction to my announcement. Most of the press was positive however there was one glaring problem. Somehow I was perceived as being soft. Some of the reporters seem to think some foreign countries wouldn't take me seriously. That was a perception I needed to change.

After an hour I could see that Nessa was getting tired and to tell the truth so was I. I told Walter and Glenora that I would be ready in the morning to head to Mississippi and Nessa and I walked out of Walter's house.

As soon as we walked outside we were greeted by four secret service agents. From this point on they are assigned to protect me. This was going to take some getting use to.

The next day as Nessa and I boarded our plane to Mississippi FBI agents walk into Dick Hilgan's house to take him into custody. Two hours later he's sitting in an interrogation room when agent Todd walks in with a folder in his hand.

"Hello Senator . . . . I'm sorry Ex Senator Hilgan. It's good to see you again."

"I should have known it was you behind this. What's the matter still mad because you couldn't hang me the last time?"

"No actually I'm quite amused at the fact that you have hung yourself."

"I don't know what you're talking about."

Agent Todd looks at Dick's lawyer. "Please explain to your client what conspiracy is."

"He already knows what conspiracy is and I don't see any proof of conspiracy."

Agent Todd takes the CD out of his folder, places it in the CD player, turns it on then sits back. Dick and his lawyer listen to the whole CD. After agent Todd turns the recorder off Dick's lawyer clears his throat.

"Even with the CD my client is only guilty of conspiracy to defraud. That carries a maximum sentence of two to four years."

Dick smiles, "And just like last time I'm not going to do any of it."

"Ex Senator Hilgan" Agent Todd emphasizes the ex part then pauses before going on. "That would be true if Senator Wright didn't have diplomatic status as well as top security clearance. Now this tape becomes a conspiracy to threaten the security of the country. And that little fact is going to keep all of your friends from helping you. None of them will want to be involved in this case. Oh by the way you will also be charged with conspiracy to impede a federal investigation. That charge carries a mandatory ten year federal sentence. Now if you add all of that together we're talking about twenty five years federal time."

Agent Todd stands up and just before walking out of the room he leans down until he's real close to Dick then he whispers.

"And this time I'm going to make sure you do every year of the twenty five you're given."

Chapter 32

When we get to Mississippi we can't stay with Ole Pop we have to get a suite at a hotel. The news service is lined up and down the highway to his house. They even had news trucks in Ole Pop's front yard but mom called the police and they made the reporters leave.

After arriving and getting settled I make arrangements for mom, Ole Pop, and Andre Jr. to be brought to the hotel. I want my whole family at the forum when I give my speech. I also want the people who support me to be there especially Glenora and Dr. Mayhew.

They all arrive an hour later and I am glad to see them especially mom. Nessa has stressed herself so much over what to wear that finally she has told me she can't find anything that will fit her so she's not going.

Nothing I say to her makes any difference she is not going and that is final. Nessa is now eight months pregnant and she's worried about her appearance. To me she is the most beautiful woman on earth but at this time I can't convince her of that.

After mom calms Nessa down and helps her pick out the right outfit mom walks into the living room to talk to me. Mom tries to explain but I just don't understand what is wrong with Nessa. Normally she isn't a vain person and it just isn't like her to be upset about something so trivial.

I'm pacing around the room. "Mom Nessa is not acting rationally. She looks fine but when I tell her that she gets mad. Why is she so upset with me? I didn't do anything and she isn't usually this fussy about her appearance."

Mom walks up to me and give me one of her "I'm tired of you" looks. Then she smacks me on the back of the head. It's not a hard smack but it can be heard around the room.

"Boy act like you have been here before. Your wife is carrying your child and she's under a lot of stress. All you have to do is make speeches. Just support her when she needs it."

Ole Pop, Jesse, Dr. Mayhew and Glenora who are all sitting in the room with us try to hold back their laughter. But Ole Pop just can't help himself. First he lets out a small laugh then he starts in on me.

"Dang son now that you are going to be the president of the United States you would think you wouldn't have to take them head smackins."

Dr. Mayhew chimes in, "Yeah son can't you do something about that. I mean aren't you going to be the one in charge of the nation? You can't let her smack the president's head like that it's not dignified."

Then it's Jesse's turn. "Naw Jackson. He may be the president but Sarah is still his mother. He's gonna have to deal wit dem head smackins as long as she lives."

And of course Glenora had to put her two cents in. "He deserved to have his head smacked. You can tell by the hollow sound his head made he wasn't thinking straight when he asked that dumb question."

And that was all that was needed for all of them to fall out laughing.

I waited until they all got through laughing.

"All of you seem to forget there are four secret service agents outside that door. I can call any one or all of them in here if I feel threatened by someone."

Ole Pop stops laughing and gives me his most serious look.

"Son don't do that."

He catches me off guard with the look and the subdued tone of his voice and I immediately am sorry for what I said.

"Ole Pop you know I wouldn't call them in here on mom or anyone else in the room."

Then Ole Pop smiles and I know I have been set up for another joke.

"That's good cause it wouldn't be very nice for the nation to see Sarah with an elm switch in her hand conversating with you on national television while your secret service agents are trying to handcuff her and keep from getting their head smacked at the same time."

We all start laughing and suddenly the situation with Nessa is no big deal. Like Ole Pop has told me many times. Laughter can keep you from going crazy.

Three hours later I take the podium to deliver my second speech as a candidate for the presidency. The speech goes over well however when it is time for the reporters to ask questions the only topic they want to talk about is the reason Glenn had to resign.

I explain that I will not answer any questions about my colleague and friend Senator Worthington and after several more question they move on to another topic.

During the question and answer period one reporter ask a question Walter and his team had prepared me for but I wasn't prepared for the manner in which it was asked.

His question is "How does it feel to be the replacement?"

The word "Replacement" caught me somewhat off guard. We had expected to have to deal with the fact that I took over for Glenn but I didn't expect this direct a question.

I answered with a simple "I plan to do the job asked of me." I didn't bother to address the replacement issue but the damage was done. The next day several news columns featured the words "The Replacement" in the story.

Of course this was not missed by my opponent Congressman Adam Dalwin who for the rest of the campaign never actually said the words himself but somehow the words managed to come out of his supporter's mouths every chance they got. This was going to be a very long primary with me fighting the "Replacement" tag for a while.

For the next two months I had to deal with the replacement issue while trying to focus on the real issues at hand. Sometimes I felt like giving up because no matter how hard I tried to focus on the issues the replacement tag loomed large over me.

In every city I stop to make a speech or shake hands there are signs are everywhere that say "America doesn't need a replacement we need the real thing."

It is very disheartening to see the signs day after day but we keep going and little by little our persistence begins to pay off. By July of that year I am almost even with my opponent.

The most perplexing thing about running for the presidency is the hate mail that I receive. Most of the time my staff keeps it from me but from time to time some of it will get through for me to read.

The first hate letter I received was from my home state of Mississippi. It simply said "There is no way a nigger should be running this nation. If I had my way all you niggers and any white man who helped you would be rounded up, put in a line up and shot in the head."

Of course there was no signature and I didn't expect one. It really didn't bother me because this is the type of letter I expected when I agreed to run for the office. I knew there were some who would disagree with my running simply because of my race. However the second letter I got floored me.

This one came from a very angry young black man. In his view I was little more than a sell out. His letter though intelligently written was full of his hostility toward me. It read like this.

> Mr. (dumb ass) Wright
>
> I hope you know that you are only being used as a pawn. I thought you were an intelligent man but I guess I am wrong. Just because you got a little white girl out of the Middle East does not mean you will be President. You have deluded yourself into thinking that because you have an education, dress white, talk and act white they will accept you. I have four words for you. "You're a damned fool."
>
> I have listened to your campaign rhetoric. I've heard your views on the economy, world diplomacy and the ecosystem but nowhere in any of your speeches have you said anything about what you are planning on doing for your people. You do remember them don't you? They are

the people who are suffering and dying in the hood every day. As far as I'm concerned you are a big sellout. You will lose the election and in another year nobody will even remember your name.

Marcus Davidson
A real black man

I wanted to write this person a letter and explain to him how wrong he was. Better still I wanted to go see Mr. Davidson in person and sit down and talk with him but Walter, Glenora and everyone in my staff advised me against it.

After reading that letter I was depressed for a few days. The campaign trail was harder than I thought. I missed my family, I hated the lonely hotel rooms and the hate mail and "Replacement" signs weren't making me feel any better.

That's when Glenora and Walter came to see me. Both of them were worried that I was thinking about dropping out of the race so they brought me something I needed to see.

It was a scrap book of their races for re-election. Walter showed me his first. I didn't know he had been in the primary race fifteen years ago. He told me no one really remembered because he had dropped out of the race after six months when he realized he had no chance of winning. He pulled one letter from his scrap book and handed it to me.

Dear Asshole

"Why are you trying to ruin the party's chances for winning in November? All you're doing is dividing the vote so that Senator Paulson won't get the support he needs. You are a real dumb ass. If you really cared for the party like you say you do you would drop out right now. You have absolutely no chance of winning the nomination especially with your voting record. I have never seen a politician vote for more ridiculous bills than you have. It's assholes like you who are weakening this great nation. If I were close to you right now I would put a bullet in your head. Listen shit head

drop out of the race for the good of the party and you own
dignity."

Of course it wasn't signed. I handed it back to Walter and he
looked at me.

"Andre no matter what you do somebody is going to be offended,
hurt or hell just be mad at you because today is Wednesday. If you
think you can lead this country and if you want to do some good stay
in the race. I believe you are the best candidate for the job. I have
always believed that from day one."

Glenora is next. She hands me a piece of paper that is old and
yellow then looks at me.

"Andre this is why I became a tough politician. I was bound and
determined that people like this were not going to stop me from
representing my state and my country as best as I could."

I opened the letter and right from the beginning this letter was a
shock and got right to the point.

"To the uppity black woman"

Why are you and others like you always messing things
up for the rest of us? Just because you got a little education
doesn't mean you should try and change things in Alabama.
Some of us like it the way it is and you are messing things
up. My husband lost his job two weeks ago. They said it was
because they didn't have any work but I know he was fired
because he told somebody at work he was going to vote for
you. Now no one will hire him all because you had to run
and make him think he was better than he is. You ain't no
better than any of us who wash their clothes and cook their
meals. You should have a job like we have and a family to
support then maybe you would understand what it is to be
truly black in Alabama. Do us all a favor and drop out before
all of us lose our jobs and houses.

Willa Mae Jenkins

I fold the paper up and shake my head. "How can people believe these types of things. Why can't she and Mr. Davidson understand that we were doing this for the benefit of our people? This is the type of thing that makes me want to rethink the whole campaign."

"Andre this country needs someone with strong character to lead it. I have known you for half of your life and I know where you come from. Your mother, Ole Pop and Jesse raised a fine young man with integrity and a belief in God. This nation needs you but you have to be willing to go through the fire to serve as its president. I know you have the will but you have to make up your mind if this is really what you want and commit to it one hundred percent then pray over it and whatever your decision is stick to it."

For the first time since I've known her Glenora leaned forward and kissed me on the forehead like mom does. I can see in her eyes that she wants me to continue but I can also see in her eyes that it has to be my decision.

Before they leave Walter walks over to me. "Without order, anarchy is the only thing that America has left. I believe you represent the order America needs to remain the great country it is. That letter you have that has made you so depressed represents Anarchy. Which one would you prefer run the country, order or anarchy?

I thought about what they told me then decided to call Ole Pop and talk to him but when Nessa answered she told me that Ole Pop had been sick for the last couple of days.

"What's wrong with him?"

"We don't know yet."

"Has he been to the doctor?"

"He's had two visits and they've run several tests on him. The doctors are waiting on the results"

"Why didn't you call and tell me? I would have flown home."

"He knew you would and that's why he told me not to tell you. He said you had work to do and now was not the time for you to be distracted. Then he made mom, Jesse and I promise we wouldn't tell you about it."

"I'll be home tomorrow."

"Andre don't come yet. Wait until we find out what's wrong. If you come now he'll think he's a burden on you. You know how he is. I will let you know when I find out something."

"I want to know as soon as you know."

"How are you doing baby?"

"I'm tired and miss you and Andre Jr. and I want to come home. Plus I just got another hate letter."

"Well you knew going into this that there would be hate mail from some white people."

"This letter didn't come from a white person."

"Really? Read it to me."

I read the whole letter before balling it up and throwing it on the bed.

"I feel like everyone is unhappy with me. It seems to me like this letter sums up what some of my own people thought of me. Some of my own people are mad at me because they think I'm a sellout and some whites are mad at me simply because I'm black. This is really becoming too much for me to handle."

Nessa was silent for a minute. Then she asked this question. "Andre do you really want this job? If so then do it like I know my Andre can do it. If not then come home to me."

"I don't know if I want the job."

"If you are not sure come home to me."

"But what about the people who have been working their butts off on my behalf?"

"They will understand and that's not why you're still there. Andre tell me why you are still there."

I had to stop and think for a moment. "There are so many difficulties in this campaign but I enjoy helping people and I really think I can make a difference."

"Then do that and stop worrying about what other people think."

"Now I know why I married you. You're a very intelligent woman but you can be kinda stubborn at times."

"Andre Wright if I had you here I would punch you in the chest."

"Well you're not here so I can say what I want to say."

"You have to come home sometimes."

"As soon as I can. I miss my Nessa."

"I miss you to honey."

I hang up the phone and get ready for bed. Tomorrow is another day and I'm going to be ready for what ever it brings.

The next day we fly to Indiana and I visit one of the orphanages there. I kiss a lot of babies and talk to several children and this one particular twelve year old child wouldn't let go of my hand so I held her hand for the whole tour.

As I was getting ready to leave she leaned up, kissed me on the cheek then whispered. "Every since I found out you were running for president you have inspired me to do better. I have raised my grades from a D to a B average and I am going to go to college. Thank you for showing me that a Black person can succeed in life."

That little speech was all I needed to move on with my campaign. That little spark pushed me on. She told me I inspired her when she was the one who pushed me on. Now I was sure I would finish this race.

Chapter 33

With a renewed purpose I entered the last stretch before the democratic convention and begin to pull closer and closer to my opponent Congressman Dalwin. It is at this point his camp told the news media they had asked for a debate but I refused to debate with them. That was a lie but the media didn't know that.

The next day in the papers and on every news program was the press release from my opponent and questions about my willingness to debate him.

My committee fired back that I had never been invited to debate Congressman Dalwin. But now that I have received his invitation whenever the good Congressman was ready I would be glad to debate the issues with him.

A neutral site was picked and our team did a great job of preparing me. The debate was watched by most of the country. He questioned my softness on defense of the country but I handled his attack then launched my own attack on his economic policy and his stand on oil prices.

The next day the majority of news services declared me the winner. By the end of the week I was even with my opponent in the polls. That's when the "replacement" ads were again saturating the airways.

But my opponent underestimated the country's consciousness. The country wasn't worried about my being a replacement they were worried about the economy and high gas prices.

We began running commercials all around the country. One of those commercials featured a young college student talking to the camera.

"Hi my name is Bill Stevens and my parents and a lot of student loans are paying my way through college. It's a struggle for them with the economy being the way it is. I'm going to vote for the first time and I want Washington to know that I don't care about replacements. I care about the economy and high gas prices. Senator Wright talks about the issues and he has a plan that I think will work. That's what I want to hear. That's someone I can vote for."

A month later the primaries began. The commercials we ran worked. America responded by giving me the first eight states. Next was Kentucky and Ohio which I lost by a slim margin. However I picked up the next three states and in the end received enough votes to win the nomination. I am now headed for the democratic convention as the presidential candidate.

In two weeks the convention will be held in California. I will give my speech there and then our party will prepare to carry our message and campaign for the presidency to the nation.

Senator David Frosh from Michigan is the candidate for the other party. He is going to be a formidable opponent but I am ready to make my run for the presidency. At least I think I am. I have no idea what is around the corner waiting on me.

The last night of the convention I walked to the podium to make my acceptance speech. There are more cameras and news media here than I have seen in one place since I have been campaigning.

Nessa is sitting to my right looking beautiful as ever eight months into her pregnancy. I told her before we left the hotel that she didn't have to come if she didn't feel up to it.

She kissed me and said, "You are about to begin your most important journey and I will be there to support you because I love you. Now go and get prepared to give the best speech of your life."

I step to the podium and wait for the applause to die down. I didn't expect this kind of positive reaction. I don't know what I expected but I didn't expect the majority of the people at the convention to be standing, cheering and clapping for me. I cleared my throat and began.

"Ladies and Gentleman I would like to thank you for the opportunity to seek the job of representing this great country. This country was built on the hard work and sacrifice of so many of our ancestors. These people were hard working honest people who took what they had and made it work. We need to go back to that spirit if we are to raise our economy to the next level. Together we can change the course of our economy and come up with alternative ways to supplement our fuel cost."

For the next forty minutes I outline our party's plan to make the economy whole again, help lower the fuel prices and move the country back to the forefront of technology. After I finish I step back, Nessa stands up and takes my hand. We wave and stand there for a few more pictures then leave the podium.

There are several reporters waiting for us at the bottom of the steps but we're ushered through the crowd without answering any of the questions until I hear one I can't resist answering.

A reporter from the Chicago Sun Times asks "Senator Wright how long before your new baby is born and what is the sex of the child?"

I slow down and turn in the direction of the question.

"I'm not qualified to answer that question. Running for president is easy. Carrying a baby is too hard for me so the expert should answer that question."

Everyone around us laughs at that response and the reporter repeats the question to Nessa. All the cameras focus in on Nessa and she gives them that room lighting one hundred watt smile that stole my heart.

"We're due to have our baby next month around the tenth and she is a baby girl."

Seizing the moment the reporter asks one last question.

"Will Senator Wright be changing his share of diapers if he wins the presidency?"

Nessa smiles once again and says "He'd better." Then our staff and secret service agents whisk us off to the hotel.

The next day the media focuses in on my speech and analyzes it to the point of boredom. Then somewhere in the middle of the analysis the media lightens the mood by showing the clips of the questions about the baby and Nessa's answer to the question about me changing diapers and suddenly Nessa is a hit.

Several days later she is invited on two national talk shows and our committee sits and helps Nessa prepare for her interviews. Since she is a teacher her whole focus is on education and during the interviews she holds her own.

Nessa is a truly intelligent, warm, gracious and engaging person and the camera picks that up easily. She also has that hundred watt smile that lights up any place she happens to be in and the camera picks that up as well.

By the end of the month she has appeared on several talk shows and one of the country's biggest fashion magazines has asked her to model maternity clothes for them.

She discusses it with me and decides to do it. The issue comes out the next month and she is absolutely beautiful. The pictures are taken with her and Andre Jr.

And the caption reads, "While her husband seeks to run the nation. She runs the family."

As soon as the first issue hits the stands Glenora buys one and calls me.

"I think we have a superstar on our hands. Vanessa looks absolutely gorgeous. The nation has fallen in love with your wife Andre."

"Yeah if the election were held today both Senator Frosh and I would lose to Nessa."

"Is she there?"

"Yes she is. Hold on a second."

"I walk into the bedroom of our suite where Nessa is lying down and hand her the phone. "It's Glenora."

Nessa takes the phone and I walk back into the living room to work on my next speech. About ten minutes after I begin working Nessa comes into the room with a strange look on her face.

"Andre mom wants to talk to you." She hands me the phone then sits on the arm of my chair.

"Hello."

"Andre Ole Pop has been diagnosed with colon cancer. He's been rushed to the hospital and the doctors don't think he has much time left."

I sit there in stunned silence. Not Ole Pop. Not the man who could pick up a car, not the old man who changed a hard headed teenager into an intelligent young man. He's not supposed to die. He's supposed to live forever.

I don't realize that I am not saying anything I'm just holding the phone while tears run down my cheeks until Nessa hugs me.

"Honey mom is still on the phone."

"Mom Nessa and I will be there in the morning."

"Andre, Nessa is due any time now do you think it's wise that she fly with you?"

"She was about to fly to Mississippi tomorrow anyway to stay with you until the baby is born."

"Okay we'll be waiting on you."

I make a few phone calls and my staff begins canceling some of my speaking engagements then Nessa and I are driven to the airport and flown to Mississippi.

We arrive at five in the morning and are at the hospital by six. When I walk into the room Jesse is sitting by the bed. He looks somehow older than he ever has. He sees me and tries to get up but his arthritic knees have gotten worse.

I motion for him to remain seated then walk over and hug him.

"How you doing Jesse?"

"Fair to middlin nephew, fair to middlin."

I look over at Ole Pop who has his eyes closed. I can't believe this man in the bed in front of me is Ole Pop. This man looks so old and tired and much thinner than the man I knew.

I have only been away from him two months. There is no way he could fall this far this fast. He opens his eyes and looks at me. I try not to look too hurt as I approach his bed but the look in his eyes tells me that he can still see into my soul.

"How you doing old man?"

"Son don't grieve for me. I have lived a long life and now it's time for me to go to the father."

"Don't talk like that old man you have a lot of time left."

"Son I tried to teach you as much as I knew and one of the things I taught you was to be realistic. I know God is in the miracle business but if it's not to be then I am ready to go. I can go now, knowing that you can take care of yourself. I can go knowing that I wasn't perfect and I'm not worthy but God loves me anyway. I am ready for what ever comes my way and I charge you with taking what you know and passing it on to the next generation of troubled youth. Don't forget where you came from and never doubt where you're headed. Keep your eyes on the Lord where your strength comes from and keep the legacy you've been given strong. I'm counting on you to make a difference."

Two days later Ole Pop passed away. We had his funeral at Mount Zion and the church was so full of people. Some of them didn't even make it inside the church but they stayed anyway.

It is hard to look at Ole Pop in that casket. So many things ran through my mind throughout the service. This man took me from a path that would have led to my death and put me on a path that may very well lead to the top job in the free world.

I tried not to let the tears fall but a few escape then I hear Ole Pop's voice in my head.

"Son what are you crying about? If I had God in my heart and he loves me and Jesus died for me then I am in a better place than you are right now. I am with the father. And if I didn't have God in my heart then I went to that other place and you can't help me so what are you crying for? Keep the good memories of me and let the rest go."

Suddenly I no longer felt like crying all I could think of was Ole Pop and Jesse sitting out on the porch singing the blues. What was that song they sung the first time I remember them singing? Oh yeah it was the apple wine blues.

I can almost see Ole Pop and Jesse on the porch singing the blues and cracking jokes and it is a good memory. For the rest of the service I smile because I can hear them singing

"Apple wine, apple wine Let's get drunk off this good ole apple wine. Apple wine apple wine another drink and everything will be fine."

Two days after the funeral I had to leave. It was the hardest thing I ever had to do. For some reason I felt if I stayed there I could keep Ole Pop's spirit alive. But if I left I would lose him forever.

The day I was to head back on the campaign trail Jesse walked into my room. He too was suffering the effects of old age. He walked real slow with his cane but his eyes were still just as intense and his brain was still sharp.

"Andre I want you to know that Buford and I couldn't have asked for a better nephew. I am proud of you and I know you will do great things. Go out there and give it all you got then go on to become the best president you can be."

We hug again and I head back for the SUV that will take me to the airport.

I didn't get the chance to campaign long before mom called and told me Nessa was in labor. I flew back to Mississippi for the birth of my baby girl. We named her Anna Marie. Her first name is Nessa's mother's middle name and her second name is my mother's middle name.

She is the most precious thing in the world. She has that same beautiful smile her mother has and when I held her for the first time I knew why I have to do the best job I can to secure a good future for our children.

After Nessa, mom and I get through holding her we hand her to Jesse. He smiles down at her and it almost looks like she wants to talk to him.

"Nessa you did good again. She is just perfect. Buford would have loved her with her little chubby cheeks."

"Hey old man you still didn't give me any credit."

"Nephew I done told you before you ain't got nothin tuh do wit this. All you can do is pay the bills. Nessa is he still paying the bills?"

"Yes Jesse he's still doing his job."

"Dat's good nephew. Keep doing your job. Your family, community and Nation need you."

I leave Nessa in the capable hands of Mom and Jesse and go back to the campaign trail but I call home every day to talk to Nessa and find out what I've missed. My family means the world to me. I will find out a little later just how much they mean.

Chapter 34

It's been two months since Ole Pop passed on and the sadness still lingers in my heart. I'm so busy with the campaign that I don't have time to really dwell on it. But at the end of the day during my quiet time I will think about him and how much I miss our conversation. Through every conversation we've had he always managed to leave me with something to think about.

With one month left before Election Day we are concentrating on the states in which my opponent has a strong hold. There doesn't seem to be enough hours in a day to make all the speeches and shake the hands of as many people as possible.

Right now the polls are too close to call and we're into the last minute push. I am living on four hours sleep a day. I didn't realize how tiring running for the Presidency would be. Days are filled with speeches, interviews and hand shaking. Nights are air travel, hotels, speech writing and learning and strategy sessions for the next city.

I am exhausted but I have to keep going. It's not very long till the end. As Ole Pop used to say, "How will you know what the end is going to be if you don't make it there?"

The end is only one month away so I journey on. My next stop is Indianapolis. According to the poles Indianapolis has thirty percent undecided voters. Hopefully several speeches in the state will swing more of the undecided votes in my favor.

It's bright and early in the morning in Ohio. I am just beginning a hand shaking and speech making session when Glenora walks over to me and while smiling says, "Andre when this is over you need to call Vanessa."

I finish my speech and hurriedly shake a few hands before making my way to the car to call Nessa.

"Hey honey I miss you."

"Andre the children and I are headed to Mississippi. You need to get there as soon as possible."

"What's wrong?"

"Andre, Uncle Jesse died this morning."

Suddenly I feel as if someone is holding their hand over my mouth and nose. I can't seem to get enough air to fill my lungs. Ole Pop is gone and now Jesse is to.

"What happened?"

"Mom said she went into his room to wake him up this morning and he wasn't breathing. She called the paramedics and when they got there they did all they could to revive him but it didn't work."

"I'll be home as quickly as I can."

It takes several phone calls and some very serious schedule juggling but Glenora and I are on the plane two hours after Nessa's phone call.

I arrive at the farm, pick up Nessa and mom leaving the children with Glenora and head to the funeral home to make the arrangements.

Three days later we have Jesse's funeral and a generation of my family ended with his passing. Now it's my turn to do my best to leave Ole Pop and Jesse's legacy as good and righteous as it is now.

Instead of being sad I go back on the campaign trail with a renewed sense of purpose. I am no longer tired and I am ready to finish taking our party's platform to the people of America. Win or lose someone is going to be affected by me and I will try to make sure it is in a positive way.

Two days later I'm back on the campaign trail. My opponent is smart enough to realize that the "Replacement" tactic won't work so it is forgotten. Instead he concentrates on my war record and the perceived notion that I'm soft on defense.

Of course we kept on the same theme we've used since I started this campaign. We hammered at the economy and the high price of living and we keep the message simple. "Together we can make it happen."

Going into the heart of the campaign our message seems to be reaching the people but we know that soon it will be time for the debates and we've seen Senator Frosh in action. He is very good at attacking his opponent's weaknesses. I am going to have to be prepared for a fight.

Two weeks before our first debate my juvenile record somehow manages to make the news. The report made it seem like I was a major dope pusher. My opponent went on the record as being totally against this new tactic which kept his hands clean. He obviously thought this would cause me to lose concentration but he was wrong.

My staff had already been briefed about my juvenile record and with the help of Walter and Glenora we formulated a plan we thought would work and now it is time to put that plan into action.

The first thing we did was get me booked on an evening news show for an interview about my past. During that interview I told the complete truth about my juvenile record and the circumstances surrounding it.

I didn't try to say I was a victim of the system. I didn't try to say I was the victim because my father wasn't around. I took full responsibility for my action and explained how much it hurt my mother and what she did to straighten me out.

Then I told the commentator about two old men who changed me from being a know it all teenager with a chip on my shoulder to a disciplined man. They also taught me what responsibility is and why I needed the drive and determination to do any job I took the correct way.

I ended the interview by looking directly into the camera and saying.

"If you don't choose to vote for me because of my juvenile record that's fine I can understand your concerns. I will still work as hard as I can for this nation and what it stands for no matter what office I hold. Lastly I will use a famous quote and bible verse. "When I was a child, I spoke as a child, I understood as a child, I thought as a child; but when I became a man, I put away childish things." Thank you.

The next day the media had their chance to dissect the interview and their consensus was I shouldn't have quoted the bible verse at the end. They thought it might hurt me more than it helped me. Again they were wrong.

In all the interviews done by the media with the average person on the street, all those who were interviewed agreed with what I was saying. One lady when asked if she thought I should have quoted the bible answered, "If he has nerve enough to let the world know he not only loves the Lord but also reads the bible even though it is going to cause him some problems with none church goers then he has nerve enough to lead this country. We need more men to step up and tell the world about God."

Of course I suffered the inevitable backlash from the citizens who had a problem with me quoting the bible and applying for the highest office the land.

At my next rally the media was ready with their questions about religion and I answered the questions with this statement.

"I believe in God and I do go to church and if that is a problem for some I am sorry. But my religion does not make me blind to the fact that as President I will be charged with serving the people and that means all the people. With the economy the way it is I think the American people have more to deal with than my religion. Let's get the economy on the right track. It's going to take the cooperation of all Americans to get this economy going in the right direction again."

After that interview the focus is put back on the economy where it belongs. In the coming weeks I keep hammering home the economy and the high cost of living and my message is beginning to reach the people. They are as tired as I am of gas prices, food prices, housing prices and the extra cost of trying to run a household and they are ready for someone to do something about it.

My next stop is Kentucky where I have two full days of speech making and hand shaking. It is here where I finally met Carl Perry, my father.

I had just finished my last speech for the day in Lexington Kentucky and I was about to get into a car and head for the airport when one of the local reporters shouted, "Senator Wright is it true that Carl Perry is your father?"

I stopped and looked at the reporter, "It is true that he is my blood father but my real father, the man who raised me is Joseph Wright."

"Have you ever met your father?"

"No I haven't."

I decide not to answer any other questions about Carl Perry. A secret service agent shuts the door after I get in the car. Outside several reporters are still shouting question about me and my relationship with my blood father.

The next day the papers are full of questions about Carl Perry. All of them want to know who he is and what he does and why he left mom and I. Glenora tells me she thinks it's an attempt at dirty tactics by my opponent. It really doesn't matter to me. He is not the one running for president.

I make two speeches in Florida then head for the airport. Ten minutes after I get on the plane Glenora walks down the aisle and sits down next to me.

"Andre someone called our headquarters in Mississippi claiming to be Carl Perry. Now do you believe me about the dirty tactics? This is too much of a coincidence not to have been arranged."

"What did he say?"

"He said he would like to talk to you."

"It's probably just another crank caller."

"I thought so too but he said tell you to ask your mother about a gold necklace with the words "Sarah Ann" on it."

I pull out my phone and call mom. "Mom do you own a necklace with your name on it?" Mom is silent for a minute before answering. "Carl Perry gave me a necklace when we first started dating with "Sarah Ann" on it. I threw it away after he left. Why do you ask?"

"Because someone called our headquarters in Mississippi and told me to ask you about the necklace. How many people knew about the necklace?"

"Just me, Ole Pop, and Jesse."

"Then it has to be him."

"Why would he call you now?"

"I don't know but when I get there next week I'm going to talk to him and find out what he wants."

I ask Glenora to contact the man and find out what he wants. One of the agents assigned to guard me changes that plan. He tells Glenora he will contact the man after they have checked him out.

Later that evening he verifies the man is indeed Carl Perry but advises me not to have the meeting. "Why shouldn't I have this meeting?"

"I have found that long lost relatives who contact a person running for office usually want something or have been paid to do something to hurt the campaign. I just don't think it is a wise idea to contact him."

"You may be right but I have to talk to this man face to face if I am to move on. Besides if I turn him down and the media finds out they will report that I didn't want to see my own father so the meeting is going to happen. However I will let you set the time and place."

Two days later, on Ole Pop and Jesse's farm I meet my blood father for the first time. It is strange standing in front of someone who brought you into the world but you have never seen.

I invite him into the living room. Mom has made some coffee and sandwiches. We walk into the room and I have a seat in Ole Pop's chair. I motion for him to sit down.

"Have a seat."

There are several secret service agents in the room and I notice he looks a little apprehensive about being here with me. That is not the only thing I notice about him. He's a very thin man of average height with a slight stoop in his stance which makes him look even shorter. He is a lot lighter than me and the little hair he has left is very curly.

I didn't resemble him at all. I guess Jesse was right when he said "If you feed a child long enough he'll start to look like you." My body and facial features looked more like Joseph Wright than this man.

Mr. Perry refuses the seat I offer him. "I'm not going to be here very long. I just wanted to see you up close. Sarah did a good job in raising you. I am sorry for running out on you. I was young and stupid."

"I don't hold . . ."

"Let me finish please before I run out of nerve to say this." I sit back in my chair and listen.

"I know you have wondered why I left you and Sarah but I have no explanation. All I can tell you is in my youth I did some very selfish things. I have no excuse just regrets. I see that you have a good strong family that loves you and supports you. That is good to know because I am experiencing the other side of that. I have no one to take care of or to take care of me. It is a lonely existence. Allow me to give you a piece of advice even though I don't deserve to. Always keep your family close they are the only people who can heal any hurt you may encounter in your life. Don't end up like me, a lonely old man with no one to turn to. If you have any anger in your heart for me let it go it will not help you run this country. And don't feel sorry for me. This is my bed, I made it and I will have to sleep in it. Thank you for taking the time to see me and good luck running the country."

With that he turns and heads for the door. I tried to talk him into staying so we could talk but he refused the invitation. He walked out the door and I have never heard from him again. I did find out later that he turned down several large offers for interviews and he even filled the air with buckshot from his shotgun when several reporters wouldn't take no for an answer.

He really didn't have to come and see me but he had a message he wanted me to hear and it was something I needed to continue on in this campaign. So I continue on this journey.

Chapter 35

When I first arrived in Washington Glenora gave me some advice. She said. "Now that you're here you're going to make enemies. The trick is not to avoid making enemies but to avoid making your friends so mad they won't help you when your enemies surround you."

Dick Hilgan either didn't understand that rule or didn't care. Now however he is in need of a friend but there is no one to help him and his enemies are about to send him away for a very long time.

Two months into my campaign Dick's trial starts and it is a very short trial. The prosecution has a solid case and his attorney is unsuccessful in trying to keep any of the evidence against him from being admitted. Dick has run out of favors and his most trusted friends have turned their back on him.

In the end he is sentenced to ten years in the federal pen for conspiracy and the prison he is sent to isn't one of those country club prisons. He's sent to the United States Penitentiary in Leavenworth Kansas.

Dick isn't a real criminal and with all the real killers and thugs as well as ex-druggies and armed robbers in the federal pen his jail time should have been very unpleasant. But Dick has a lot of money at his disposal and he's good at reading and manipulating people.

He wasn't in prison a week before he knew which guards could be paid to look the other way. In a month's time and after two visits from his attorney Dick had several guards on his payroll. By the end of the second month he became the inmate other prisoners came to if they needed money or cell phones or cigarettes.

Being able to get this illegal property pass the guards brought Dick a lot of protection in the pen so he didn't have to worry about anything bad happening to him. The cell phones allowed him to make phone calls and conduct his business as if he were a free man.

Two months after Dick enters Leavenworth Drake Orton stops by to see him. Dick called Drake because he needed someone he could trust to do him a very special favor. Actually Dick needed someone who was dumb enough or desperate enough to take the fall if anyone found out about the plan.

The only person who hated me more than Senator Hilgan was Drake Orton. He blamed me for everything that had happened to him in the last year. What he didn't know was his troubles were just now beginning.

In Mississippi word had gotten around that Councilman Orton was the reason the FBI had taken Senator Hilgan into custody the first time. The other council members knew about Orton's obsession over trying to get me out of the council. They also knew he was the one who convinced Senator Hilgan to use Jarrett Singler to frame me.

After the FBI took Senator Hilgan into custody Drake's political backers all walked away from him. They were no longer willing to risk their position to help him. However he still had very powerful friends so he enjoyed a very profitable business.

His company still got most of the government contracts for highway improvement or renovations and sometimes small building projects in the down town area so he wasn't in very bad shape or so it seemed.

Unfortunately for Drake he had a problem. He was an obsessive gambler. His gambling addiction was so strong it caused him to lose his wife and family and without the help of his powerful friends he would have lost his business sooner than he did.

Drake would sometimes spend days in Tunica Mississippi gambling and losing as much as eighty to ninety thousand dollars in one weekend. Then he would come home and do some very creative bookkeeping to hide the lost.

Several times while he was still in the council he got dangerously close to losing all he had. Each time he gambled his money away his friends would bail his company out putting him deeper into their debt which is how he got himself caught up in the city contracts scam.

After his friends on the council abandoned him he still knew enough inside dirt to keep his powerful friends from abandoning him. Plus the fact his company was still useful in handling different projects that were still being illegally handed to construction companies for kickbacks.

However his addiction eventually led his financial supporters to view him as a huge liability. Suddenly he was no longer needed or wanted by his powerful friends and with his gambling addiction it wasn't long before his business was in trouble again.

Two years after he left the council his run was at an end. He found out this out after he lost two hundred thousand at the poker tables in Tunica. When he tried to get a loan to help his business none of his friends would return his phone calls. The last person he called was David Hawkins.

David Hawkins was the owner of the biggest construction company in the southeast and as ruthless as they come. His company sometimes did work as far away as Japan. He was only pennies shy of being a billionaire. He got his money by playing politics but on a scale Drake couldn't even imagine.

He and Senator Hilgan were best friends and he was not happy when Senator Hilgan was caught by the FBI. Not because they were friends but because he lost a very powerful ally in the national senate. People like Senator Hilgan were hard to come by and losing him meant losing money.

Drake went to David simply because he knew confidential information about David's business that could possibly get him sent to jail. However this time David didn't return his calls.

Finally one day after receiving notice of foreclosure on his business Drake drank himself into some courage and as a last resort he went to David Hawkins house to see if he would give him a loan.

Drake pulled up to the gates of David's huge estate and pressed the button. The butler answered.

"Can I help you?"

"I need to see Mr. Hawkins."

"May I ask who this is?"

"It's Drake Orton." A few seconds go by before the butler comes back. "I'm sorry sir but Mr. Hawkins isn't available right now."

Drake is at the end of his rope. He needs help so his whiskey fueled courage.

"You tell David that he had better talk to me or I will talk to the FBI."

Minutes later the large wrought iron gates swing open and Drake drives up the highway to the house.

After the butler leads Drake into David's study he sits there and waits for thirty minutes. He's about to get up and tell the butler to go find David when the doors open and David walks in with two very large bodyguards.

David closes the doors behind them and without saying a word they all quickly cross the distance between them and Drake. The two body guards pull Drake up by the shoulders and hold him while David drives a hard left into his stomach.

David's bodyguards strip Drake down to his boxers. They take off everything including his watch and wallet. Now David is satisfied Drake is not wearing a wire and with his guards still holding Drake, David slams another right into his gut then grabs him by the chin and raises his head.

"The only reason you are living right now is because I don't know who knows you are here. But if you ever threaten me or even come by this neighborhood again I will have you killed and dumped into the Mississippi river."

David motions to his guards and they drag him out to his car and throw him on the ground beside it then drop his clothes beside him. It takes a few minutes for him to get in his car and when he does he speeds out of David's yard almost running into the gate as he leaves.

David has his bodyguards follow Drake for the next few weeks to make sure he isn't talking to anyone. If he had talked they had orders to kill him. However Drake got the message and kept his mouth shut.

Shortly after that visit Drake lost his business got into some trouble with the law for writing bad checks and was placed on probation for five years. He's just inches away from going to jail or dying but he still can't stop gambling.

Now Drake is just desperate enough to do whatever Dick needs him to do. However Drake is in such bad shape Dick has to have his attorney wire him some money. It has been a long fall for Drake Orton and he will do anything to get back to the top.

When Drake gets to Kansas he is a far cry from the man who ran the council. The man who ran the council was a slender man with a head full of hair, white teeth and a winning smile fit for a popular politician. Now Drake has a receding hairline, a few teeth are missing and he has put on eighty pounds.

Since the lost of his job and friends he has drifted all over the south looking for the quick score that will allow him to get back his wealth and possibly put him back into politics. He has a score to settle with me and in his mind the only way he can settle it is to get back into politics. But hard times seem to follow him around.

He's worked as a carpenter, a brick layer, a construction sight supervisor and the manager of an industrial waste management company. He lost all those well paying jobs because of his addiction to gambling.

Gambling is what leads him back to Tunica and large losses of money. The losses cause him to borrow from less than reputable money lenders followed by the inability to pay. Now he's on the run and trying to make enough money to pay his lenders back so he won't mysteriously disappear.

Drake walks into the visitors room, signs the visitor's role then sits down and picks up the phone. Dick is sitting on the other side of the glass with a phone to his ear.

"How's it going Dick?"

"How the hell do you think it's going in here?"

"You are the last person I would have thought would end up in a place like this."

"I don't have time for the bullshit. I need you to do me a favor. Is the "Watering hole" still open?

"Yeah what about it?"

"Go see my lawyer tomorrow. He will tell you what I need."

"Alright is that all you wanted?"

"Yeah."

Dick hangs up the phone, stands up and a guard takes him back to his cell.

Drake walks out of the visitor's room wondering what Dick
wants him to do. If he's lucky he might have a job for him and if he's
really lucky it might be something political.

The next day Drake walks into the lawyer's office and sits down.
Dick's lawyer gives him a brand new cell phone.

"What's this for?"

"Dick said to take this cell phone don't use it unless you are
talking to him."

"What does he want with me?"

"I don't know but I'm supposed to tell you that when the time
comes what you need will be at the watering hole."

Dick's lawyer gives Drake five thousand dollars and a plane ticket
back to Tennessee.

"Dick told me to tell you not to gamble his money away. This
money is to pay your personal expenses. Dick will contact you in a
month or so. Do not get yourself into trouble and stay away from the
casinos."

Drake takes the money, gets in a cab and heads for the airport.
As soon as Drake's plane hits the runway he rents a car, heads to
Tunica Mississippi and gambles the money away.

It is now three weeks before the election and the pace has
increased. During the beginning of the week I shake hands and hug
babies and smile for pictures until I am almost dizzy. However at one
rally I am met with a pleasant surprise.

I give a speech in North Carolina and after the speech there is
another round of hand shaking and posing. In the middle of the
hand shaking a little hand reaches out from the crowd. I shake it
then start to move on when I hear,

"Have you learned to speak Arabic yet Senator Wright?"

I look down and there is Crystal Ashton standing with her
mother. I stoop down and hug her and she smiles.

"I didn't think I would ever see you again. I was happy that you
were coming to this city."

"I am glad to see you Crystal."

I look at her mother. "How are you doing?"

"I am doing fine."

One of my staff touches me on the shoulder. "Senator we need to go now."

"Okay."

I hug Crystal again and head for my car. It is good to see her. She is just one more reason I want to win this election. I want to keep this country safe for our children.

The next day my opponent Senator Frosh gives an intense speech about our country's defense and what is needed to keep the country strong against our enemies. The speech is well written and his delivery is excellent. He did a great job of underlining his point about my weakness on the defense of our country.

As soon as he finished our staff went to work on the speech that would answer his and the next afternoon at a rally in Oregon I gave that speech in which I explained that I believed in diplomacy first but I would not hesitate to defend our country with all the resources available to me.

I delivered the speech with more passion than I had ever delivered on defense. It was full of fire and determination and it came from my heart. While delivering this speech, thoughts of my children and children like little Crystal Ashton filled my head.

I end the speech by saying, "We must keep this country safe for our children's future."

Glenora told me later that it was the best speech I had ever given on my stance on the defense of our nation.

"I think you got the country's attention with that speech."

We finish the week with visits to three key support states. I am so tired I can barely remember what state we're in. It has been a long campaign and I am ready for it to be over. When Sunday comes Nessa and I go to church in Boston then head back to the hotel where I sleep for the rest of the day.

On Monday two weeks before the election we began work on my last speech before the election. Glenora and Walter tell me it has to be the best speech I have ever given. My speech writers work overtime to put everything in the speech our party wants to emphasize. They write it and re-write it until Walter and Glenora are satisfied.

Monday thru Saturday we go through the same campaign routine of shaking hands and smiling for the cameras then Sunday we go to church. After church we head to Tennessee for a rally on Tuesday at Vanderbilt University.

After finishing my speech, taking a few pictures and shaking a few hands we will fly to Mississippi. This is the last week before the election and I will give my last and most important speech in my home state at Ole Miss.

We arrive in Mississippi at three in the afternoon. I've decided that Nessa and I are going to stay at Ole Pop and Jesse's house which is now my house. Mom joins us there and we reminisce about Ole Pop and Jesse and the jokes they had.

At four-thirty I kiss mom on the cheek and head for the hotel so I can began getting ready for the most important speech of my life.

That evening when we sit down at our last strategy session Glenora makes me go over the speech several times while she and the staff made corrections in everything from my inflection to my posture. It is eleven o'clock when my head finally hits the pillow. We have one week to go.

It takes several days of hitchhiking for Drake to get back to his small run down trailer in Paris Tennessee. He's totally out of money and all his utilities have been turned off. He needs money to survive.

He uses Dick's cell phone to call Ken Links. Ken has used Drake on a couple of jobs before. The jobs weren't exactly the legal type but it was good money. Ken answers the phone and tells Drake about a job in Camden, Tennessee.

Two agents sitting in a van two blocks down the street listen to Ken's conversation with Drake. They have been monitoring Ken for the last two weeks making a list of his contacts. Now they have Drake on their list. Drake told Dick to call him on the phone and not use it for anything else. Drake didn't listen.

The next morning Ken picks Drake up and drives to a house out in the woods where Drake meets Adam Lancaster. For the next couple of weeks Drake is paid a thousand dollars a run to make several deliveries to Dayton Ohio.

Each time the SUV is loaded with taped boxes. Drake has no idea what is in the boxes he's carrying and he really doesn't care. Three runs have put three thousand dollars in his pocket. Now he can go back to Tunica and that's all he cares about.

When he gets back from his third run Adam tells Drake he has one last run. This is the last run for the next two weeks. Drake smiles, now he can go and gamble his money away. He loads the SUV, gets in and heads for the interstate. In about seven and a half hours he'll be in Ohio.

As soon as he hits the highway Drake turns on his favorite radio station and opens a can of beer. Then he settles in for the long drive to Dayton. The only thought in his head is getting back to Tunica.

Every so often as Drake heads toward Dayton a couple of DEA agents will fall in behind him and follows him for several miles then pulls off the interstate. They are making sure the tracking device Drake has on him is still working. Drake doesn't know about the device in his traveling bag. It was put there by a very pretty young lady who happened to bump into him while he was gambling several nights ago.

After she bumped into him he invited her for drinks. One thing led to another and they ended up in his room. Drake was hoping to get lucky and it looked like he was about to until he went to the bathroom. When he came back she was gone. He checked his bag but everything was still where he left it so he finished his coffee laid down and went to sleep. The next morning he headed for Dayton.

Drake arrives in at the warehouse in Dayton just after dark and is in the process of unloading the boxes into a van that will move the drugs to another location for distribution. The DEA is going to follow that truck in hopes that it will lead them to the man in charge.

At nine o'clock lights are out in the prison and the guards walk the corridors once a shift sometimes using a flashlight to look into certain inmates cells. Dick uses his cell phone to make a call to Drake.

Drake has just gotten back in the SUV and is pulling out of the parking lot when his phone rings.

"Hello."

"Drake I don't have much time to talk. I want you to take care of a problem you and I have had for the last eight years. I want you to kill Senator Wright. There is no way he's ever going to be the President of the United States."

"You want me to do what! Dick I hate the nigger as much as you do but I ain't no killer."

"Look Drake sometimes you have to make sacrifices to keep this country great."

"I know but can't this be done some other way?"

"You've seen the polls just like I have. He is going to win the election. There is no way the dumb sombitch he's running against can win. Somebody has to kill Senator Wright and that someone is you."

"I don't know Dick I don't think I could kill him even if I wanted to."

"I thought you and I understood what it took to keep America safe. I guess I was wrong about you."

"You aren't wrong I agree with you but killing the man is more than I think I can do."

"You and I both know this country will go to hell in a hand basket if he gets in office."

"Yeah you're right but how am I going to do it. Now that it looks like he might win the election security around him is going to be really tight. There is no way I'm gonna be able to get close enough to him to kill him."

"If you're scared about getting caught don't be. I have the whole thing planned out. I just need someone I can trust to get it done for me."

"I don't know about this."

"When you get the job done I will pay off the debt you owe to Stubbs and Charlie. Those are some pretty bad boys I would hate to think what they will do to you if they find you."

"How did you find out about that?"

"Don't worry about it. Do the job and I'll take care of the rest. He's going to speak at the University of Mississippi. Go to the old watering hole everything you need will be there waiting for you. All you need to do is handle the job. I will call you back in two days and tell you exactly where the things you need are."

Dick hangs up the phone and Drake straightens himself up in the seat. He has a lot to think about on his way back to Tennessee. Killing a man in cold blood is something he doesn't think he can do but Dick is right there is no way Senator Wright is going to be the next President of his country.

At a checkpoint five miles ahead of Drake the DEA is waiting to stop and arrest him. With enough pressure they hope he will turn against the leader of the drug operation. Lead DEA agent Chris Oakland has been listening in on Drake's conversation with a person named Dick.

After hearing the beginning of a conspiracy to shoot a U.S. Senator and possibly the next President of the United States, Chris tells his unit to stand down. They may have stumbled onto something really big.

Drake's truck passes the DEA checkpoint and heads for the interstate. As he passes the checkpoint Chris takes out his cell phone and makes a call to local FBI office.

Special agent Stanley Davidson answers agent Oakland's call. After being briefed about Drake Orton, agent Davidson calls special agent Bobby Todd's office in Washington and explains the situation to him. An hour later there are several unmarked FBI cars following Drake to Tennessee.

Chapter 36

FBI agents Larry Williams and David Hall have taken up residence at the house in Camden, Tennessee. They are waiting for Drake to bring the SUV back.

The house has been cleaned of all evidence of the gun battle. The plan is to convince Drake that the owner left the two agents in charge and told them to tell Drake to keep the SUV until he has to make another run.

Drake arrives in Camden and is surprised as well as suspicious to see two new people working in the house.

"Where is Adam?"

"He has another house in Memphis he has to check on. He told us to tell you to keep the SUV and he will call you. Oh and here's some money. He said that's for doing a good job."

Drake takes the money and counts it. Adam has paid him another thousand dollars. That is enough to get him to Mississippi. He gets back in the SUV and heads for Memphis. Several FBI agents follow him using the tracking device in his bag. They hang back a couple of miles so Drake never spots them.

Just before Drake gets to Memphis he pulls off the interstate, finds a nice hotel and checks in for the night. The clerk gives him his room key, he grabs his bag out of the SUV, opens the door to his room and walks in.

Two FBI agents, one male and one female check into the same hotel asking for the room right beside Drakes. Their excuse for wanting the room is they spent the first night of their honeymoon there.

The clerk smiles and gives them the key to room three seventy one. The agents get their bags, walk into the room and set up their surveillance equipment.

Twenty minutes after ten Drake's phone rings. He rolls over on the bed, picks it up and answers it

"Hello."

"Where are you?"

"Just outside of Memphis. I should be in Oxford by tomorrow afternoon."

"Good. The things you are going to need will be placed in the watering hole tomorrow morning. The vantage point from there is excellent. You can see all over the coliseum. The people that are working for me even saw Senator Wright walking into one of the coach's offices. This is going to be very easy."

"Are you sure I'm not going to get caught?"

"Trust me Drake. No one even knows where the watering hole is. Once you get the job done you'll be home free."

Dick hangs up the phone. "That dumb sombitch ain't got the brains of a hummin bird. That's alright I'm gonna take care of that too."

Dick dials another number and the phone rings several times before someone answers.

"Hello."

"The target will come out of the door just above the red section. It looks like a Janitor's closet but inside the closet behind the brooms and mops is a small door that leads to a small room. Only I and a few other people know about it and have the keys to it. You can kill him there then wait until everybody leaves."

"Gotcha."

"Make it clean. I don't want any witnesses."

Dick closes his phone and lies back on his cot. There is no way anyone can pin this on him. No one is going to believe an inmate pulled off the assassination of a presidential nominee.

The two agents relay what they've just heard to Agent Bobby Todd at Ole Miss. He and several other agents walk around the coliseum until they find the room but they don't open it. They will wait until tomorrow.

I wake up Sunday morning anxious. Tomorrow is going to be the last time I get to talk to the voters. I want to make sure that I cover all the things I want to say. If I lose the election I don't want it to be because I didn't do everything in my power to get my ideas across.

I walk into the sitting area of our hotel room and Andre Jr. is playing in his play pen while Nessa feeds Anna. I stand there for a few minutes watching the family I never thought I would have and realize that it doesn't matter if I win or lose God has blessed me beyond measure

I barely have time to eat breakfast before Glenora is knocking on the door.

"Alright Andre let's go over everything one more time."

"Glenora don't you think we've been over this enough."

"Andre I want you to feel and look as comfortable as you can when you deliver this last speech."

"I will be fine."

"Okay then go over it one more time for me."

"Nessa will you tell this woman to relax?"

"Nope."

"Is that all you have to say?"

"Yep."

"I thought you were on my side."

"Honey Glenora is right. Just go over it one last time to make us happy."

"Slave driver."

"Wuuuuv you."

Glenora has never heard Nessa say that to me and she starts laughing.

"So those are the golden words huh?"

"Don't you start Glenora."

"What, I'm not doing anything."

"Yes you are. You're agitating just like Ole Pop and Jesse would be doing."

Glenora turns her back to me but I can still see her laughing. After a few seconds she manages to look at me with a straight face.

"I don't know what you're talking about. Now let's hear this speech one more time.

I rehearse the speech one last time and Glenora and Nessa both nod their heads in approval after I finish. Then Glenora and I go over the latest poll results.

The polls have me in the lead by a slight margin but no one really knows what tomorrow night will bring. All I know is after tonight all the election work will be over.

At ten o'clock we head to our cars. It's time for me to go home. It's good to go home and get some fortification for the journey ahead. Home is Mount Zion Primitive Baptist church.

When we arrive service has already started. I can hear the Dr. Watts hymn being sung by the congregation. The women in the mother's board are in rare form today. The singing has reached the roof of the church and is now ringing through the surrounding countryside.

After we enter and get seated Deacon Leroy Hall gets down on one knee, places his head in the chair and begins to pray.

"Most holy and wonderful father it is once again we come to you praising you for allowing us to rise this morning. Father we know we are not worthy but your grace is sufficient to cleanse us of our sins. We pray that you continue to let your grace and mercy rain down on us and that you continue to keep us in your loving arms. And Lord I want to pray a special prayer for one of our children who is striving to take on the responsibility of running this great country of ours. Lord, guide him to the path you would have him walk. Keep your spirit in his heart Lord and he will be able to handle what ever his future holds for him. And Lord let him know that we love him and we support him."

While Deacon Hall is on his knees as per usual the other deacons are pushing him on saying things like "Let him know bout it son" and "Say it straight son" and Tell it like it needs to be told." I had forgotten how much I enjoyed my home church's service.

After the prayer the new pastor, reverend Joseph Brooks delivered the sermon. It was a well-delivered sermon about following the purpose the Lord has for you and the consequences of not following God's plan. It was a good service and my spirit felt renewed when we left.

The rest of the day was spent going over the speech and being briefed by the secret service on the rout, time and venue for the meeting with the press. After that I had time to wrestle around on the floor with Andre Jr. then it was time for bed. Tomorrow is the day.

Monday morning finds me trying to relax and get my thoughts together but by eleven o'clock I was ready to do something. I am so anxious I can't keep still.

I decide to go to our old weight room and work out but after finding out the secret service would have to disrupt every one else's routine just to make sure its secure I decide against it.

It's been a long time since I've been back to Ole Miss. I have had great times here. Most of the coaches who worked with me are gone but some of the guys I played football with have moved up into the coaching ranks. I decide to call them rather than disrupt their routine with a visit.

I do however go to see my best friend John "Bubba" Frakes. Of course the arrangements have to be made through the secret service. I am still trying to get use to the fact I can't go anywhere without a prearranged plan. Still it will be nice to see Bubba so I wait until the agents secure everything.

Until I met Bubba Ole Pop was the biggest man I had ever seen but even he wasn't as big as Bubba. Bubba is six foot ten and back in the day he weighed four hundred and twenty pounds.

He was the reason I became an all American linebacker. It took a whole offensive line to stop him once he got going. That gave me room to move through the offensive line and either sack the quarterback, knock the pass down or tackle the running back. He would have gone pro if it hadn't been for his bad knees.

The sign on his door says John Frakes Defensive line coach. The Secret Service enters and checks the room out first then I enter. I hate to visit an old friend with all the Secret Service around me but it can't be helped.

When I walk into his office he's sitting behind his desk with a shirt, tie and coat on looking like someone squeezed him together and put him in a suit. He still had that same smile and surprisingly he still wore his blonde hair in the same style as when we used to room together.

During our college days I used to cut his hair along with several of my team mates and a couple of coaches. Ole Pop taught me how to cut hair my senior year in high school. I made a nice little bit of change that year especially during prom time.

Bubba's hair always had to be high and tight. His father was in the military and that's the way retired Marine Colonel Bob Frakes taught his son to wear his hair. Honor is also something the Colonel taught his son and the lesson stuck. I can't think of too many people who are as honorable as Bubba.

Of course the suit was something different. The only other time I have seen Bubba in a suit was when I got married. We had a heck of a time finding a tuxedo to fit him. I don't think I've ever seen anyone so uncomfortable in a suit.

"How you doing Bubba?"

Bubba stands, extends his hand and says in a very formal voice, "Hello Senator Wright how are you doing?" I shake his hand then shake my head and smile. "Bubba what's with the suit and the formal tone?"

"This is the way you're supposed to dress and talk when you could be addressing the next president of the United States."

"Bubba you are my best friend. We were roomies in college. Besides I may not be the next president and even if I do win the election good friends are hard to come by so let's drop the formalities."

Bubba smiles, walks around his desk and in front the secret service agents wraps his big arms around me, picks me up and gives me one his patented country boy hugs. His bear hug locks my arms in place and squeezes the air out of my lungs.

"How is the baddest man on the planet?"

While trying to breathe I manage to gasp out the words, "I could be better if your big butt would put me down."

Bubba smiles that big ole country smile of his and puts me down. The two secret service agents in the room with us try their best to conceal the fact they want to laugh. I straighten myself out and walk over to a chair beside Bubba's desk and sit down.

"I see you're still as strong as a mule."

"Yeah but at thirty-eight the knees and legs are getting worse by the day. You know I had hip surgery a couple of months ago."

"I didn't know that. How are you doing and how is our team going to do this year?"

We sit and talk for the next hour and I catch up on what has happened to everyone.

While he and I talk over old times the officials of the university are getting the C.M. Smith Coliseum ready for my speech. People are cleaning and setting up chairs and stages.

The sound crew is working on the P.A. and security is reviewing plans to make sure I and every one else on stage are secure. In six hours I will be on that stage making my last pre-election speech.

At noon Dick Hilgan's contact walks up the walkway to the janitor's closet with a small satchel in his hand. He unlocks the door and steps in then shuts it behind him.

After moving two brooms out of the way he locates the small door and opens it. He bends over, walks in then straightens up and turns on the light then suddenly becomes very still.

FBI agents Larry Williams and David Hall are standing in front of him with their guns drawn.

"Put the case down slowly and place your hands over your head."

"I was just coming to clean the place up."

Agent Williams takes a step forward and raises his gun until it's pointing right between the courier's eyes.

"I said put the case down and slowly place your hands over your head."

The courier does as he's told and agent Williams places the cuffs on him. Agent Hall opens the bag and finds a high powered rifle with a scope inside. He radios Agent Todd.

"We've got him in custody and we've got the gun."

"Put our security cameras in place, unload the gun, put it back in the case and leave it there. Then quietly take the prisoner out of the coliseum."

Drake Orton has just pulled into the parking lot of the coliseum and locked his SUV. He has an ID provided to him by Dick's lawyer. All he has to do now is get to the watering hole and do the job.

He slowly makes his way across the parking lot to the door. An agent checks his ID. He tries to look calm but inside he's panicking. His heart is racing so fast he can feel it in his chest.

The agent lets him pass and after passing several more check points he makes his way up the steps until he gets to the janitor's closet.

After he walks into the watering hole he picks up the case, takes out the gun then walks over to the cabinet beside the couch, takes out a bottle of scotch and pours himself a glass.

He takes a drink then puts the glass down and begins to check the gun to make sure it works and to get use to the feel of it. While he checks the gun agents are closing in on the room. Another agent in a truck in the parking lot is watching Drake on the monitor screen. He relays where he is in the room and what he is doing.

"He has the gun in his hand."

Drake pulls back the bolt on the gun and is about to check it when the door to the room flies open and three FBI agents enter the room with their guns drawn. In a few minutes they bring Drake out in handcuffs.

They quietly take him to a break room in the basement of the coliseum and sit him down in a chair in front of a table. Agent Todd sits down across the table from him and places a tape recorder in front of them.

"Mr. Orton you are going to go to jail for a very long time. We have you talking to Dick on tape about a conspiracy to carry out an assassination attempt on Senator Wright's life. Now you can go to a medium security prison or you can go a maximum security prison with Dick. Of course the maximum security prison is quite a bit rougher than the medium security prison. I don't really know how long you would last there."

Before Drake can say anything agent Todd presses the play button on the tape recorder and the whole conversation Drake has with Dick replays while Drake sits there staring at his hands.

"Mr. Orton what's it going to be? Do you serve hard time or do we make a deal?"

"If I give you what you want I don't want to do any jail time."

Agent Todd leans in close and looks Drake in the eyes.

"No Drake that is not how it works. You will give me the information I want or I will put you in prison with the most ruthless serial killers and murderers in the country. Now, one last time what's it going to be?"

"What do you want to know?"

"Who is your contact person?"

"His name is Kendall Otley, he's Dick's lawyer."

"Where is his office?"

"Downtown Leavenworth."

"Is there anyone else involved in this?"

"Not that I know of."

Agent Todd stands up, walks across the room and takes out his cell phone. After giving some instructions to an agent in Leavenworth he closes his phone and walks back to the table.

"An hour and a half from now I want you to call Mr. Otley and tell him the package hasn't arrived yet."

Thirty minutes after agent Todd's phone call the lights flicker then go out in the building where Kendall Otley's law office is located. Thirty minutes later several repairmen show up and check the building including Kendall's law office. They find the problem and soon the lights are back on.

Exactly an hour and half later agent Todd takes Drake's phone out of his pocket and hands it to him. Drake takes the phone and makes the call.

"Hello."

"This is Drake. The package isn't here."

"Are you sure?"

"I'm in the watering hole right now and it's not here."

"I'll call you back." Drake closes the phone and hands it back to Agent Todd

Its four o'clock and we should be heading to the coliseum but we're going to be late. Nessa walks into our bedroom still in her robe. I look at her and shake my head. My wife is beautiful, intelligent, charming and loving. All of these are good things to have in a wife but I wish she was a little more time conscious. We have to leave in an hour and she's not close to being ready yet.

"Uh Nessa you know we have to leave in an hour."

"I'll be ready but are you going to wear that tie?"

"What's wrong with the tie?"

"It doesn't go with the suit."

"Nessa, the staff stylist picked out the suit and the tie."

"Well I like the suit but the tie is a mistake."

"Fine. What tie do you think I should wear?"

"Wear the royal blue one. Blue always looks good on you."

"Are you saying that as the voting public or as my wife?"

"Both." She helps me with the tie and kisses me then begins to get dressed.

At five o'clock we get into our car and our caravan of staff and agents head off to the coliseum. Nessa takes hold of my hand.

"Andre no matter what tomorrow brings I will always love you and be there for you."

"I know you will Nessa. I didn't think this meant that much to me but my heart is racing and my throat is dry. I know this is my last chance and I'm scared I might make a mistake."

"You won't make a mistake. You are very good at making speeches. You learned it from Ole Pop."

"You're right that old man could make a speech and he would be right about whatever he was speaking about."

"Just walk up to the podium and make that speech like Ole Pop would and you will be fine."

With the support of my wife and family and the memories of Ole Pop and Jesse and what they stood for in my head I am ready. I will make this the best speech I have ever made and hopefully if the American public is willing I will be their next president.

Kendall call's Dick's phone and his answering service picks up.

"Dick this is Kendall. You need to call me as soon as you get this message. Drake called and said the package isn't there."

Fifteen minutes later Kendall's phone rings. "Hello."

"What do you mean the package hasn't been delivered? It was supposed to be there two hours ago. Call Frank and find out what happened."

"I tried but he's not answering his phone."

"Then call Jerry Dawson and tell him to deliver another package and tell Drake to meet him in the parking lot."

Kendall hangs up the phone and calls Jerry Dawson. After telling Jerry what Dick wants him to do Kendall hangs up and calls Drake back.

"Drake, another package is going to be delivered to you but you're going to have to go outside and pick it up in the parking lot. The courier will have on a red Kansas city Chiefs hat and a blue bag."

"Okay."

Chapter 37

Ten minutes after Drake leaves the room Agent Todd's phone rings.

"Hello."

"We got every word and you were right there is someone else involved."

"Do you have a name?"

"His name is Jerry Dawson and he's going to deliver another weapon to Drake Orton. What do you want us to do?"

"Pick the lawyer up and tell agent Jackson to see if he can get any information out of him. If there is someone else involved in this I want to know."

After putting his phone in his pocket Todd sits down in front of Drake.

"I want you to go to the parking lot and pick up the package then walk away. Don't try to run you won't make it more than a few feet."

Another agent walks into the room carrying a large tool box. He places on the table in front of Todd and leaves. Todd slides it over to Drake.

"Take this with you. You're a maintenance man you should look like one."

It's now five thirty and we have arrived at the coliseum. We walk into the coliseum and go directly to Bubba's office. The whole hallway that leads to Bubba's office is shut down and full of FBI and secret service agents.

My secret service agents flank Nessa and me on both sides as we walk down the hall. When we get to Bubba's office the agents walk into the room and check it out before allowing Nessa and me to walk in.

Bubba is sitting behind his desk but this time he has on a coach's jersey and he looks a great deal more comfortable. He stands up and walks around his desk.

"Hey Andre so this is what it's like not to have a life."

"Ha, ha, ha very funny big man."

I am about to say something else to him but he's not paying attention to me. He's too busy hugging Nessa. His big arms swallow her up whole.

"Hey Nessa it's been a long time. When you gonna divorce this buzzard so we can get married."

Nessa hugs Bubba back, hits him in the ribs then laughs.

"Now Bubba I told you I love Andre and stop calling him a buzzard."

"He ain't nothing but a raggedy old line backin buzzard. Besides I remember you told me on your wedding day if he hadn't been around you would have married me."

Nessa puts her finger to her lips and half whispers.

"Shhhhh Bubba he wasn't supposed to know that."

I put a fake frown on my face. "Watch it big man. There are too many secret service agents around here. Something bad could happen to you."

Bubba smiles that big ole country boy smile. "See that. One day from the presidency and already his head is swelling and he's pushing people around. I told you he's a buzzard." Even the secret service people laugh at that one.

I give Bubba my best fake angry glare. "Just unwrap your arms away from around my wife so there won't be a problem."

He lets Nessa go but has to get one last jab in. He bends down and kisses Nessa on the cheek and with that big old grin on his face he says, "Nessa if this buzzard messes up you know where to find me"

Nessa gives me the evil eye then looks at bubba. "I'll remember that."

Now it's my turn to give the evil eye to bubba.

"Big man you and I are about to have a serious problem."

Bubba winks at Nessa and walks back around behind his desk. We all sit down and Bubba and I immediately start talking football and Nessa rolls her eyes. Glenora walks in shortly after that and she and Nessa begin talking. It is now one hour before I am to give my speech and I am relaxed. It is a blessing to be around family and good friends.

———————————

At six thirty Mississippi time FBI agents walk into Kendall Otley's office and take him into custody. He has no idea why they are arresting him and he protests as they take him out to their car.

At ten after seven Mr. Otley is led to an interrogation room in the local police station. Ten minutes later agent Jackson walks in, places a tape recorder in front of Kendall and sits down. Kendall doesn't wait for agent Jackson to question him. Kendall has a few questions of his own.

"What am I being charged with?"

Agent Jackson doesn't say anything he is busy finishing his paper work or so it seems. Actually all he is doing is doodling on a pad while letting Kendall sweat.

"I said what am I being charged with?"

Agent Jackson looks up, "Just a minute Mr. Otley I need to finish this paperwork."

"Look I'm a lawyer and I know my rights."

Without looking up this time agent Jackson says, "Yes sir I know you do."

"Then I have the right to know what I'm being charged with."

By this time Kendall has lost his patience and is about to reach the frantic point. If he had been arrested by the police then he wouldn't be so frantic but this is the FBI. They know he's a lawyer so they wouldn't have arrested him without solid evidence to back it up.

Agent Jackson takes another few minutes to doodle on his pad then closes his folder turns on the tape recorder and sits back in his chair. The first voice that comes from the recorder is Kendall's.

Kendall sits there for a few moments then stands up. "You know this tape is not admissible in court?"

"Mr. Kendall please have a seat."

Agent Jackson allows the tape to continue playing and watches Kendall as he listens. All the details of Dick's plot to assassinate a Senator and candidate for the Presidency of the United States is on the tape. Kendall tries not to show it but he knows he's in trouble.

After a few very long minutes agent Jackson turns the tape off then sits back and allows a long exasperated exhale to flow from his lips as if he's disappointed in Kendall. He shakes his head as he begins to talk to the attorney.

"Mr. Otley we have a big problem here."

"As I said that tape is not admissible in court."

Agent Jackson shakes his head once again in disappointment then picks up the tape recorder and changes the tape. This time Kendall hears Drakes voice then his own. Drake is explaining that the package hadn't arrived yet. After that conversation ends agent Jackson turns the tape player off and sits back.

"Now before you say this tape is inadmissible in court you need to know that Drake has already been arrested with the gun in his hands. He has confessed to being a part of a conspiracy to assassinate a U.S. Senator and implicated you. He also agreed to allow us to tap his phone when he called you. Your conversation with him was all we needed to get a writ to place surveillance equipment in your offices. That equipment allowed us to tape the previous conversation. Now I'm not the lawyer you are but I'm pretty sure these tapes along with Drake's confession and implication of you will be admissible in court."

Suddenly Kendall is nervous. "I don't know anything about a conspiracy. All I did was relay instructions from my client. I'm just a messenger and you can't prove anything different. I didn't know what was being delivered. At best I will get a year's probation."

"That's not actually true Mr. Otley. Those messages are part of the conspiracy which is punishable by a mandatory sentence of three years minimum."

"Good luck proving that." Kendall stands up to head for the door.

"Sit down Mr. Otley unless you want to go to jail right now for obstruction of justice."

Kendall sits back down but still has some fight in him. "You can't prove that either."

"No but I can put you in one of the worse cells downtown and accidentally lose your paperwork for a while. Now let's see by the time we find the paper work, get it to the police precinct and they process it you could be there for a month. Oh and incidentally we already have two of the guards in custody who allowed Dick's cell phone to slip into the prison. They aren't the lawyer you are so I'm pretty sure they're going to want a deal especially after they find out they can and will be charged as a part of the conspiracy to assassinate a U.S. Senator. If they give you up you're done. You will do a maximum of fifteen years and I will make sure you and Mr. Hilgan are in the same prison. Oh, and this time there won't be any cell phones or money reaching either of you."

Kendall is a smart lawyer. He knows there is no way he can beat this especially since it's the FBI. He sighs and looks at agent Jackson.

"What do you want from me?"

"I want to know if there is anyone else involved in this."

"What do I get in return?"

"You get to take Mr. Hilgan's place in a medium security prison."

Kendall shakes his head this is not what he was expecting when he woke up this morning.

"His name is Saul "Turk" Reardon. He's supposed to kill Drake after Drake kills Senator Wright. He is somewhere in the coliseum."

"What happens if Drake doesn't show up?"

"He's been instructed to take the shot himself then find Drake and kill him."

"Have you ever seen this man?"

"Yes."

"I'm going to need a description of him."

Kendall gives a full description of the other assassin then Agent Jackson stands up, walks out of the room, immediately pulls out his cell phone and calls agent Todd.

"Hello."

"Bobby there's another shooter in the building. He's supposed to kill Drake after he takes the shot but he will take the shot if Drake doesn't make it to the watering hole. I'm sending you his name and a description now."

Agent Todd receives the information on his cell phone. After looking at the picture he heads for Bubba's office.

380 A. R. McKnight

The secret service agent in front of Bubba's door opens it and allows agent Todd to walk in. He gets right to the point.

"Senator there is a sniper in the building. We are going to hold the program up until we find him."

"How do you know there is a sniper in the building?"

"We caught Drake Orton with a gun in a secret room at the top of the coliseum. We also have taped conversations between him and Dick Hilgan planning the conspiracy."

"Are you saying that Dick Hilgan and Drake Orton were conspiring to kill me?"

"Yes sir and there is another shooter set to take Drake's place if he doesn't succeed. That's why we're going to hold up on your speech until we find him."

I look at Todd for a second with the look Ole Pop used to give people who made the mistake of thinking he couldn't figure them out.

"Now let me get this straight. You caught Drake but there is another sniper in the building so you want me to delay my speech until you find him. Now agent Todd you and I both know that you are planning on using Drake for bait for the other sniper. I'm pretty sure you have enough agents to find him so I'm going to make this speech without any delays."

"But Senator Wright we might not catch the other sniper in time."

"Agent Todd I have seen you in action. I'm sure you will find this person."

Agent Todd sticks his hand out to shake mine. "I thought you would say that. Senator Wright I will do my best."

I shake his hand. "Thank you agent Todd I know you will."

After he leaves I walk over to Nessa. "I don't want you on stage with me tonight."

"Andre Wright if you go up on that stage I am going with you."

"Nessa I am not going to argue about this. We have two children who need their mother."

"We have two children who need both mother and father. If you think this is safe then I am going with you. If you think it's not safe then you don't need to go either."

I turn to Glenora, "Glenora will you help me out here."

"I'm sorry Andre as per usual her logic is flawless. Now unless you delay or postpone the speech we're both going on stage with you."

I look at Bubba for a little support but he shakes his head.

"Sorry little fella you're on your own or don't you remember what Ole Pop used to say?"

"Yeah I know. There's nothing more determined than a woman trying to change a man's ways."

"Nope that's not it. The one I'm talking about is, "A smart man knows when to stay out of the affairs between a man and a woman. I'm sorry son I can't help you this time."

"Yeah thanks a lot big man."

"Hey I'll knock down big ole offensive linemen for you but I'm scared of Nessa."

Nessa starts laughing, "You'd better be."

I look at Bubba and laugh. "Yeah, so am I."

I hug Nessa like it's going to be my last time. I love her so much.

At seven o'clock the program begins. The Ole Miss "Pride of the South" band performs one song then plays our school fight song. Nessa and I stand and sing and clap.

Nessa sings with her beautiful soprano voice and I sing out of key of course and smile. It has been a long time since I've been on the football field but the fight song brings it all back just like it was yesterday.

Several city councilmen then the University President gives his speech in which he talks about change and making strong country through academics. The band plays one last song and its time for Dr. Mayhew the dean of the Ole Miss School of Law to introduce me.

His speech is excellent and he ends it by saying, "This strong and intelligent man was one of my most promising students and the next president of the United States, ladies and gentleman Senator Andre Wright."

At seven o'clock I start my speech. It is going very well and I have managed to make a spirited push for our party's ideas and the direction we think the country should move for the future.

At ten after seven Drake makes his way to the watering hole and shuts the door behind him. Agent Todd has explained to Drake exactly what he has to do but before he does he gives Drake some bad news to him.

Todd pulls up a chair and sit down in front of Drake. After shaking his head he looks Drake straight in the eyes.

"Drake did you know that Dick hired someone to kill you after you shot Senator Wright?"

"Dick wouldn't do that."

"He would to keep from going to a maximum security prison for the next forty years. You were the only link to him. He had to get you out of the way. Now here's the problem. The person he hired to kill you will try to kill Senator Wright if you miss. We need to know where this person is. So here's what I want you to do. Go to the watering hole and sit there so we can draw him out."

"No way! There is no way you're going to use me for bait."

"Look Drake we know you're not the leader of this conspiracy but you're going to go down for it if we don't get everyone involved in this. All you have to do is sit in the room and wait for our agents to come and get you."

Drake sits down and shakes his head. How in the hell did he end up in this situation. It wasn't too long ago he was a powerful councilman with more money than he knew what to do with now he's being used to bait a killer out into the open.

At seven forty five Turk begins working his way toward the door to the watering hole. He has a nine millimeter with a silencer in his coat. As soon as Drake pulls the trigger Turk will take him out, leave the gun on the floor and that will be the end of it.

Turk doesn't realize just inside the door are two agents with ear pieces listening to another agent who is looking at him through a set of binoculars.

"He's in position take him now."

Turk walks up to the, door puts his hand in his pocket and waits. A few seconds later the door suddenly swings open and Turk is looking at two federal agents with their guns drawn. He turns to run but comes face to face with agent Todd and his gun.

"Put the gun down, lie down on the floor face down and place your arms out to your sides. If you don't follow my instructions exactly I will kill you."

Turk lies down on his stomach and one of Todd's men puts the cuffs on him while the other picks up Turk's gun and hands it to agent Todd. After cuffing Turk the agent pulls him up off the floor and reads him his rights while leading him down the ramp and out the back of the building.

I finish my speech to a round of enthusiastic applause then wave to the crowd and head back to Bubba's office. The secret service won't allow me to stop and shake hands they hurriedly get us all off stage.

When we are secure in Bubba's office agent Todd walks in again. "Senator that was a very brave thing you did out there."

"I was doing the job I was asked to do."

"Well we got the other sniper."

"I knew you would and thank you for keeping us safe."

"That's the job I was asked to do."

We shake hands and he walks out the door but returns.

"Oh by the way the next time we meet could it be under circumstances other than someone pointing a gun at you."

I smile. "I will try to make sure that happens."

Chapter 38

Somehow the media finds out about the assassination attempt and the next morning instead of focusing on the speech and the issues the only thing on every channel is the capture of several men in a conspiracy to assassinate me.

The last thing I wanted was for this to come out. I wanted the day of the election to focus on our party's policies and the plan we have for moving into the future. Unfortunately when the polls opened the only thing on everybody's mind was the assassination attempt.

People wanted to know who was behind it, was it racially motivated and some wanted to know if it was a hoax to get more votes. I sat at home and shook my head.

Ole Pop once told me. "No matter how much good you try to do someone is always going to do their best to point out what they think is bad about it."

All I can do now is sit in our hotel room and wait. After about an hour I turn off the television, walk into the bedroom, shut the door, open my bible and began to read. Reading the bible always makes me correct myself when I get off balance.

At seven o'clock the latest reports have my opponent ahead by a small margin. However we aren't worried because the polls in several of our key states are still open. It will be a waiting game for several more hours.

At eight our caravan heads for the downtown convention. Soon it will be time for me to address our party as the President-Elect or to give my concession speech. Either way the long journey is over and tomorrow will bring a new direction.

We arrive in the lounge to find a table set up with several different appetizers, chips, cookies and drinks. I'm too nervous to eat so Nessa, our children and I go to the private lounge set up for us.

The lounge has a couch and two plush chairs along with a portable bar stocked with cold water and drinks. I have told the committee that I don't want a television in the room. I don't want to see the projections, all I want to know about is the final results.

While I sit in the room playing with Andre Jr. Glenora walks in with two pieces of mail. Both of them have been opened by the secret service. One of them is post marked Chicago Illinois and the other is from Seattle Washington.

I pull the card out of the one with the Chicago post mark first. It's from little Crystal Ashton.

Dear Senator Wright.

I saw you on television last night. My mother let me stay up and watch the whole thing. I like what you said about education and the future. I would like to be an interpreter just like my mom and I am going to need as much education as I can get. I hope you are able to make gas less expensive. We didn't get a chance to go on our vacation this year because the gas prices are too high. Well I guess that's all I have to say now. Good luck. I hope you win.

Crystal Ashton

I smile as I place the card back in the envelope. I hope I can win so that I can help secure a future for the young ones coming along behind me. I hope I can pass on to them the wisdom, love and compassion shown to me by two intelligent, strong black men.

Nessa walks in and I give Crystal's letter to her and she reads it while I take the other card out of its envelope. This one is blank except for the Roman numerals on it.

It's from Amir, Farrah and Amira. I'm glad to know they are alright but I'm concerned that writing me this way may put them in jeopardy. Glenora touches me on the arm then leans over and whispers, "Don't worry it wasn't mailed by them. It was mailed to your favorite CIA director Simon Blakely. He had it mailed to you from Seattle."

Once again I smile and wonder even if I do win the presidency will I ever really know all that is going on in the departments under my jurisdiction. Well as Ole Pop used to say. "Worry about your job and let every one else do theirs and usually things will work just fine."

My mind is on nothing in particular when Walter walks in with a very down look on his face.

"Andre you need to come out and see the final results."

I guess we didn't get it done. It's hard to walk out and face the people who have worked so hard for this campaign. Somehow "Thank you" just doesn't seem to be enough.

As I walk out into the main room everyone is standing still and quiet. Walter turns around with a big smile on his face and says.

"Congratulations Mr. President."

I blink twice then look at him with a very quizzical look on my face. "Did you just call me Mr. President?"

"Yes I did."

I stand there stunned as all of our campaign workers and secret service agents applaud. Is this really happening? Am I really the president of the United States?

Nessa takes my hand and leads me over to the big screen television. The CNN news anchor is reporting.

"At the closing of the last polls Senator Wright is far enough ahead to be projected as the next President of the United States."

Glenora walks over to me and gently pushes me toward the podium. "Don't keep your committee and all the people who supported you waiting."

As I walk into the main ballroom with Nessa by my side there is thunderous applause. My head is still spinning with the fact that in a few days I will be sworn in as the President of the United States.

After I step to the podium it takes several minutes for the applause to die down and it takes several more minutes before I can speak. I suddenly realize that I am no longer running for the office. I am now in office and the people of this great country are expecting me to live up to my promises. From here on I had better do the best that I can to do just that.

After I finish my speech and shake what seems like an endless amount of hands I can finally go back to the hotel and rest. I didn't realize I was that tired. Before I know it morning is here and it is time to go to D.C.

Two weeks later I am sworn in as president. Two days after that my friend Senate Minority Leader Walter Bowens introduces me for my first speech to the nation. I step to the mike take a deep breath and start my prepared speech, but after speaking several well written words I close up the prepared speech and speak like African Americans have always done, "From the heart."

"I have a prepared speech in front of me, a speech that our staff of speechwriters have taken a great deal of time to write and while it is a nice speech it's not what I truly want to say on this special evening. I could stand up here and say it is an honor and a privilege to be the second African American President of the United States but that should already be obvious. I could say that I will strive to keep America's life and values strong and continuing but I hope that is obvious also. So instead I want to tell you a story about a confused child, a child who saw no future and didn't care about his past.

The African saying that "It takes a village to raise a child," is indeed true, especially in the case of this child. You see I was the child on his way to nowhere. I'm the child who can stand here and tell you that while there are still a lot of things that need to be straightened out in America, we still have a value system that works. I am a product of that system and I can assure you that it does work." I speak for thirty minutes and in those thirty minutes I explain our parties perspective on the path we think the United States should be following. In thirty minutes I have just done what every political partner and worker I've ever known has said is the kiss of death. I've spoken from my heart.

After I get through there is silence and I think, "Well that ends my career." Then there is thunderous applause. I turn to my left and look at my wife. She is clapping and there are tears in her eyes.

Epilogue

I walk off the podium amid the applause and Nessa is waiting for me.

"How did I do?"

"The speech was fantastic. Ole Pop and Jesse would be proud of you and I know mom is."

Glenora smiles and whispers, "I knew you were the right one for the job."

Walter shakes my hand and several people on my staff congratulate me.

Nessa's phone rings as we are walking away from the press conference. She answers it then hands it to me, its mom.

"Hey mom, how are the kids?"

"They are fine."

"What did you think of my speech?"

"Your speech was great. If you live up to half of what you said out there you'll make an excellent President. Just remember to put God before you in every decision you make."

"I wish Ole Pop and Jesse could be here now."

"They are with you in spirit and I know they are as happy for you as I am. Now go make me proud."

I close the phone and hand it back to Nessa. Then in front of every one standing in the hall I hug her and whisper "I love you." I take her hand and we turn and walk into the Oval office. It's a lot to take in and both of us stand there looking around then it hits me.

It's hard to wrap my brain around the fact that I am expected to govern this great country for the next four years. Never in my life have I shouldered such responsibility. However as the leader of this great nation I must do the best I can in making laws that are just and right.

It's a great responsibility and it's going to be hard work but I believe this is the greatest country in the world and I will do the best I can to see that it keeps moving in the right direction.

Nessa lets my hand go, looks at the desk then at me. She smiles, nods her head toward the desk and whispers. Mr. President don't you have work to do? I smile back at her then walk to the chair and sit down behind the desk that so many great men have sat behind and say a silent "Thank you Lord." It is indeed time to go to work.

Inspirations

First and foremost I have to acknowledge and give honor to God. Without him none of this would have been possible. I want to thank him for blessing me with the ability to write and I hope this book is pleasing in his sight.

Second of all I'd like to acknowledge my mom and pops. This book was written for them. Both have gone home to glory but their words continue to inspire me to greater heights than I ever could have imagined.

And now, as the saying goes, "Behind every good man is a good woman or in my case a Great woman. A special thank you goes out to my wife Renna. I love you sweetheart and I always will.

And much appreciation to Paulette Thompson. Thank you so much for putting my words in order. I couldn't have done this without you. Love you sis.

A man cannot become a positive role model without the positive being modeled for him first. Clay has to be placed in a mold to become a statue. We as Black men need to become better molds for our younger generation . . .

I have been blessed to have several family members, teachers and friends as role models in my life. They have inspired me to become the man I am. I hope I have been as positive a role model to those I've met as these men have been to me.

These men are my father William F. McKnight, my brother William B. Lockridge, brother in law Stanley T. Marshall, Uncle Leroy Green, father in law Alonzo C. Newbill, Uncle Alvin Hall,

392   A. R. McKnight

Uncle Ernest Hall, Uncle George Jamison, Uncle Hershel Hall and
Uncle Thomas Lane.

My friends are Jay Shoemaker, Dwight Bond, Bill Transley,
Bobbye Sherrell, Donald Pulliam, Barry Scott and I can't forget my
big partner Michael Andre Baines (also gone home to Glory).

My teachers and administrators are Mr. John Green Sr., Mr.
Donald Barrett, Mr. Ralph Thompson, Dr. Edward Lewis and Mr.
Robert Churchwell.

Pastor Charles Fitzgerald Nance Jr., the pastor of Ole Pop's
church was modeled after the influential preachers in my life. They
are Reverend Charles R. Williams Jr. (my baptismal Minister),
Reverend John Nance and Reverend Charles Fitzgerald.

I would also like to thank my cousin Duane Rhodes for the
inspiration to write again. Duane I had almost given up on writing
until I was inspired by your books. Keep doing what you do. You
never know where your influence will spread.

I'd better stop now before I start counting my blessings and
never be able to stop writing. And to all the young men out there
struggling, don't forget "Life is going to kick your butt, but if you
keep standing while it kicks you, life will have to kick up and the
harder life kicks you the higher you're going to climb."

A. R. McKnight

You can email Ricky McKnight at
abericky@hotmail.com

CLOC II